Theoretical and Practical Understanding of the Integral Reordering of Canon Law

THEORETICAL AND PRACTICAL UNDERSTANDING OF THE INTEGRAL REORDERING OF CANON LAW

Patricia Smith

Roman Catholic Studies
Volume 16

The Edwin Mellen Press
Lewiston•Queenston•Lampeter

Library of Congress Cataloging-in-Publication Data

Smith, Patricia, 1947-
　Theoretical and practical understanding of the integral reordering of canon law / Patricia Smith.
　　p. cm. -- (Roman Catholic studies ; v. 16)
　Includes bibliographical references and index.
　ISBN 0-7734-7264-9
　1. Canon law. 2. Revocation. 3. Effectiveness and validity of law. I. Title. II. Series.

KBU2196 .S64 2002
262.9'4--dc21

2001044555

This is volume 16 in the continuing series
Roman Catholic Studies
Volume 16 ISBN 0-7734-7264-9
RCS Series ISBN 0-88946-240-X

A CIP catalog record for this book is available from the British Library.

Copyright © 2002 Patricia Smith

All rights reserved. For information contact

The Edwin Mellen Press
Box 450
Lewiston, New York
USA 14092-0450

The Edwin Mellen Press
Box 67
Queenston, Ontario
CANADA L0S 1L0

The Edwin Mellen Press, Ltd.
Lampeter, Ceredigion, Wales
UNITED KINGDOM SA48 8LT

Printed in the United States of America

TO MY PARENTS

TABLE OF CONTENTS

PREFACE i
FOREWORD v
ACKNOWLEDGMENTS vii
INTRODUCTION 1

1. THE CONCEPT ON INTEGRAL REORDERING IN CANON LAW 7
    1.1.   CLARIFICATION OF TERMS 9
        1.1.1. *Ex/de integro; ordinare* 9
        1.1.2. *Lex* and *ius* 11
    1.2.   CANON 6 14
        1.2.1. Initial codification of ecclesiastical law 14
        1.2.2. Canon 6, *CIC/17* 16
        1.2.3. Revision of *CIC* 18
        1.2.4. Canon 6, *CIC/83* 20
            1.2.4.1. In relation to postconciliar laws 21
            1.2.4.2. Role in code 23
            1.2.4.3. Scope and contextual understanding ... 24
        1.2.5. Canon 6, *CCEO* 25
    1.3.   CANON 20 27
        1.3.1. Source of the canon 27
        1.3.2. Simplification of terms 29
            1.3.2.1. Abrogation/derogation 29
            1.3.2.2. *Ius speciale* 29

	1.3.3. Cessation of law 31
	1.3.3.1. Express revocation 33
	1.3.3.2. Tacit revocation 33

1.4.   INTEGRAL REORDERING 36
       1.4.1. Mind of the legislator 37
       1.4.2. Extent of integrity 38
       1.4.3. Formal integral reordering 39
              1.4.3.1. The Ecumenical Directory 40
              1.4.3.2. Tone of document 42
       1.4.4. Doubt of revocation: canon 21 44
       1.4.5. Verification 46

1.5.   JURIDIC DOCUMENTS AND INTEGRAL REORDERING 48
       1.5.1. Complexity of juridic norms 49
       1.5.2. Practical working model 49
              1.5.2.1. Hierarchy of juridic documents 50
                      1.5.2.1.1. Legislative documents 52
                      1.5.2.1.2. Administrative documents
                              for the community 53
                      1.5.2.1.3. Administrative documents for
                              executors of the law 53
              1.5.2.2. Practical implications of model 54

2. **PRINCIPLES OF INTEGRAL REORDERING** 57
   2.1.   INTEGRAL REORDERING OF NORMS 58
   2.2.   PRINCIPLES REGARDING INTEGRAL REORDERING 62
       2.2.1. Abrogation/derogation 63
       2.2.2. Distinct for direct contrariety 65
       2.2.3. Reordering of entire document/juridic institute .. 66

  2.2.4. Hierarchy of juridic documents 67
    2.2.4.1. Level one documents 68
    2.2.4.2. Level two documents 69
    2.2.4.3. Level three documents 70
    2.2.4.4. Further implications of principle 71
  2.2.5. Proof required 72
  2.2.6. Tenor/circumstances of law; mind of legislator .. 74
  2.2.7. Change in tone or forcefulness 76
  2.2.8. Independence of new norm 77
2.3. Summary of principles 78
2.4. Model of integrally reordered norms 79
  2.4.1. Examples of emendations 83
    2.4.1.1. Direct contrariety 84
    2.4.1.2. Change of competent authority 86
    2.4.1.3. Substantive addition 87
    2.4.1.4. Change in tone 89
    2.4.1.5. Complex norms; juridic institutes 92
  2.4.2. Significance of examples 96

3. Application of Principles to Religious Law 101
3.1. Scope of the study 103
3.2. Expressly abrogated documents 105
  3.2.1. *Ecclesiae sanctae* 105
  3.2.2. SCRIS decrees 106
  3.2.3. *Renovationis causam* 107
3.3. Juridic documents not expressly revoked 108
  3.3.1. *Pastorale munus* 109
  3.3.2. *Cum admote* 112
  3.3.3. *Religionum laicalium* 115
  3.3.4. *Cum superiores generales* 116
  3.3.5. *Venite seorsum* and *Verbi sponsa* 117

        3.3.6. *Clericalia instituta* 121

        3.3.7. *Clausuram papalem* 123

        3.3.8. *Mutuae relationes* 123

                3.3.8.1. Integrally reordered norms 126

                3.3.8.2. Doubt of revocation 128

                3.3.8.3. Norms not compatible with *CIC/83* .. 131

        3.3.9. SCRIS plenary documents 132

        3.3.10. "Essential Elements" 134

        3.3.11. Transitional CRIS decrees 135

        3.3.12. "Procedures for the Separation of Members from Their Institute" 136

        3.3.13. *Potissimum Institutione* 137

        3.3.14. "Fraternal Life in Community" 139

   3.4.   RELIGIOUS LIFE: THE *IUS VIGENS* 140

   3.5.   ANALYSIS OF PRINCIPLES AS APPLIED TO DOCUMENTS . 141

AFTERWORD 149

APPENDIX 157

SOURCES AND SELECT BIBLIOGRAPHY 161

GENERAL INDEX 177

INDEX OF AUTHORS 179

PREFACE

Canon law governs the institutional life of the Roman Catholic Church and that of its one billion members worldwide. Canon law is a dynamic, changing system. New laws are regularly promulgated and old ones revoked by the various legislators of the Church (the pope, ecumenical and particular councils, conferences of bishops, diocesan bishops). Although the Church holds that some of its laws are of divine origin, it readily acknowledges that most are human laws, capable of emendation and abrogation. Indeed, during the twentieth century many thousands of universal ecclesiastical laws, some quite ancient, were revoked outright or replaced by new laws to suit contemporary needs and changing circumstances.

The first *Code of Canon Law* of the Church, promulgated in 1917, revoked a substantial part of the enormous, and often confusing, corpus of law that had grown ever larger and more unwieldy over the course of nineteen centuries. The code provided rules for the revocation of old law by new law to assure greater clarity for the future concerning what constitutes the *ius vigens*, the actual law in force. Accordingly, laws may be totally revoked (abrogation) or partially revoked (derogation) in three ways: (1) A later law revokes a former law when it expressly states that it is doing so. (2) A new law revokes an old one when the later law is directly contrary to an earlier law. (3) A later law revokes an earlier law by integrally, or completely, reordering the entire subject matter of the previous law. These same rules are repeated in the revised code of 1983, and they have also been taken up in the first code for Eastern Catholics, the *Code of Canons of the Eastern Churches* of 1990.

Express revocation rarely results in any doubt about which law is in force. It is clear from the wording of the new law that a former law is revoked. Likewise, when a new law is directly contrary to a previous law, the legislator's intent to revoke the old law is evident. The revocation of law by the integral reordering of its subject matter in later law is also obvious in some cases, for example, when a new document is entirely revised, replacing a previous document on the same subject. In many cases, however, there is no such clarity. Most canonical commentators cite obvious examples of the integral reordering of law, but they fail to tackle the more difficult problems, in particular, determining when a new text of laws has integrally reordered some of the norms of a previous document, while leaving the rest in force.

This problem has been especially acute since the promulgation of the revised code of 1983. During and following the Second Vatican Council (1962-1965), the Holy See issued several hundred juridic documents to implement the reforms decreed by the Council. Some of these documents were expressly revoked when the code went into effect, but many others were not. The revised code, to a greater or lesser extent, touches on the subject matter of these documents, but seldom on the entire subject matter. This gives rise to doubts: Which norms within these many documents remain in force? Which norms are abrogated or derogated? The answers to these questions impact both canonical scholarship and the practice of the Church itself, because they determine what is the *ius vigens*, the law that must be applied and observed throughout the Church.

These questions have been very difficult to answer, even for experts in the law, because objective, scientific criteria and practical tools were lacking for assessing whether a later law integrally reordered an earlier law, particularly in the many cases when certain laws of a document are affected by later law but others are not. This major theoretical and practical problem for the canonical science and the Church at large has now been resolved in this comprehensive and masterful study by Dr. Patricia Smith.

Dr. Smith reviews and analyzes the canonical doctrine on integral reordering of law and develops eight principles to guide the scholar and practitioner of the law in determining when a later law has abrogated an earlier law or derogated from it. She then verifies the objective basis for her principles by demonstrating how they were implicitly operative in the work of a commission appointed by the Holy See whose task was to determine which of the liturgical laws were affected by the 1983 code and were in need of revision or deletion from the liturgical books. Having thus established the soundness of her eight principles, she then applies them to a particular juridical institute, or body of law, namely, that governing persons consecrated by vows of poverty, chastity, and obedience in religious institutes, commonly known as religious orders or religious congregations. Her results are surprising: the post-conciliar juridical documents on religious life–which are well known and frequently still cited by canonists, Church officials, and religious themselves–have mostly been revoked by the code or by later law.

Dr. Smith's determination of what constitutes the *ius vigens* for religious life is in itself a valuable accomplishment. However, the lasting contribution of this work is the method she has developed, which can be used to determine the *ius vigens* of *any* juridical institute of canon law, and even to determine whether a single law has been totally or partially revoked by a subsequent law. This is a major and, very likely, enduring achievement of great theoretical import and practical benefit for both the canonical science and the Church at large.

John M. Huels, O.S.M., J.C.D.
Professor of Canon Law
Saint Paul University, Ottawa

FOREWORD

I chose to research the concept of the integral reordering of the subject matter of a law because I believe that it is both a pressing and a timely concern in the church today. With the exception of several commentaries English speaking canonists have written little on canons 6 and 20 of the 1983 *Code of Canon Law*, which deal with the abrogation and derogation of laws. While some Spanish and Italian canonists have made contributions to the canonical doctrine on the extrinsic cessation of law and, in particular, the exploration of the concept of integral reordering, they have not treated this topic comprehensively.

The integral reordering of the subject matter of a law is a most common way by which ecclesiastical law is revoked. Thus, it is essential that canonists fully understand the concept of integral reordering.

This is especially important today. Numerous juridic documents issued between the Second Vatican Council and the promulgation of the revised code have not been expressly revoked. Likewise, numerous juridic documents have been issued by the Holy See since 1983. What is the status of these earlier documents?

No one should be in doubt about which juridic norms are in force. Yet the revocation of law by integral reordering is seldom obvious, even to those versed in canon law. The determination of precisely what is the *ius vigens* – and what is not – is a technical exercise that necessitates skilled canonists who have proper tools at their disposal for reaching the right judgment.

Laws prior to the code that are not directly contrary to its prescripts or laws whose subject matter was not integrally reordered by the code remain part of the *ius vigens*, unless they have subsequently been integrally reordered by a later legislative text. Ascertaining the *ius vigens* then requires a thorough understanding of the concept of integral reordering as a means of abrogation or derogation of law.

I believe that the research that follows, particularly the principles that emerge from this study, provide such clarification. Additionally, the application of these tenets to a given body of law both validates them and models their effective use. This is the major achievement of this research.

I believe that canonists and others with an interest in ecclesiastical law will find these principles beneficial. It is my hope that this book will engender further reflection and discussion, and perhaps lead to refinements in the ideas presented here.

Patricia Smith, osf
Wilmington, DE
May 15, 2001

ACKNOWLEDGMENTS

I am grateful to the many people who supported and encouraged me in this endeavor. I thank especially the members of my family, my religious community, the Sisters of St. Francis of Philadelphia, and my friends.

Likewise. I extend appreciation to those I encountered within the faculty of Canon Law at Saint Paul University in Ottawa, particularly, Dr. Roch Pagé, Dean, and Professors Augustine Mendonça, Francis G. Morrisey, Lynda Robitaille, William Woestman, and the late Michel Thériault. I also thank Dr. James A. Coriden of Washington Theological Union, Washington, DC, for his insight and suggestions regarding this work.

Finally, I am especially grateful to Professor John Huels for his direction in writing this book that was originally presented as a doctoral dissertation. His unique ability to challenge and motivate was continually complemented by encouragement and support. John's enthusiasm for this work as well as his generous sharing of time and talent energized me. His expertise, insight and suggestions, reflected in this book, are greatly valued.

INTRODUCTION

Throughout its history the Church has assumed a conservative posture regarding the extrinsic cessation of law. As a result, ecclesiastical legislation has at times become multi-layered, cumbersome and even confusing. If this is acknowledged by those versed in canon law, so much the more is it true for those whose knowledge of the law is limited. In the Apostolic Constitution that promulgated the *Code of Canon Law* of 1917 (= *CIC/17*), Benedict XV reiterated this fact, stating that the laws of the Church were so numerous, separated and scattered that many of them were unknown not only to the people, but to eminent scholars, as well.[1] Thus, *CIC/17* had among its prime purposes that of clarifying the status of ecclesiastical legislation by issuing in one collection the Church's legal corpus.[2]

The lack of clarity that accompanied ecclesiastical law before the promulgation of the initial code was partly due to the fact that, throughout the first nineteen centuries of the Church, abrogation was sparingly used. The earliest attempt to bring clarity to a complex ecclesiastical system of laws by means of abrogating past laws was the papal Bull, *Rex pacificus*, issued in 1234, which accompanied the promulgation of the Decretals of Gregory IX. However, the express revocation contained within the bull, while eliminating some previous collections of law, did not deal with the status of others. Canonists were still left with questions regarding what

---

[1] See BENEDICT XV, Apostolic Constitution, *Providentissima Mater Ecclesia*, 27 May 1917, in *Acta Apostolicae Sedis* (= *AAS*), 9, Part II (1917), p. 6: "Accedit etiam, quod leges canonicae ita numero creverant, tam disiunctae dispersaeque vagabantur, ut satis multae peritissimos ipsos, nedum vulgus, laterent."
[2] See PIUS X, Motu proprio, *Arduum sane munus*, 19 March 1904, in *Acta Sanctae Sedis*, 36 (1903-1904), p. 550.

laws remained in force.[3] Thousands of laws remained "on the books" in the *Corpus Juris Canonici*, consisting of the *Decree of Gratian*, the Decretals of Gregory IX, the *Liber Sextus* of Boniface VIII, the *Clementinae*, the *Extravagantes* of John XXII and the *Extravagantes communes*. To this collection the decretals of subsequent popes as well as the disciplinary decrees of various councils continued to be added.[4]

Thus, at the time the 1917 *Code of Canon Law* was promulgated, c. 6 represented the most extensive use of express abrogation in Church history. While seeking to retain for the most part the discipline in force, c. 6 of *CIC/17* nonetheless abrogated all universal and particular laws contrary to its prescriptions, unless other provision was made in regard to particular law; all penalties not included in the code; and all disciplinary laws that were neither explicitly nor implicitly contained within the canons. In regard to future cessation of law, c. 22 outlined the three ways in which abrogation or derogation could occur. These included express revocation of a law by the legislator, direct contrariety of a new law with a former one, and the integral reordering of the subject matter of an earlier law by a later one. Thus *CIC/17* offered clearer understanding of the *ius vigens* as well as a means of preventing the corpus of the law itself from becoming unwieldy in the future.

Overall, this initial codification had a stabilizing effect on ecclesiastical law. Although at the time of the promulgation of *CIC/17* the legislator provided for the possibility of its amendment and the addition of further canons,[5] this mechanism was rarely used for the first fifty years of the code's existence.

---

[3] See N.J. NEUBERGER, *Canon 6*, Canon Law Studies, no. 44, Washington, DC, Catholic University of America, 1927, pp. 2-10; see also C. AUGUSTINE, *A Commentary on the New Code of Canon Law*, vol. 1, St. Louis, MO, Herder, 1931, pp. 36-40.

[4] See NEUBERGER, *Canon 6*, pp. 10-16 and AUGUSTINE, *A Commentary on the New Code of Canon Law*, pp. 38-49.

[5] See BENEDICT XV, Motu proprio, *Cum iuris canonici*, 15 September 1917, in *AAS*, 9 (1917), p. 484. English translation in *Canon Law Digest* (= *CLD*), 1, pp. 56. According to the motu proprio, the Roman Congregations were to enact no new general decrees, unless urgently required. If a new general decree was needed, the appropriate Congregation would draw up the decree and inform the pope if it was not in agreement with the code. After approval by the pope, the same Congregation would present it to the Code Commission which, in turn, would decide whether a new canon or canons should be inserted into the code and how they would be appropriately numbered. The changes would then be published in the *Acta Apostolicae Sedis*.

The Second Vatican Council, which ushered in a period of *aggiornamento* in the Church, generated an extensive utilization of c. 22. The sixteen documents that were the fruit of the council abrogated or derogated from many canons of *CIC/17*. These constitutions, decrees and declarations, in turn, generated a multitude of ecclesiastical documents needed for their implementation. Many of these subsequent documents embodied matter of a juridic nature that served as part of the *ius vigens* until the promulgation of the *Code of Canon Law* of 1983 (=*CIC/83*).

The revised code did not have the same intent of unifying ecclesiastical legislation as did the initial codification. Many postconciliar documents were not expressly abrogated or even derogated when *CIC/83* came into force. Thus, the question is raised: what is the status of the juridic documents that were issued before the promulgation of the code? Furthermore, this question has arisen on a regular basis in the years subsequent to the revised code's coming into force as documents of a juridic nature implement *CIC/83* or pre-code documents that have remained part of the *ius vigens*. How do the more recently issued documents affect previous ones or the norms within them, or even the contents of the code itself? These questions provide the impetus for the chapters that follow.

Canon 6 of *CIC/83* reiterates overall criteria for the abrogation of prior laws. It sets parameters for dealing with ecclesiastical legislation, postconciliar and earlier, which was in force at the time the revised code took effect. Canon 6 expressly abrogates *CIC/17* and penal laws issued by the Apostolic See that are not contained within the code. However, it is §1, 2° and particularly §1, 4° of this canon that are significant to this work. The former abrogates universal or particular laws contrary to the prescriptions of *CIC/83* unless the particular laws are expressly provided for within the code; the latter abrogates universal disciplinary laws concerning matters integrally reordered by the code itself. These two sections of c. 6 are key in determining which postconciliar juridic matters remain the *ius vigens* and which have been revoked.

Likewise, these two means of revocation pertain to future law. Canon 20, like its predecessor, c. 22 of *CIC/17*, outlines three ways that abrogation or derogation of law can occur: express revocation, direct contrariety, and the integral reordering of the subject matter of a prior law. Express revocation is evident. The legislator indicates that a certain law is repealed. Although express revocation can occur in several forms, its intent is nonetheless clear.[6] Similarly, revocation is usually apparent when a new law is in direct opposition to a former one. However, the integral reordering of the subject matter of an earlier law by a later one as a means of abrogation or derogation is often not obvious. Thus, this work seeks to clarify and deepen the understanding of the concept of revocation by means of integral reordering. The integral reordering of law may be understood as its tacit revocation by a later law that treats anew the entire matter of the earlier law, thus resulting in an incompatibility between the two laws.[7]

This book includes three chapters. The first explores integral reordering in the *traditio canonica*, with *CIC/17* as the starting point, as well as its contemporary understanding in light of *CIC/83* and the *Code of the Canons of the Eastern Churches* (= *CCEO*). The initial chapter also presents a hierarchical model for evaluating juridic documents and the norms within them, which can assist in determining whether or not integral reordering has occurred.

Chapter 2 develops principles that serve as indicators of whether a given law has been integrally reordered. These tenets are verified through their application to the liturgical emendations that were necessitated as a result of the promulgation of the revised code.

Chapter 3 applies the principles formulated in the previous chapter to religious law. Focusing on the area of consecrated life pertaining to religious, it answers the questions that are at the heart of this work: what is the status of the juridic documents that were issued before the promulgation of the code? How do juridic documents

---

[6] Express revocation is treated in Chapter 1.
[7] This definition is explained and illustrated in the chapters that follow.

issued after *CIC/83* affect these previous documents, the norms within them, or even the code itself? This chapter also provides a model of how these principles can be applied to other areas of law as well as to individual documents.

The afterword offers a conclusive definition of integral reordering in the canonical tradition. It likewise challenges the reader by posing four areas for further reflection and research.

CHAPTER 1
THE CONCEPT OF INTEGRAL REORDERING
IN CANON LAW

The *Code of Canon Law* of 1983 is unequivocal in stating in canon 7 that "a law is established when it is promulgated."[1] In its subsequent canon, furthermore, *CIC/83* leaves no doubt as to what this promulgation entails, outlining the specifics of how and when this occurs for both universal and particular law.[2] Yet, the Code has no succinct corollary for the cessation of a law. In accord with the conservative posture toward abrogation that the Church has assumed throughout the centuries,[3] *CIC/83* deals only with the revocation of law by the competent authority. However, even the criteria for revocation put forth in the code are not always clear. The abundant juridic documents that ensued from the Second Vatican Council as well as those that continue to be promulgated today often lead to questions concerning the *ius vigens*.

---

[1] *Codex iuris canonici, auctoritate Ioannis Pauli PP. II promulgatus*, Vatican City, Libreria editrice Vaticana, 1989. *Code of Canon Law*, Latin-English Edition, new English translation prepared under the auspices of the Canon Law Society of America (= CLSA), Washington, DC, CLSA, 1999. English translation of canons are derived from this source.

[2] See *CIC/83*, canon 8.

[3] See S. WOYWOD, *The New Canon Law: A Commentary and Summary of the New Code of Canon Law*, 3rd ed., New York, NY, J.F. Wagner, 1918, pp. 14-15. See also J. GAUDEMET, *La doctrine canonique médiévale*, Brookfield, Vermont, Ashgate Publishing Company, 1994, pp. 9-13. Gaudemet describes the domain of canon law after the Council of Trent as very limited, its development essentially a commentary on the Decretals of Gregory IX. He believes that this stance was reflected in the *Code of Canon Law* of 1917. See also A. CICOGNANI, *Canon Law*, authorized English version by J. O'HARA and F. BRENNAN from the Latin original, 2nd rev. ed., Philadelphia, Dolphin Press, 1935, p. 500. Cicognani notes that even the general abrogation brought about by *CIC/17* only impacted laws which were opposed to the code.

This first chapter highlights one principal way in which a law ceases through revocation: that is, by the integral reordering of its subject matter. This most efficient and common way that laws cease extrinsically today, is also been termed the most difficult means of revocation to identify.[4]

The concept of integral reordering was formally introduced into canonical legislation with the promulgation of the *Code of Canon Law* of 1917 in c. 22. However, it was most extensively and effectively employed in the years following the Second Vatican Council.[5] Its importance in dealing with postconciliar laws was highlighted with the *Code of Canon Law* of 1983 which incorporated integral reordering into c. 6 in addition to retaining it as a means of revocation of ecclesiastical law in c. 20.

It is important at the outset to clarify some terms fundamental to the concept of integral reordering. Following this an overview of cc. 6 and 22 of the *CIC/17* and cc. 6 and 20 of *CIC/83* as well as cc. 6 and 1502 of the *Code of Canons of the Eastern Churches* will provide a contextual understanding for the discussion of integral reordering.[6] While the source and history of the concept will be considered, its purpose and interpretation today is of primary focus. The doubt of revocation of law, treated in c. 21, will also be discussed. The chapter concludes with an examination of the nature of juridic texts subject to integral reordering or capable of integrally reordering. A model for evaluating juridic documents and the norms within them will be presented.

---

[4] See J. OTADUY, "Normas y actos juridicos," in *Manuale de derecho canónico*, obra a cargo del INSTITUTO MARTÍN DE AZPILCUETA, Pamplona, Ediciones Universidad de Navarra, 1988, p. 254.

[5] M. CABREROS DE ANTA, *Vigencia y estado actual de la legislación canónica*, Pamplona, Ediciones Universidad de Navarra, S.A., 1974, p. 23: "Los casos de revocación de la legislación canónica por reorganización completa de determinados institutos jurídicos, hecha en virtud de disposiciones conciliares o por ordenamientos pontificios posteriores al Concilio, son ya no pocos y de no escasa importancia."

[6] Relatively little has been written on cc. 6 and 20 of *CIC/83*. Because both canons are derived directly from their predecessors, commentaries dealing with *CIC/17* prove helpful.

1.1 — CLARIFICATION OF TERMS

A brief explanation of the concepts *ex/de integro* and *ordinare*, as well as *lex* and *ius* enables a more expeditious treatment of this topic.[7] In light of c.17, *CIC/83*, these terms will be considered according to their proper meaning in their text and context. References to parallel places, to the purpose and circumstances of the law and to the mind of the legislator will be employed as needed in this initial clarification. However, these alternatives will be further developed throughout this book.

1.1.1 — *Ex/de integro; ordinare*

The adjective *integer* is found in some 26 canons in *CIC/83*.[8] It is most commonly translated in the Code as "full," "whole," "intact," "entire, " "complete" or "integral." Only in cc. 6 (*ex integro*) and 20 (*de integro*) is the ablative case used with a preposition. The *Oxford Latin Dictionary* lists 14 meanings for *integer*. The third entry specifically cites *a/de/ex integro*, defining this phrase concisely as "afresh, anew."[9] Sources from classical Latin writings illustrate this. Works of first century authors, among others, provide evidence of the use of this expression in a variety of settings and circumstances. *A/de/ex integro* connoted a new beginning, a complete change, a fresh approach – in essence, a starting from scratch.[10]

English translations of the code of 1983 render *ex integro ordinatur* in c. 6 and *de integro ordinet* in c. 20 as "integrally reorders," with the exception of the most

---

[7] This section presents an overall description of these terms in order to establish a framework for the discussion that follows. *Lex* and *ius* will be further discussed later in this chapter in considering the nature of juridic matter that can integrally reorder another law or itself be integrally reordered.

[8] See X. OCHOA, *Index verborum ac locutionum Codicis iuris canonici*, 2nd ed., Roma, Commentarium pro Religiosis, 1984, p. 232. Ochoa gives 28 references for *integer* found in some 26 canons. One reference (c. 212, §2), however, actually refers to *integrum est*, a separate heading, comprising thirteen canonical citations. It appears to be mis-catalogued here.

[9] See P. GLARE et al., *Oxford Latin Dictionary*, Oxford, Clarendon Press, 1968, p. 934.

[10] See TITUS LIVIUS, *Ab urbe condita libri*, English and Latin trans. by B.O. FOSTER, Cambridge, MA, Harvard University Press, 1970 -1991, pp. 60-61; LUCIUS JUNIUS MODERATUS COLUMELLA, *De re rustica*, English and Latin, ed. and trans. by H.B. ASH, Cambridge, MA, Harvard University Press, 1968-1993, pp. 208-209; CORNELIUS TACITUS, *Historiae*, trans. by C.H. MOORE, Cambridge, MA, Harvard University Press, 1992, pp. 428-429.

recent translation that uses the phrase "completely reorders."[11] French, Italian and Spanish translations concur in using similar expressions: *entièrement réorganisée/ réorganise entièrement; ordinata integralmente/riordina integralmente; se regulan por completo/ordena completamente* for cc. 6 and 20 respectively.[12]

In both canons *de/ex integro* is coupled with the Latin verb *ordinare*. Most translators apply this sense of "entirely, integrally, completely" to the verb itself. Of the various meanings and uses of *ordinare* given in both classical and ecclesiastical dictionaries, the translation "reorders" never appears.[13] Of the 34 times that *ordinare* is used in the code, only in cc. 6 and 20 is it translated as "reorders." This additional emphasis seems necessary for clarity in the context of both canons. For "integral reordering" implies that a law is not merely ordered again but that something wholly

---

[11] See *Code of Canon Law,* new English translation, CLSA, 1999. Although this translation uses the term "completely reorders" for both *ex integro ordinatur* of canon 6 and *de integro ordinet* of c. 20, the term "integrally reorders" will be used throughout this work for several reasons. First, it is the more common term used in other English translations. See for example, E. CAPARROS, M. THÉRIAULT and J. THORN (eds.), *Code of Canon Law Annotated, Latin-English Edition of the Code of Canon Law and English-language Translation of the 5th Spanish-language Edition of the Commentary Prepared under the Responsibility of the Instituto Martín de Azpilcueta* (= *Code of Canon Law Annotated*), Montréal, Wilson & Lafleur Limitée, 1993; G. SHEEHY et al. (eds.), *The Canon Law: Letter & Spirit: A Practical Guide to the Code of Canon Law,* prepared by the Canon Law Society of Great Britain and Ireland in association with the Canadian Canon Law Society (= *Letter & Spirit*), Collegeville, MN, Liturgical Press, 1995; and J.A. CORIDEN, T.J. GREEN and D.E. HEINTSCHEL (eds.), *The Code of Canon Law: A Text and Commentary,* commissioned by CLSA, New York, Mahwah, New Jersey, Paulist Press (= *CLSA Commentary)*, 1985. (The translation in this commentary is inconsistent in its treatment of the phrase. Canon 6 uses the Latin original *ex integro* while c. 20 translates it as "entirely reorders.") Second, the word "integral" is more akin to the Latin root. Third, as will be demonstrated, integral reordering results from either abrogation or derogation. The word "completely" used in the sense of derogation could prove to be confusing.

[12] See cc. 6 and 20 in *Code de droit canonique, texte officiel et traduction française par La Société internationale de droit canonique et de législations religieuses comparées avec le concours des Faculté de droit canonique de l'Université Saint-Paul d'Ottawa, Faculté de droit canonique de l'Institut catholique de Paris,* Paris, Éditions Centurion, Cerf, Tardy, 1984; *Codice di diritto canonico, testo ufficiale e versione italiana, sotto il patrocinio della Pontificia Università Lateranense e della Pontificia Università Salesiana,* Roma, Unione editori cattolici italiani, 1983; and L. DE ECHEVERRIA, (ed.), *Código de derecho canónico, edición bilingüe comentada por los professores de la Facultad de Derecho canónico de la Universidad Pontificia de Salamanca,* 7th ed., Madrid, Biblioteca de Autores cristianos, 1986.

[13] See GLARE, *Oxford Latin Dictionary,* pp. 1265-1266. See also L.F. STELTEN, *Dictionary of Ecclesiastical Latin,* Peabody, Massachusetts, Hendrickson Publishers, 1995, p. 182.

new has replaced it despite any similarities which appear to exist between the former and the present law.

1.1.2 — *Lex* and *ius*

Canon 6, §1 speaks of *leges sive universales sive particulares*, *leges pœnales and leges disciplinares universales* while §2 speaks of *canones huius Codicis, quaetenus ius vetus referunt*. Canon 20 likewise refers to *lex posterior*, *lex prior* and *lex universalis*. However, the second part of the canon uses the word *ius*: *sed lex universalis minime derogat iuri particulari aut speciali, nisi aliud in iure expresse caveatur* (emphasis added). English versions of the code translate both *lex* and *ius* as "law," but other modern languages use a distinct word for each. Thus *Codex iuris canonici*, translated as the *Code of Canon Law* in English, is more precisely determined in its French, Italian, Spanish and German titles.[14]

The word *lex* appears nearly 200 times in *CIC/83*; *ius*, however, is used much more frequently.[15] In the title *Codex iuris canonici*, *ius* is the genus. *Lex* is a species of *ius*. This is evident in the systematic arrangement of the first five titles of Book I which deal with various forms of *ius* – ecclesiastical laws, customs, general decrees and instructions, singular administrative acts, and statutes and ordinances.

Lex and *ius* appear together in numerous canons often seeming somewhat synonymous. At times throughout the code it is difficult to distinguish between their different uses.[16] Neither *lex* nor *ius* is defined in *CIC/83*.[17] However, the definition of

---

[14] Each of these translations has a separate word for *lex* and *ius*. Thus the titles *Code de droit canonique*, *Codice di diritto canonico*, *Código de derecho canónico* and *Codex des kanonischen Rechtes* include *lex* in the broader concept of *ius*.

[15] See OCHOA, *Index verborum*, pp. 258-261 and 248-253.

[16] See, for example, cc. 335 and 349. The former refers to the *leges speciales* when the Roman See is vacant or impeded; the latter speaks of the Cardinals electing the Roman Pontiff in accordance with the *ius peculiare*.

[17] See H. EIJSINK, "Some Striking Changes in the Code of Canon Law since April 1982," in J.H. PROVOST and K. WALF (eds.), *Studies in Canon Law Presented to P.J.M. Huizing*, Leuven, University Press, 1991, pp. 4-5. Eijsink notes that a definition of law was discussed in the preparation of *CIC/83* and that a definition is given in the *Schema novissimum*. He finds it somewhat surprising that there is no definition in the final redaction since the Code is not reluctant to provide definitions. See also PONTIFICIA COMMISSIO CODICI IURIS CANONICI RECOGNOSCENDO,

general decrees given in canon 29 can be understood as a description of *leges*, namely, "common provisions ... issued by a competent legislator for a community capable of receiving a law." J. Huels notes that this definition applies not only to general decrees but equally to canons, prescripts, norms, rubrics, etc. – all of which are species of *lex*, which in turn is a species of *ius*.[18]

A. Cicognani outlines three explanations of *ius* in regard to its causal, subjective and objective senses. He identifies the causal meaning as principal since the other two are founded on it.[19] From this perspective Cicognani states that: "*ius* denotes 'a sum of laws' (a complete collection of laws and customs) of one and the same character, for instance ... the canon law. The meaning of the term embraces both written and unwritten law." This understanding is rooted in the Roman understanding of *ius* – a norm which regulates a person's relationship with others.[20] A similar yet simpler understanding is presented by Huels, who holds that *ius* has two meanings:

Codex iuris canonici: schema Patribus commissionis reservatum, Romae, Citta del Vaticano, Liberia editrice Vaticana, 1980. Canon 7 read, "Lex, norma scilicet generalis ad bonum commune alicui communitati a competenti auctoritate data, instituitur cum promulgatur." See *Communicationes*, 14 (1982), p. 131. At the October 1981 meeting of the Code Commission the only objection raised regarding the definition was that it was too general: "Definitio legis, quae in canone data est, *nimis generalis* est et melius videtur ut supprimatur definitio." The Secretariat, however, responded that it was needed for juridic certitude: "Aliqua requiritur definitio, securitatis iuridicae causa. Determinare oportet quandonam vere habeatur lex."

[18] See J.M. HUELS, "A Theory of Juridical Documents Based on CC. 29-34," in *Studia canonica*, 32 (1998), p. 347.

[19] See CICOGNANI, *Canon Law*, pp. 10-12. *Ius* in its subjective or formal sense is regarded as a "right," that is, a moral or legal faculty conferred by law for doing, possessing, omitting or exacting something. In its objective or material sense *ius* is the object of justice, what is due, that which is just. In a contemporary study dealing with *lex* in the *ius canonicum*, L. WÄCHTER, likewise speaks of the subjective and objective understanding of *ius* in *CIC/83*. He describes the subjective concept as those rights which flow from the objective norm of the law. In its objective sense *ius* is the ordering of the law embracing a variety of contexts. Mostly, he believes *ius* refers to the general ordering of the law itself. This seems to parallel Cicognani's schema, in that the objective sense described by Wächter embraces both the formal and the causal sense described by Cicognani. See *Gesetz im kanonischen Recht: eine rechtssprachliche und systematisch-normative Untersuchung zu Grundproblemen der Erfassung des Gesetzes im katholischen Kirchenrecht*, Münchener theologische Studien, III, Kanonistische Abteilung, Bd. 43, St. Otilien, EOS Verlag, 1989.

[20] See CICOGNANI, *Canon Law*, p. 10.

in the subjective sense it is a "right;" in its objective sense *ius* consists of norms for the community that may be *leges*, customs, general administrative norms and other kinds of written norms such as statutes and ordinances.[21]

Both *lex* and *ius* are further delineated in canon law as being universal, particular or special. The difference between universal and particular *lex* is obvious. The scope and formalities of each are outlined in cc. 8, 12 and 13.[22] *Lex specialis* is not so clearly specified. *CIC/83* refers to this term only twice.[23] However, the code also uses *lex peculiaris* that has a connotation similar to *lex specialis*.[24] L. Wächter concludes that the terms *lex peculiaris* and *lex specialis* are used in the same way to describe separate laws for a definite class of people or a community. He sees this demonstrated in factual terms in c. 13, §2, 1° in its application to *peregrini* who are not bound by the particular laws of their own territory unless the laws are personal.[25]

---

[21] J.M. HUELS, "Back to the Future: the Role of Custom in a World Church," in *Proceedings of the Fifty-ninth Annual Convention*, Washington, DC, Canon Law Society of America, Catholic University of America, 1997, p. 7. These concepts and their juridical implications will be further discussed in a later section of this chapter.

[22] Canon 8, §1 prescribes the norms for promulgating *leges ecclesiasticæ universales*; §2 delineates the same for *leges particulares*. Canons 12 and 13 deal with those bound by universal and particular laws.

[23] See OCHOA, *Index verborum*, p. 260. Canon 335 speaks of the *leges speciales* to be observed when the Roman See is vacant or completely impeded; c. 596 refers to the *lex specialis* governing military chaplains. Canon 359 refers to the special law (*lex peculiaris*) that is granted to cardinals; c. 360 cites the *lex peculiaris* that governs the Roman Curia; c. 997 makes reference to the *lex peculiaris Ecclesiæ* concerning indulgences; c. 1403, §1 deals with the *lex peculiaris pontificia* having to do with cases for canonization.

[24] The English translations cited in n. 11 above consistently translate *peculiaris* as "special." Spanish and Italian versions use the word *peculiar/peculiare*, respectively which means unique or special; while the French translation is rendered *particulière*. Its use within the code supports the meaning of "special," that is, a set of laws applicable to a particular juridical institute or circumstance.

[25] See WÄCHTER, *Getsetz im Kanonischen Recht*, p. 15: "Die Begriffe 'lex peculiaris' bzw. 'lex specialis' werden ebenso einheitlich zur Bezeichnung eines Sondergesetzes für bestimmte Personenklassen und Gemeinschaften gebraucht." Wächter gives as examples cc. 359 and 360 that deal with *lex peculiaris* for the college of cardinals when the Apostolic See is vacant or impeded and the structure and competency of the Roman Curia, respectively. He further extends this concept to institutes in citing the *lex peculiaris* for indulgences referred to in c. 997 or for canonization of saints in c. 1403, §1.

Ius parallels *lex* in its universal and particular scope. However, *ius speciale*, found in cc. 20 and 565, poses some difficulty that will be noted in dealing with c. 20.[26]

This preliminary understanding of the terms *ex/de integro* and *lex* and *ius* will be further developed in this study. These concepts will be contexualized by examining cc. 6 and 20 of *CIC/83* and their antecedents, cc. 6 and 22 of *CIC/17* in order to provide insight into integral reordering as a means of abrogating law.

1.2 — CANON 6

In both *CIC/83* and *CIC/17* c. 6 serves an introductory and defining role. Together with the five preceding canons, it establishes the parameters of the codified law. Specifically c. 6 deals with the relationship between the former law and the law contained within the code. It reflects the very purposes of codification, which in turn shed light on the notion of integral reordering.[27]

1.2.1 — Initial codification of ecclesiastical law

The first codification of ecclesiastical law evolved from the need to identify and simplify the *ius vigens* as the Church entered the twentieth century. At the time of the first Vatican Council bishops were already asking Pope Pius IX for both the modification and codification of Church law.[28] In the years preceding the promulgation of *CIC/17* ecclesiastical legislation had become most confusing. Innumerable laws were obsolete; yet these were organized in compilations side by side

---

[26] Canon 565, which deals with appointment of chaplains by the local Ordinary, uses the word *ius* twice. It is translated as "law" and "rights" respectively in the English translations, to convey the broader meaning of the word. The use of the term in this canon differs from that in c. 20.

[27] Some canonists have referred to *CIC/17* as an example of law that has integrally reordered previous law. For example, see A. VAN HOVE, *De legibus ecclesiasticis*, vol. 1, Romae, H. Dessain, 1930, p. 357. This is also true of *CIC/83*. See J. OTADUY, "Introducción: cc. 1-6," in *Comentario exegético al Código de derecho canónico*, vol. 1, obra coordinada y dirigida por A. MARZOA, J. MIRAS and R. RODRÍGUEZ-OSCAÑA, segunda edición, (= *Comentario exegético*), Pamplona, Ediciónes Universidad de Navarra, S.A., 1997, p. 283.

[28] See E. JOMBART, *Manuel de droit canonique conforme au Code de 1917 et aux plus recéntes décisions du Saint-Siége*, Paris, Beauchesne, 1958, p. 20. Jombart explains how the bishops of France, because they found the ecclesiastical laws too numerous, obscure and difficult to know, requested a commission to publish a *Corpus iuris* adapting church law to the present era. This was echoed by German and Italian bishops who demanded some type of collection of the laws in force.

with the *disciplina vigens*. Adding to this disarray was the fact that some laws were arranged chronologically while others were systematically ordered in the same collection.[29]

In response to these problems Pope Pius X in his 1904 Motu proprio, *Arduum sane munus*, called for a compilation of ecclesiastical law, clearly ordered and brought together in one collection suitably adapted to the times.[30] Some thirteen years later this was realized when *CIC/17* was promulgated by the Apostolic Constitution, *Providentissima Mater Ecclesia*.[31] The code that became the *ius vigens* achieved both the primary and secondary purposes outlined by Pius X. It was a systematically ordered collection of ecclesiastical law that abrogated obsolete laws; and it adapted those laws remaining in force to the present time.[32]

While codification was a highlight in the Church's legal history, the legislation it produced was not a new entity per se. Rather the code was a unification of the law already in force, modified and better accommodated to the times.[33] Nonetheless, *CIC/17* did introduce innovations which revised the previous law. It organized and adapted that law to actual necessities and to juridical science.[34] The changes embodied in the code in themselves were neither few nor sparing but, relative to the total codification, the actual modifications comprised only a minor part.[35]

---

[29] See NEUBERGER, *Canon 6*, p. 17. Tracing the existence of a law was a project in itself. Laws could be found in authentic or in private collections. Particular law existed side-by-side with general legislation. It was nearly impossible to discover whether a law had been abrogated or derogated by a later enactment.

[30] See *Arduum sane munus*, in *ASS*, 36, p. 550.

[31] See *Providentissima Mater Ecclesia*, in *AAS*, 9, pp. 5-8.

[32] See A. CRNICA, *Commentarium theoretico - practicum Codicis iuris canonici*, vol. 1, Sibenik, Typis Typographie, 1940, p. 9.

[33] See E. EICHMANN, *Manual de derecho eclesiástico a tenor del Codex juris*, trans. by T. GÓMEZ PIÑÁN, vol. 1, 3rd ed., Barcelona, Librería Bosch, 1931, p. 29.

[34] See L. MIGUÉLEZ DOMINGUEZ, S. ALONSO MORÁN and M. CABREROS DE ANTA, *Código de derecho canónico y legislación complementaria, texto latino y versión castellana, con jurisprudencia y comentarios*, 9th ed., Madrid, Biblioteca de autores cristianos, 1974, p. 6.

[35] See B. OJETTI, *Commentarium in Codicem iuris canonici*, vol. 1, Romae, Apud Aedes Universitatis Gregorianae, 1927, p. 7. The fact that the code brought about relatively little material change should not minimize its impact on the canonical history of the Church. See also M. CABREROS DE ANTA, *Nuevos estudios canónicos*, Victoria, Editorial Eset, 1966, p. 103: "... el año 1917, la máxima de adaptación de la disciplina ecclesiástica que simultáneamente y con un solo acto

1.2.2 — Canon 6, *CIC/17*

Canon 6 of *CIC/17* states:

The Code for the most part retains the discipline previously in force but makes some opportune changes. Thus:

1° All laws, whether universal or particular, that are opposed to the prescriptions of this Code are abrogated unless some other provision is made in favor of particular law;
2° Those canons which restate the old law in its entirety, must be interpreted in accord with the authority of the old law, and therefore according to the interpretations of the approved authors;
3° Those canons which agree with the old law only in part, must be interpreted according to the old law in so far as they agree with it, and in light of their own wording in so far as they differ from the old law;
4° When it is doubtful whether some provisions of the canons of the Code differ from the old law, the former law must be upheld;
5° As regards penalties not mentioned in the Code, whether spiritual or temporal, medicinal or vindictive, as they are called, whether incurred by the act itself, *latae sententiae* or *ferendae sententiae*, they are to be considered as abrogated;
6° If there is anything among other disciplinary laws previously in force, which is neither explicitly nor implicitly contained in this Code, it must be held to have lost all force unless it is found in approved liturgical books or unless it is of divine right, positive or natural.[36]

---

promulgatoria se ha llevado acabo en toda la historia de la Iglesia. Solamente la reforma introducida por el Concilio Tridentino puede compararse con la renovación de la disciplina impuesta por la Constitución Apostólica *'Providentissima Mater Ecclesia'* de Benedicto XVI. La reforma disciplinar del Concilio Tridentino fue más profunda en su fondo o contendido; la renovación producida por el Código de Benedicto XV fue, en cambio, más extensa, más orgánica, más formal que material o sustantivo, sobre todo, por haber adoptado la forma moderna de codificación."

[36] *Codex iuris canonici, Pii X Pontificis Maximi iussu digestus, Benedicti Papae XV auctoritate promulgatus*, Romae, Typis polyglottis Vaticanis, 1917. English translation of canons adapted from AUGUSTINE, *A Commentary on the New Code of Canon Law*, and S.WOYWOD, *A Practical Commentary on the Code of Canon Law*, vol. 1, revised by C. SMITH, New York, NY, J.F. Wagner, 1948. Canon 6: "Codex vigentem huc usque disciplinam plerumque retinet, licet opportunas immutationes afferat. Itaque: 1° Leges quaelibet, sive universales sive particulares, praescriptis huius Codicis oppositae, abrogantur, nisi de particularibus legibus aliud expresse caveatur; 2° Canones qui ius vetus ex integro referunt, ex veteris iuris auctoritate, atque ideo ex receptis apud probatos auctores interpretationibus, sunt aestimandi; 3° Canones qui ex parte tantum cum veteri iure congruunt, qua congruunt, ex iure antiquo aestimandi sunt; qua discrepant, sunt ex sua ipsorum sententia diiudicandi; 4° In dubio num aliquid canonum praescriptum cum veteri iure discrepet, a veteri iure non est recedendum; 5° Quod ad poenas attinet, quarum in Codice nulla fit mentio, spirituales sint vel temporales, medicinales vel, ut vocant, vindicativae, latae vel ferendae sententiae, eae tanquam abrogatae habeantur; 6° Si qua ex ceteris disciplinaribus legibus, quae usque adhuc viguerunt, nec explicite nec implicite in Codice contineatur, ea vim omnem amisisse dicenda est, nisi in probatis liturgicis libris reperiatur, aut lex sit iuris divini sive positivi sive naturalis."

17

This canon reflects both the novelty of the codified law as well as its intent to preserve ecclesiastical discipline. The opening sentence attests to this specifying that the code generally retains the discipline previously in force, while making some changes. The majority of commentators agree that in essence the code materially retained the old law even as it was formally substituted for it. Because *correctio iuris est odiosa*, canonists were quick to point out the stability of law in the newly promulgated code.[37] *CIC/17* was not a transformation of the previous law, but rather flowed from its progressive evolution. It reproduced the old law so as to better understand, perfect and determine it.[38] The *fontes* of *CIC/17* confirm this. Its sources include some 8500 references to the *Decree of Gratian*, 1200 to the ecumenical councils, 4000 to the constitutions of the Roman Pontiffs, more than 11,000 to the Sacred Congregations and 800 to the liturgical books.[39] However, as law must always be adapted to human life, the amelioration of canonical legislation was also evident in the fitting changes which c. 6 introduced.

Most obvious among these innovations was the canon's broad use of abrogation. Neuberger notes that such "wholesale abrogation of laws was unknown" in the Church. While partial revocations existed, they too were seldom utilized. The abrogating scope of c. 6 was unique in the history of ecclesiastical law.[40] Although

---

[37] See J. CREUSEN, "L'abrogation de l'ancien droit," in *Nouvelle revue théologique*, 50 (1923), p. 196.

[38] See F. BLANCO NÁJERA, *Código de derecho canónico traducido y comentado*, vol. 1, Cadiz, Establecimientos Cerón y Libreria Cervantes, S.L., 1942, p. 6.

[39] See M. CABREROS DE ANTA, A. ALONSO LOBO and S. ALONSO MORÁN, *Comentarios al derecho canónico*, vol. 1, Madrid, Biblioteca de Autores Cristianos, 1963, p. 85. See also M. RAMSTEIN, *A Manual of Canon Law*, Hoboken, NJ, Terminal Printing and Publishing Co., 1947, p. 40. Annotated editions of *CIC/17* include approximately 26,000 references to the former law.

[40] See NEUBERGER, *Canon 6*, pp. 2 and 19. Neuberger notes that the *Corpus iuris canonici*, in particular the Gregorian Decretals and the Decretals of Boniface VIII, made the first attempts to abrogate other collections of law. However, widespread abrogation was not part of Church tradition. Abrogation was usually connected with the bull of promulgation of a new law that would revoke former legislation. For other innovations, see CICOGNANI, *Canon Law*, p. 501. In reference to c. 6, 1°, he notes that prior to *CIC/17* abrogation of particular law could only take place if the particular law was explicitly named. See also G. MICHIELS, *Normae generales juris canonici: commentarius libri I Codicis juris canonici*, editio altera, vol. 1, Tournai, Desclée, 1949, p. 127. Michiels explains that *CIC/17* no longer saw "opposition" to law as meaning only the directly contrary; but also, in accord with c. 22, when something totally reordered the matter of the previous law.

it did not include the concept of integral reordering, commentators on the code of 1917 frequently linked c. 22, which included integral reordering, with various segments of c. 6. This will be developed in subsequent discussion.[41]

1.2.3 — Revision of *CIC*

The revised *Code of Canon Law* originated in an historical context different from that of its predecessor. By the middle of the twentieth century the need for renewal was obvious to many, not only of law, but of the Church itself. On 25 January 1959, Pope John XXIII, shortly after assuming the papacy, announced that the *Code of Canon Law* would be revised and that a Roman synod and an ecumenical council would be held.[42] Between this declaration and the promulgation of *CIC/83*, the purposes of the code's renovation were highlighted and clarified by the experience of the Second Vatican Council.

Despite the fact that the legislator kept the format of a code, the differences between *CIC/17* and *CIC/83* are vast.[43] Fundamentally it might be said that *CIC/83*

---

[41] Because commentators frequently linked c. 22 with sections of c. 6, the canon provided a natural context for this concept in c. 6 of *CIC/83*. See, for example, MICHIELS, *Normae generales*, pp. 121 and 127.

[42] JOHN XXIII, Allocution, *Ad Emos Patres Cardinales in urbe praesentes habita*, 25 January 1959, in *AAS*, 51 (1959), pp. 65-69.

[43] See E. CORECCO, "Theological Justifications of the Codification of Canon Law," in M. THÉRIAULT and J. THORN (eds.), *The New Code of Canon Law, Proceedings of the 5th International Congress of Canon Law Organized by Saint Paul University and Held at the University of Ottawa, August 19-25, 1984*, vol. 1, Ottawa, Faculty of Canon Law, Saint Paul University, 1986 (= *Proceedings, 5th International Congress*), pp. 69-71. Corecco cites differences in the purposes of the codifications. In this light he offers suggestions as to why a code might not be the most practical form for ecclesiastical law today. He lists several reasons: the lack of practical need for juridic security that accompanied *CIC/17*, even with the abundant postconciliar legislative documents that followed Vatican II; that *CIC/83* did not intend to give the same scientific structure to church law as did the former code; that *CIC/83* codified more recent laws which had not been tested by experience over a significant period of time; that the revised code did not proceed from a homogeneous model of Church, thus it is difficult to express the laws which proceed from various models in the same form; that *CIC/83* was promulgated in a pluralistic society in an era of transition; and the fact that a code is associated with a European cultural experience. Despite these drawbacks, Corecco acknowledges that there are *post factum* reasons that support the code today. He defines these as the new epistemological criterion, through which theological principles have been more integrated into *CIC/83*, specifically in Books II, III and IV; the constitutional character of the code, in that the universal church embraces the particular churches and reinforces their legislative

effected a material change of law in contrast to the largely formal change brought about by *CIC/17*. Whereas the earlier code actually sought to preserve the existing legislation, *CIC/83* revised the legislation in force.[44]

The revised code can only be understood within the context of the Second Vatican Council. Pope John Paul II in the Apostolic Constitution, *Sacræ disciplinæ leges*, states: "... it is very much hoped that the new canonical legislation will be an effective instrument by the help of which the Church will be able to perfect itself in the spirit of the Second Vatican Council, and show itself ever more equal to carry out its salvific role in the world."[45]

J. Hervada emphasizes that the revised code must be interpreted in constant relation with the conciliar documents. The purpose of *CIC/83*, the light in which its redaction must be understood, is the ordering and structuring of the Church according to the conciliar directives.[46] The code is based not merely on the change of law according to social and cultural conditions but on a change of ecclesiology effected by the Council.[47]

---

autonomy, including less borrowing from Roman and private law; and the importance of the individual member of the faith community highlighted in the juridical system.

[44] See P. LOMBARDÍA and J.I. ARRIETA, *Codice di diritto canonico: edizione bilingue commentata*, vol. 1, Italian ed. by L. CASTIGLIONE, Rome, Logos, 1986-1987, p. 56. See also F.J. URRUTIA, "Il libro I: le norme generali," in J. BEYER et al., *Il nuovo Codice di diritto canonico*, Leumann (Torino), Editrice Elle di CI, 1985, pp. 37-38.

[45] JOHN PAUL II, Apostolic Constitution, *Sacræ disciplinæ leges*, 25 January 1983, in *AAS*, 75, Part II (1983), p. xiii: "Quibus omnibus consideratis, optandum sane est, ut nova canonica legislatio efficax instrumentum evadat, cuius ope Ecclesia valeat se ipsam perficere secundum Concilii Vaticani II spiritum, ac magis magisque parem se præbeat salutifero suo muneri in hoc mundo exsequendo." English translation in the *Code of Canon Law Annotated*, p. 55.

[46] J. HERVADA, *Vetera et nova — cuestiones de derecho canónico y afines (1958-1991)*, vol. 1, Pamplona, Servicio de Publicaciones de la Universidad de Navarra, S.A., 1991: "Ordenar y estructurar la Iglesia según las directrices conciliares: ésta es el fin del nuevo CIC, a cuya luz debe entenderse en constante redacción. Por eso, el nuevo *CIC* debe interpretarse en constante relación con los documentos conciliares." This is echoed by other commentators. See also L. CHIAPPETTA, *Il Codice di diritto canonico: commento giuridico-pastorale*, vol. 1, Roma, Edizioni Dehoniane, 1996, p. 41; R. POTZ, "The Concept and Development of Law according to 1983 *CIC*," in *Concilium*, 185 (1986), p. 15; A. MENDONÇA, "Book I: General Norms, Canons 1-95," in *Letter & Spirit*, p. 5.

[47] See J. HERRANZ, *Studi sulla nuova legislazione della Chiesa*, Milano, Guiffrè Editore, 1990, p. 66. *CIC/83* presents an ecclesiology of communion and co-responsibility. See also J.A. ALESANDRO, "The Revision of the *Code of Canon Law*: A Background Study," in *Studia canonica*, 24 (1990), p. 93-94. At the outset it was not anticipated that the code would depend on the results

The differences between the motivating causes of the two codes has been described by J. Otaduy as a move from "codification" to "reconciliation." Using the word "reconciliation" intentionally but not technically, he maintains:

> ... *CIC/83* has attempted to reconcile, to make congruent, the old legislation with the new, and the new legislation is precisely that of the Council. We will encounter few claims that the new code is exhaustive; there is a codification as is logical, but in a mitigated way ... [*CIC/83* reflects] ... a more improved and balanced system; the choice for simplicity and brevity; the desire to gather the original and basic juridic assumptions of the institutes.[48]

1.2.4 — Canon 6, *CIC/83*

Canon 6 of *CIC/83* states:

> §1. When this Code takes force, the following are abrogated:
> 1° the Code of Canon Law promulgated in 1917;
> 2° other universal or particular laws contrary to the prescripts of this Code, unless other provision is expressly made for particular laws;
> 3° any universal or particular penal laws whatsoever issued by the Apostolic See, unless they are contained in this Code;
> 4° other universal disciplinary laws regarding matter which this Code completely reorders.
> §2. Insofar as they repeat former law, the canons of this Code must be assessed also in accord with canonical tradition.[49]

---

of Vatican II. The two were viewed as somewhat autonomous events, similar to the first Vatican Council and *CIC/17*. However, as the Council unfolded, it became clear that it would be the primary source for the revision of ecclesiastical law. Its pastoral nature would impact the very character of the revised law.

[48] J. OTADUY, "El derecho canónico postconciliar como *ius vetus* (c. 6 §1)," in *Proceedings, 5th International Congress*, p. 117: "... el *C.I.C.* de 1983 ha pretendido conciliar, hacer congruente, la anterior legislación con la nueva, y que la nueva legislación ha sido precisamente la del Concilio. Pocas pretensiones de exhaustividad encontraremos en el nuevo Código; la 'codificatio' existe, como es lógico, pero mitigada. Los motivos de la amortiguación del aspecto codificador son también claros: una sistemática mas perfecta y equilibrada; una opcíon por la sencillez y la brevedad; por último, el fundamentalismo: la voluntad de recoger los presupuestos jurídicos originarios y fundantes de las instituciones."

[49] "§1. Hoc Codice vim obtinente, abrogantur:1° Codex Iuris Canonici anno 1917 promulgatus; 2° aliae quoque lege, sive universales sive particulares, praescriptis huius Codicis contrariae, nisi de particularibus aliud expresse caveatur; 3° leges poenales quaelibet, sive universales sive particulares a Sede Apostolica latae, nisi in ipso hoc Codice recipiantur; 4° ceterae quoque leges disciplinares materiam respicientes, quae hoc Codice ex integro ordinatur. §2. Canones huius Codicis, quatenus ius vetus referunt, aestimandi sunt ratione etiam canonicae traditionis habita."

This canon reflects the purposes of the revised codification. Although §2 affirms a continuity with canonical tradition, §1, which speaks only of abrogation, indicates that a significant change has occurred in the law.[50] Unlike its predecessor, c. 6 is not primarily concerned with safeguarding the existing legislation. This is evident in §1, 1° that abrogates the *Code of Canon Law* of 1917.[51] The overall simplification of c. 6 reinforces the fact that it attempts neither to collect nor to embody all the existing legislation.[52]

1.2.4.1 —In relation to postconciliar laws

Canon 6 does not allude specifically to conciliar/postconciliar legislation, yet the *coetus* which studied and prepared general norms was aware of that dimension in its redaction. At its January 1976 meeting, the proposed draft of what was to become c. 6 included the term *ex integro* in §4. However, a consultor asked that it be removed because of the difficulty in determining whether a given matter was reordered *ex integro* or *ex parte*. This was accepted by the *coetus*.[53] Nevertheless, at its session in May 1979, it was proposed that the phrase *ex integro* be reinserted in c. 6, §1, 4°. The

---

[50] Canon 6 of *CIC/17* combined principles of both abrogation and interpretation of law. Some commentators of the Pio-Benedictine code believe this amalgamation of the two principles weakened the canon. See M. FALCO, *Introduzione allo studio del "Codex iuris canonici,"* Torino, Fratelli Bocca, Editori, 1925, p. 50, n. 1. Canon 6, *CIC/83*, separates these components in two distinct paragraphs.

[51] See *Communicationes*, 14 (1982), p. 129. A member of the *coetus* had suggested eliminating this statement from the canon because of its obvious nature. The other members, however, believed it was necessary to abrogate the former code for clarity, if not in this canon, then in the decree of promulgation. Otherwise the new code would only derogate from what is contrary to the code of 1917. See also OTADUY, "Introducción: cc. 1-6," p. 280. Otaduy notes that the codifiers received a mandate to reform or revise *CIC/17*. Yet, from the formal point of view it is evident that a full substitution of one code for another was produced as the immediate abrogation of *CIC/17* indicates.

[52] *CIC/17* sought to bring together ecclesiastical law in one collection. This was reflected in the prescriptions of c. 6, which elaborated in great detail how laws were included in the code. That this was not the purpose of *CIC/83* is evident in the redaction of c. 6.

[53] See *Communicationes*, 23 (1991), p. 120. The initial draft of canon 6, §1, 4° put forth by the *coetus* read: "Ceterae quoque leges disciplinares quae materias respiciunt quae hoc Codice ex integro ordinantur." "Ill.mus sextus Consultor ... quaerit ut expressio «ex integro», n. 4, tollatur ne difficultates stabiliendi quod ex integro est vel ex parte oriantur. (Placet)."

motion was not accepted because the formula was deemed broader without the addition.[54]

At the meeting of the Code Commission in October 1981, as the revision neared completion, the view was expressed that the formulation of the canon was more radical than *CIC/17* especially in light of the abundance of postconciliar legislation. One member recommended that another paragraph be added, similar to what was expressed in §2, but specifically in regard to the decrees of Vatican II. In response to this, the Secretary of the Commission clarified that §1, 4° was such a transitional norm. In effect it reiterated the general principle of c. 20 (c. 22, *CIC/17*) that would be valid for all law even if it were not mentioned specifically in c. 6. However, to remove doubts, it was agreed to insert the expression *ex integro* after the phrase *hoc Codice*.[55]

Canon 6 of *CIC/83* reflects the purpose of the code itself: to bring about a renewal of discipline in the spirit of Vatican Council II. Likewise, it reconciles new legislation with the former law. While not maintaining that the code presents a comprehensive collection of the law, the canon defines the parameters of the *ius vigens*.

---

[54] See *Communicationes*, 23 (1991), pp. 145-146: "Rev.mus primus Consultor proponit sequentem textum: «materias respicientes quae in hoc Codice ex integro ordinantur.» Tamen suffragatione peracta (3 contra 6), additio verbi «ex integro» non admittitur. Rev.mus Secretarius Ad. proponit ut loco «ex integro» dicatur «quatenus hoc Codice ordinatur», sed propositio reicitur quia formula sine additione amplior est."

[55] See *Communicationes*, 14 (1982), pp. 130-131: "§1, n. 4 nimis videtur generalis et radicalior quam Codex a. 1917 qui abrogat praecedentem legislationem. Saltem relate ad decreta Conc. Vat. II alia desideratur § in quo similis norma ac in § 2 statuatur .... §1, n. 4 est simplex applicatio, tamquam norma transitoria, praescripti generalis canonis 20 (= can. 33 C.I.C.), quod praescriptum valet pro omni lege, etiam si in can. 6 non statueretur. Ad omne tamen fugandum dubium, addatur post «hoc Codice» locutio «ex integro». Notetur quod Codex vigens severior est, nam abrogat omnes leges universales disciplinares praeter legem («...quae ... nec explicite nec implicite in Codice contineantur»: can 6, n. 6 C.I.C.). Prae oculis vero habeatur quod praescriptum Schematis (quod ex natura ipsa rei profluit, ob necessariam certitudinem iuridicam), tantum respicit leges disciplinares, quarum materia ex integro in Codice ordinatur (n. 4) aut ipsi sint contrariae (n. 2) ..."

1.2.4.2 — Role in code

Canon 6 establishes the criteria to be applied to laws which existed before the promulgation of the new code. It delineates the *ius vigens* by specifying what is abrogated and prescribing how to interpret the contents of the new code in conformity with the previous law. That its focus is to bring forth something new is clear. Paragraph 1 succinctly lists four categories of law no longer in force: the *Code of Canon Law* of 1917; other universal or particular laws contrary to the provisions of the code, unless in the case of particular law the code prescribes otherwise; all penal laws enacted by the Apostolic See unless they are restated in the code; and any other universal disciplinary laws whose subject matter has been integrally reordered by the code.[56]

Paragraph two notes that, to the extent that canons in *CIC/83* reproduce the former Code, they are to be assessed in light of canonical tradition. This statement, which simplifies c. 6, nn. 2 - 4 of *CIC/17*, represents a significant change. For the text of *CIC/83* is qualified by the word *etiam*.[57] Thus even canons in the revised code that are identical to those in *CIC/17* might be interpreted differently in light of the teachings of Vatican II.[58]

Canon 6, §2, unlike its predecessor, does not delineate how the *ius vetus* might be contained in the canons of the code. Paragraph 2 maintains that recourse to canonical tradition is obligatory, yet it states this in a way quite different from that mandated in the former code. For assessing a law in light of the *traditio canonica* is

---

[56] See L. ÖRSY, "Book I, General Norms (cc. 1-203)," in *CLSA Commentary*, p. 28. Örsy states that by implication the following laws remain in force and continue to bind: all universal and particular laws not contrary to the code; and all particular norms contrary to the code, provided the code itself grants them exception.

[57] The prescriptions of c. 6 of *CIC/17* stated that canons which referred to the *ius vetus ex integro* were to be interpreted in accord with the authority of the ancient law and also in light of approved authors; canons which agreed with the former law *ex parte* were to be interpreted according to the *ius vetus* in the parts in which they agree; and whenever it was doubtful whether a canon differed from the *ius vetus* the former law was to be upheld. However, c. 6, §2 of *CIC/83* simplifies this by stating that to the extent the canons refer to the *ius vetus* they are also to be assessed in light of *canonica traditio*.

[58] See *Code of Canon Law Annotated*, p. 83, (translator's note).

much broader than interpreting it in regard to the authority of the *ius vetus* and the *auctores probati* called for in c. 6, 2° of *CIC/17*. The *traditio canonica* of c. 6, §2 of *CIC/83* embraces not only the historical, classical and current law but also the many commentaries on the first codified law.[59]

1.2.4.3 — Scope and contextual understanding

"Although c. 6 speaks only of *leges*, the purpose of the canon and the circumstances of its development allow one reasonably to conclude that it is not speaking of law (*lex*) in a strict sense, but of all written norms proceeding from ecclesiastical power."[60] This is borne out in the *coetus*' discussion regarding this canon. The 1976 draft of canon 6, §1, nn. 2 and 4 referred to *leges... sive universales sive particulares* and *leges disciplinares* respectively. The *coetus*, however, agreed to replace *leges* with *normae* so that a broad rather than strict interpretation of law would be understood.[61] Yet, by the time of the 1980 schema of the revised code, the word *leges* had been restored.[62] However, there is no further indication that the *coetus* considered that the understanding of *leges* was to be strictly interpreted. Rather discussions imply the broader understanding of the term in light of the decrees of Vatican II and the postconciliar legislation which followed it.[63]

With the exception of penal law, c. 6 outlines two ways for the abrogation of universal disciplinary law: contrariety to the provisions of the code and the integral reordering of the subject matter of a law by the code. L. Örsy interprets "laws contrary to the prescriptions of this code" as those in "clear conflict" with its norms

---

[59] See OTADUY, "Introducción: cc. 1-6," p. 287.

[60] Ibid., pp. 279-280: "Aunque el c. 6 dice siempre 'leyes' a finalidad del canon y las circunstancias de su elaboración permiten inducir razonablemente que no ser está hablando de ley en sentido estricto, sino de todas aquellas normas escritas procedentes de la potestad eclesiástica."

[61] See *Communicationes*, 23 (1991), p. 120: "Rev.mi secundus, quartus et primus Consultores postulant ut in n. 2 et n. 4 loco «leges» dicatur «normae», ita ut etiam quae stricte formaliter leges non sunt comprehendantur. Quod placet aliis."

[62] See PONTIFICIA COMMISSIO CODICI IURIS CANONICI RECOGNOSCENDO, *Codex iuris canonici: schema Patribus commissionis reservatum*, Romae, Città del Vaticano, Libreria editrice Vaticana, 1980, p. 4.

[63] See *Communicationes*, 14 (1982), p. 131.

and "integrally reordered laws" as those whose "subject matter has been entirely revised" by *CIC/83*.[64] However, most commentators do not deal with the distinction between contrariety and integral reordering in treating this canon; often they reference c. 20 for information.[65] In line with this, these ways of tacit revocation will be further examined in light of c. 20.

Both direct contrariety and integral reordering are especially urgent in light of postconciliar legislation for they are the means for clarifying the *ius vigens*. More than 400 documents of various natures and forms containing juridic or parajuridic matters were issued between the end of the Second Vatican Council and the promulgation of *CIC/83*. The many norms in these documents surpass the volume of the code several times.[66] While c. 6, §1, 2° revokes those laws that are contrary to the code, c. 6, §1, 4° declares that those universal disciplinary laws are abrogated whose matter has been integrally reordered by the code. Thus all universal disciplinary laws which are not contrary to the code maintain their force unless their matter has been integrally reordered by the code.[67]

1.2.5 — Canon 6, *CCEO*

Having referred to the simplification of c. 6 in *CIC/83*, it is noteworthy that the canon has been even further simplified in the *Code of Canons of the Eastern Churches*.[68] Canon 6 of *CCEO*, which parallels cc. 5 and 6 of *CIC/83*, states:

---

[64] See ÖRSY, "General Norms," p. 28.
[65] See, for example, OTADUY, "Introducción: cc. 1-6," p. 281. Otaduy speaks of direct contrariety as the sole means of implicit revocation of particular law but does not define what contrariety means. See also CHIAPPETTA, *Il Codice di diritto canonico*, pp. 41-42; URRUTIA, "Il libro I: le norme generali," p. 13; and MENDONÇA, "Book I: General Norms, Canons 1-95," p. 5.
[66] See OTADUY, "El derecho canónico postconciliar," p. 115.
[67] See ibid., p. 117.
[68] *Codex canonum Ecclesiarum orientalium, Ioannis Pauli PP. II auctoritate promulgatus*, Vatican City, Typis Polyglottis Vaticanis, 1990. English translation prepared under the auspices of the CLSA, Washington, DC, CLSA, 1992. English translation of canons are derived from this source.

Once this Code goes into effect:

1° all common or particular laws are abrogated, which are contrary to the canons of the Code or which pertain to a matter *ex integro* regulated in the Code;
2° all customs are revoked which are reprobated by the canons of this Code or which are contrary to them and are neither centenary nor immemorial.[69]

The formulation of this canon, in the seven year time span between the promulgations of the two codes, emphasizes the importance of integral reordering as a means of abrogation for the Eastern Churches, not only in dealing with the postconciliar legislation, but also in the clarification of the *ius vigens* for each church *sui iuris*.

The terminology of the canon expands the use of integral reordering as a means of abrogation of law in the Eastern Churches. Canon 6, 1° speaks of *leges* of the *ius commune* and *ius particulare* that are abrogated. Like the Latin code, it refers to *lex*. However, also like the Latin code, an earlier schema of the canon indicated a broader understanding of law in speaking of the abrogation of *leges ac normae*.[70] In addition, the phrase "*quae materiam respiciunt in Codice ex integro ordinatam*" is much more encompassing than the comparatively restrictive application of integral reordering to "*leges disciplinares universales*" in c. 6, §1, 4° of *CIC/83*.[71] Moreover, in the Eastern code, unlike *CIC/83*, the integral reordering of a matter can abrogate particular law,[72] except for those areas referred to in cc. 3, 4 and 5.[73] Acknowledging

---

[69] "Codice vim obtinente: 1° abrogatae sunt omnes leges iuris communis vel iuris particularis, quae sunt canonibus Codicis contrariae aut quae materiam respiciunt in Codice ex integro ordinatam; 2° revocatae sunt omnes consuetudines, quae canonibus Codicis reprobantur aut quae contrariae sunt nec centenariae vel immemorabiles."

[70] See *Nuntia*, 19 (1984), p. 21: "Hoc Codice vim obtinente, abrogatae sunt omnes leges ac normae a quacumque Auctoritatae editae quae materias respiciunt quae hoc Codice ordinantur."

[71] See F.J. URRUTIA, "Canones praeliminares Codicis (CIC). Comparatio cum canonibus praeliminaribus Codicis canonum Ecclesiarum orientalium (CC)," in *Periodica*, 81 (1992), pp. 169-171: "Canon CC etiam sonat multo simplicior quam canon CIC: leges enim praecodiciales abrogat omnes '*canonibus Codicis contraria[s]*;' et, inter non contrarias, eas quae respiciunt materiam in Codice ex integro ordinatum .... Quod leges '*quae materiam respiciunt in Codice ex integro ordinatam*', discrimen notatur quatenus CIC has leges qualificat, amplitudinem abrogationis restringendo, '*leges disciplinares universales*'."

[72] Canon 1493 of CCEO provides a definition of common and particular law: "§1. Beyond the laws and legitimate customs of the universal law, this Code also includes by the designation 'common law' the laws and legitimate customs common to all Eastern Churches. §2. Included in the

the Eastern and Latin codes as two distinct entities, it is obvious that *CCEO* applies the concept of integral reordering more extensively than does *CIC/83*.

1.3 — CANON 20

Canon 6 of *CIC/83* as an introductory and defining canon is especially important in assessing the *ius vigens* of the postconciliar period before the promulgation of *CIC/83*. Its counterpart c. 20 takes on a similar role in regard to post-code legislation. Canon 20 is located in Title I of General Norms, *De legibus ecclesiasticis*, which provides fundamental rules governing ecclesiastical law. The canon states:

> A later law abrogates, or derogates from, an earlier law if it states so expressly, is directly contrary to it, or completely reorders the entire matter of the earlier law. A universal law, however, in no way derogates from a particular or special law unless the law expressly provides otherwise.[74]

It parallels c. 22 of *CIC/17*, which it reiterates with minor changes, dealing with the revocation of law, its stipulations and extent.

1.3.1 — Source of the canon

At the time of the initial codification of ecclesiastical law, the Church relied on the structure of civil codes already established.[75] Canon 22 of *CIC/17* reads:

---

designation 'particular law' are all the laws, legitimate customs, statutes and other norms of law which are not common to the universal Church nor to all the Eastern Churches."

[73] See J.D. FARIS, *Eastern Catholic Churches: Constitution and Governance According to the Code of Canons of the Eastern Churches*, New York, Saint Maron Publications, 1992, p. 114. Canons 3, 4 and 5 treat liturgical matters; agreements between the Apostolic See and nations or political societies; and acquired rights and privileges, respectively.

[74] "Lex posterior abrogat priorem aut eidem derogat, si id expresse edicat aut illi sit directe contraria, aut totam de integro ordinet legis prioris materiam; sed lex universalis minime derogat iuri particulari aut speciali, nisi aliud in iure expresse caveatur."

[75] This was in accord with ecclesiastical tradition that since earliest times has incorporated concepts from civil legal systems, especially from Roman law. Much of the material in Book I of both *CIC/17* and *CIC/83* has parallels in secular systems.

A later law given by the competent authority obrogates an earlier one if it expressly says so or if it is directly contrary to it, or wholly reorders the subject matter of the older law; however, canon 6, 1° of this Code remains in force, that is to say, a general law in no way derogates from the law in force in particular places or with regard to particular persons unless the contrary is expressly provided therein.[76]

The first part of the canon was borrowed nearly verbatim from Article V on the "Dispositions of Publications" of the Italian Civil Code which stated, "Laws are not abrogated except by later laws by express declaration of the legislator, either because of the disagreement of the new dispositions with those preceding, or because the new law regulates entirely a matter already regulated by the prior law."[77] While c. 22 introduced the concept of integral reordering into ecclesiastical legislation, commentators were quick to point out that integral reordering had been used as a means of abrogation throughout the history of the Church. The principle was borrowed because it reflected what already was the experience of the Church in regard to the ways in which laws are revoked [78]

---

[76] "Lex posterior, a competenti auctoritate lata obrogat priori, si id expresse edicat, aut sit illi directe contraria, aut totam de integro ordinet legis prioris materiam; sed firmo praescripto can. 6, 1°, lex nullatenus derogat locorum specialium et personarum singularium statutis nisi aliud in ipsa expresse caveatur."

[77] See CICOGNANI, *Canon Law*, p. 643. Also cited in J. OTADUY, "De las normas generales: Título I de las leyes eclesiásticas," in *Comentario exegético*, pp. 400-401: "Le leggi non sono abrogate che da leggi posteriori per dichiarazione espressa del legislatore, o per incompatibilità tra le nuove disposizioni e le precedenti o perchè la nuova legge regola l'intera materia già regolata dalla legge anteriore."

[78] See VAN HOVE, *De legibus ecclesiasticis*, pp. 352 and 355. The principle of integral reordering, new in *CIC/17*, is consonant with the nature of ecclesiastical law. It is a determination of the more general principle *"Lex posterior derogat priori,"* put forth by Boniface VIII in the *Sexto*, c. I, *de constitutionibus*, I, 2. See also J.A. MARTINS, *Instituiçoes de direito canónico*, 3rd ed., Braga, Escola Tip. De Oficiana de S. José, 1955, pp. 70-71.This canon of the Sexto presumes the legislator is aware of all general laws that have been promulgated *in scrino pectoris*. Consequently when he promulgates a norm contrary to or irreconcilable with a former law, it is presumed that he has revoked it. See also C. BERUTTI, *Institutiones iuris canonici*, vol. 1, Taurini, Romae, Marietti, 1936, p. 95-96. Berutti refers to c. 106 of *CIC/17* as an example of integral reordering that completely revises the *ius* regarding precedence of persons in the Church; consequently the norms previously in force were abrogated.

1.3.2 — Simplification of terms

Canon 20 of *CIC/83* reflects the overall efforts of the Code Commission to simplify terminology throughout the code. Despite its basic similarity with c. 22 of *CIC/17*, the changes it embodies are important to note.

1.3.2.1 — Abrogation and derogation

An obvious example to clarify language is the replacement of the word *obrogare* used in c. 22 of *CIC/17* with the clearer terms *abrogare* and *derogare* in the present code. Abrogation denotes total revocation of a law; derogation is used when the revocation is partial.[79] Frequently found in *CIC/17*, *obrogare* alluded to the substitution of one law for another. In the revision process the word disappeared from the terminology on the revocation of law.[80] Although some commentators on *CIC/17* noted differences between the two terms, many considered *obrogare* as used in c. 22 to be synonymous with *abrogare*.[81]

1.3.2.2 — *Ius speciale*

The Code Commission, in redacting c. 22 of *CIC/17*, also simplified the language of the final clause. The last part of c. 20, *CIC/83* states that a universal law does not derogate from particular or special laws.[82] However, as alluded to previously, this specification has posed some difficulties in its interpretation.

---

[79] See *Communicationes*, 14 (1982), p. 131.

[80] See OTADUY, "De las normas generales: título I," p. 401. The word *obrogare* is still retained in *CIC/83* in cc. 53 and 1739 in reference to administrative acts.

[81] See CICOGNANI, *Canon Law*, p. 629. Cicognani explains abrogation as total revocation; derogation as partial revocation; subrogation as something added to an existing law; and obrogation as the change of a law by a contrary law. However, he believes that in c. 22 the word *obrogare* is synonymous with *abrogare*. See also R. NAZ (ed.), *Dictionnaire de droit canonique*, vol. 1, Paris, Letouzey et Ané, 1935-1965, p. 116; and F. BLANCO NÁJERA, *Código de derecho canónico traducido y comentado*, vol. 1, Cadiz, Establecimientos Cerón y Liberia Cervantes, S.L., 1942, p. 40.

[82] The phrase "iuri particulari aut speciali" of c. 20, *CIC/83* replaced the words "locorum specialium et personarum singularium statutis" used in c. 22, *CIC/17*.

Canon 20 states that *"lex universalis minime derogat iuri particulari aut speciali, nisi aliud in iure expresse caveatur."* Yet when *lex specialis/peculiaris* or *ius speciale* is used in other places in the code it appears that a universal law could indeed derogate from the *lex specialis/ius speciale*.[83] For "special law" can be particular as well as universal. A survey of the work of the *coetus* preparing this section of the code provides no additional insight into the specific meaning of *ius speciale* in c. 20.[84]

Debate centers on whether *ius speciale* of c. 20 is to be equated with *locorum specialium et personarum singularium statutis* of c. 22 of the 1917 code. However, the use of the conjunction *aut* in the present text clearly distinguishes the term from particular law.[85] F. Urrutia and Otaduy entertain possible interpretations of the use of *ius speciale* in c. 20.[86] Urrutia notes that it is equated at times with the *ius proprium* of juridic persons (*universitates personarum* or *universitates rerum*).[87] However, Otaduy argues that if this were the case the legislator would have used the terms *statuta* or *ius proprium*. This perspective maintains that *ius speciale* does not allude to the statutes of juridic persons referred to in c. 94 precisely because the canon omits any reference to persons or statutes.[88] Otaduy proposes that the use of *ius speciale* has to do with a unique type of juridical matter. He contends that the term, unlike its

---

[83] See OCHOA, *Index verborum,* pp. 252 and 304. The use of *ius peculiare* sheds little light on this issue. The terms *ius peculiare/norma iuris peculiaris* are used nine times in regard to synodal law in cc. 346, §§ 1(twice), 2 and 3; 344, §§ 2, 3; 348, §1; and 349. See also WÄCHTER, *Gesetz im kanonischen Recht*, p. 32. Wächter concurs that *ius peculiare/speciale* is not used unambiguously in the code. He notes that this term was not found at all in the 1980 schema of *CIC/83*.

[84] The 1977 schema read: "... derogat locorum iuri particulari nec personarum specialibus statutis ..." By the time of the 1980 schema this had been modified to "... derogat iuri particulari nec specialibus statutis ..." The 1981 schema contains the redaction which ultimately became canon 20 of *CIC/83*: "... derogat iure particulari aut speciali ..."

[85] The final clause of c. 20 refers to "iuri particulari *aut* speciali." The use of *aut* indicates that these are two distinct categories of law.

[86] See F.J. URRUTIA, "De quibusdam quaestionibus ad librum primum Codicis pertinentibus," in *Periodica*, 73 (1984), pp. 298-300 and OTADUY, "De las normas generales: título I," pp. 405-407.

[87] See URRUTIA, "De quibusdam quaestionibus, " p. 300.

[88] The final part of canon 22 of *CIC/17* reads: "... lex generalis nullatenus derogat locorum specialium et personarum singularum statutis, nisi aliud in ipsa expresse caveatur." The last clause of canon 20 omits any reference to persons or statutes.

other uses in the code, describes a special kind of juridical matter not about categories of persons, institutes, or territory. Such a juridic entity would require an express indication of revocation rather than being affected by a more abstract and general law.[89]

While the term *ius speciale* is not totally clear in c. 20, the change from "statutes" in c. 22 of *CIC/17* to *ius speciale* in its counterpart in *CIC/83* could indicate that the legislator intended a broader meaning than statutes. In that case *ius speciale* could refer not only to the written laws of a juridic person, but to its legal customs, as well.

CCEO avoids this difficulty by omitting the concept of *ius speciale* in c. 1502, the parallel of c. 20 *CIC/83*. It states:

> §1. A later law abrogates a former law or derogates from it if it expressly states so, if it is directly contrary to it, or if it entirely re-orders the subject matter of the former law.
> §2. A prescription of common law, unless the law expressly provides otherwise, does not derogate from a particular law nor does a norm of particular law enacted for a Church *sui iuris* derogate from a more particular norm in force in that same Church.[90]

Thus it reiterates the methods of revocation put forth in c. 20 of *CIC/83*. *CCEO* does, however, retain the term *lex specialis* in other canons.[91]

1.3.3 — Cessation of law

Canon 20 pertains to the revocation of law. Laws cease to bind in various ways. L. Chiappetta notes that merely ecclesiastical laws, like any human laws, have

---

[89] See OTADUY, "De las normas generales: título I," pp. 406-407. Although Otaduy provides no examples, this could refer to some special laws such as unpublished norms that regulate the internal administration of the various dicasteries of the Roman Curia.

[90] "§ 1. Lex posterior abrogat priorem aut eidem derogat, si id expresse edicit aut si illi est directe contraria aut totam de integro ordinat legis prioris materiam. §2. Lex iuris communis vero, nisi aliter in ipsa lege expresse cavetur, non derogat legi iuris particularis nec lex iuris particularis pro aliqua Ecclesia sui iuris lata derogat iuri magis particulari in eadem Ecclesia vigenti."

As noted in discussing c. 6 of *CCEO* above, particular law includes all laws, legitimate customs and other norms of law that are not common to the universal Church nor to all the Eastern churches. Thus particular law would include the concept of *ius speciale* in its various interpretations.

[91] See, for example, *CCEO*, c. 47, which parallels c. 335, *CIC/83*.

a stable character, but are not absolutely unchangeable. While the Church has always valued the stability of law, nevertheless, as doctrine unfolds and evolves, so too laws can be modified and cease.[92]

A law ceases to bind in two ways: intrinsically by the termination of the purpose of the law; and extrinsically through revocation by the legislator or by contrary customs.[93] The code does not treat cessation *ab intrinseco* per se. This occurs when a law becomes positively harmful, unreasonable or is injurious to fundamental ecclesiastical rights; or, if the law is morally impossible to observe; or, if due to changed circumstances, its purpose has ceased for all or a major part of the community.[94] Likewise, c. 20 considers neither cases of singular cessation which result from natural excusing causes such as ignorance, doubt or *epikeia,* nor reasons, such as privileges and dispensations, brought about by singular administrative acts.[95]

---

[92] See CHIAPPETTA, *Il Codice di diritto canonico,* p. 72. See also L. ÖRSY, *Theology and Canon Law: New Horizons for Legislation and Interpretation,* Collegeville, Minnesota, A Michael Glazier Book, The Liturgical Press, 1992. Örsy reiterates this progression in outlining the life cycle of a human law: it is conceived, born, lives and dies or fades away. The death or cessation of the law can be by abrogation or derogation. It could also occur through custom or desuetude when the law is judged unnecessary by the people of God. See pp. 40-42.

[93] See F. DELLA ROCCA, *Manual of Canon Law,* translated by A. THATCHER, Milwaukee, The Bruce Publishing Company, 1959, p. 69. See also F.M. CAPPELLO, *Summa iuris canonici in usum scholarum concinnata,* 4th ed., vol. 1, Romae, Apud Aedes Universitatis Gregorianae, 1945, pp. 78-79. The schema of cessation of law used by some commentators can be quite detailed, listing various modes of cessation of law. In addition to *ab intrinseco/ab extrinseco,* Cappello subdivides cessation into absolute and relative or *ex integro* or *ex parte* and the ceasing of the law's obligation and the ceasing of the law itself. These classifications are intermingled in numerous possibilities for the cessation of law. See also CABREROS DE ANTE, *Comentarios al Código de derecho canónico,* pp. 169-170 and E.F. REGATILLO, *Institutiones iuris canonici,* vol. 1, Santander, Sal Terrae, 1941, pp. 67-68. For the purposes of this work, the classification of *ab intrinseco* and *ab extrinseco* with some qualifications will suffice. However, it should be noted that laws that cease *ab intrinseco* still remain "on the books" as laws.

[94] See CHIAPPETTA, *Il Codice di diritto canonico,* p. 72 and T.L. BOUSCAREN, A.C. ELLIS and F.N. KORTH, *Canon Law: A Text and Commentary,* 4th rev. ed., Milwaukee, The Bruce Publishing Company, 1966, p. 36.

[95] See OTADUY, "De las normas generales: título I," p. 399.

1.3.3.1 — Express revocation

Canon 20 of *CIC/83*, like its antecedent c. 22 of *CIC/17*, deals only with cessation of law *ab extrinseco*, that is, repeal by the competent legislator.[96] Express revocation is the first of the three means of abrogation put forth in the canon. Revocation is express when it is stated as such by the legislator. Abrogation or derogation can be decreed in unequivocal words as is obvious in c. 6, §1, 1° which abrogates the code of 1917; or, as is more commonly the case, through a generic clause. While a general formula abrogates universal laws, even particular or special laws may be repealed if the provision so specifies.[97] Canon 6, §1, 2° exemplifies this in abrogating universal or particular laws contrary to the code, unless the particular laws are expressly provided for.

1.3.3.2 — Tacit revocation

Canon 20 presents two additional ways by which the legislator can revoke a law: direct contrariety with a former law or the integral reordering of the subject matter of an earlier law. Canonists have traditionally categorized these two as means of tacit or implicit revocation by the legislator.[98] J. Arias Gomez describes revocation

---

[96] See OTADUY, "De las normas generales: título I," p. 399. Although revocation assumes by definition the power of the legislator, the legislator is not in the strict sense the "master of the law." A law is also influenced by the community for which it is intended, by judges and administrators, by the doctrine that interprets it, and by the other norms that accompany it. However, it is ultimately the legislator who has the power to determine or revoke the law's force.

[97] See J.A. ABBO and J.D. HANNAN, *The Sacred Canons, A Concise Presentation of the Current Disciplinary Norms of the Church*, rev. ed., vol. 1, St. Louis, MO, B. Herder Book Co., 1957, pp. 45-46. A phrase such as "non obstante quacumque lege vel consuetudine in contrarium faciente" would abrogate particular and special *ius*.

[98] See, for example, DELLA ROCCA, *Manual of Canon Law*, p. 69: "Tacit abrogation is indicated when the new law is incompatible with a preceding one either because it is contrary to it, or because it takes up and entirely reorders the subject matter of the old law." Likewise, CABREROS DE ANTE, *Comentarios al Código de derecho canónico*, pp. 170-171, speaks of tacit revocation by direct contrariety or by integral reordering of the subject matter of a law. Similar descriptions of tacit revocation are given by many commentators, including CICOGNANI, *Canon Law*, p. 629; CAPPELLO, *Summa iuris canonici*, p. 45; CHIAPPETTA, *Il Codice di diritto canonico*, p. 73 and F.J.URRUTIA, *Les normes générales: commentaire des canons 1-203*, Paris, Éditions Tardy, 1992, pp. 73-74. However, MICHIELS, *Normae generales*, p. 654, uses the word "implicit" but acknowledges that some commentators call this means of revocation "tacit." He states: "Vi hujus canonis revocatio legis, sive totalis sit sive partialis, *vel directa est seu explicita*, cum scilicet legislator voluntatem revocandi

as implicit, in the same sense that other commentators use tacit, "when the content of the past law is suppressed by incompatibility with the suppositions of the new law."[99] He then proceeds to outline the ways in which this incompatibility is brought about by the later law: by direct contrariety with the past law or by the integral reordering of its subject matter.[100] Yet the distinction between these two modes is not absolute. Some commentators describe *directe contraria* as incompatibility and do not apply the term "incompatible" to integral reordering.[101] Urrutia, for example, notes that the Italian Civil Code, on which the canon is based, used the word *incompatibilità* for *directly contrary* and because of this he equates direct contrariety with incompatibility.[102]

---

expresse manifestat per verba aperte vel aequivalenter revocatoria, vel *indirecta seu implicita* (quae a quibusdam dicitur tacita), cum legislator, expressa voluntatis revocandi mentione omissa, factum ponit quod revocationem virtualiter includit."

Most commentators of *CIC/83* use neither "tacit" nor "implicit" but describe the three modes of revocation as express, direct contrariety with a former law, and the integral reordering of the subject matter of a law. See, for example, MENDONÇA, "Book I: General Norms, Canons 1-95," p. 20; ÖRSY, "General Norms," p. 38; and OTADUY, "De las normas generales: título I," pp. 402-404. It should be noted that Otaduy, while not applying the word "tacit" or "implicit" to revocation by direct contrariety or integral reordering, uses "implicit" to describe express revocation done by the legislator through a generic clause rather than the explicit referral to the past law. GLARE, in the *Oxford Latin Dictionary*, pp. 847 and 1921 cites distinct meanings for *"implicite"* and *"tacite."* *Tacite* includes the definition "without express statement." *Implicite* is explained as "in a complicated or confused manner." However, the entries of present day English dictionaries see the terms as synonymous with each other. See, for example, *Webster's Third New International Dictionary* and *Funk's New Standard Dictionary*. It is important to note that there is not general agreement among commentators of *CIC/17* or *CIC/83* on the use of "tacit" and "implicit." Throughout this work, the word "tacit" will be applied to revocation by the legislator which is not expressly given, unless the author being cited uses the word "implicit."

[99] J. ARIAS GOMEZ, "Revocación, irretroactividad y derechos adquiridos," in *Ius canonicum*, 21 (1981), p. 724: "La revocacíon es implícita cuando el contenido de la ley anterior se suprime por incompatibilidad con el supuesto de hecho de la nueva ley."

[100] See ARIAS GOMEZ, "Revocación, irretroactividad y derechos adquiridos," p. 724.

[101] See OTADUY, "De las normas generales: título I," pp. 403-404. See also CHIAPPETTA, *Il Codice diritto canonico,* p. 44; MENDONÇA, "Book I: General Norms, Canons 1-95," p. 20; CABREROS DE ANTA, *Comentarios al Código de derecho canónico*, p. 170; CICOGNANI, *Canon Law*, p. 631. Cicognani notes that the incompatibility must be evident.

[102] See F.J. URRUTIA, *De normis generalibus adnotationes in Codicem: liber I*, Romae, Pontificia Universitas Gregoriana, 1983, p. 21. However, in a later work Urrutia states that direct contrariety is when two norms, an earlier and a later, cannot be observed at the same time. See URRUTIA, *Les normes générales*, p. 74.

Commentators on *CIC/17* expanded this notion of revocation by a contrary law by speaking of direct and indirect contrariety.[103] However, even before the promulgation of *CIC/83* the meaning of indirect contrariety was being questioned.[104] Since the promulgation of the revised code, all incompatibility is considered as contradiction.[105]

A succinct description of *directe contraria* is provided by Örsy who understands this notion as the diametric opposition between a former and a later law. As such they cannot coexist as a guide for the community.[106] This explanation avoids using the generic description of tacit revocation as "incompatible" for the specific way in which incompatibility is accomplished through direct contrariety. Thus, direct contrariety, understood in the sense of diametric opposition, will be helpful in seeing this means of revocation in light of its counterpart. For integral reordering likewise implies an incompatibility, though at times less obvious, with the former law.[107]

Otaduy points out that revocation by a contrary law is relatively similar to express revocation by means of a general revocatory clause. Both are not total revocations, for both derogate only that which is opposed to their prescriptions. The

---

[103] See MICHIELS, *Normae generales*, pp. 656-657. The contradiction is considered "direct" between two laws of the same kind and the same extent; "indirect" contrariety occurs when the new law is opposed to the former only obliquely, that is, the object of both is formally diverse but they maintain between them a certain connection of effective dependency. See also VAN HOVE, *De legibus*, p. 353 and A. VERMEERSCH and J. CREUSEN, *Epitome iuris canonici cum commentariis ad scholas et ad usum privatum*, 8th ed., revised by A. BERGH and I. RECO, Museum Lessianum, Section Théologique, no. 5, Mechliniae, H. Dessain, 1963, p. 151.

[104] See ARIAS GOMEZ, "Revocación, irretroactividad y derechos adquiridos," p. 725.

[105] See OTADUY, "De las normas generales: título I," p. 402: "Si la contrariedad se entiende efectivamente como incompatibilidad no parece que valga la pena discutir, como hace buena parte de la doctrina, sobre el carácter directo o indirecto que debe tener la contrariedad: toda incompatibilidad es contradicción directa."

[106] See ÖRSY, "General Norms," p. 38.

[107] This research supports the theory that when c. 22 was introduced canonists, while attributing integral reordering of law to juridic institutes (as will be further discussed), felt more comfortable in seeing tacit revocation in terms of that which was "directly contrary." This could explain why a more elaborate scheme of the understanding of contrariety was developed. It will be demonstrated how the concept of tacit revocation was broadened and a greater emphasis was put on integral reordering in light of the documents of the Second Vatican Council and the many postconciliar juridic documents that implemented them.

key difference between revocation by a contrary law and by an express general revocatory clause is that the former cannot affect the derogation of particular law.[108]

The other means of tacit revocation put forth in c. 20 is the integral reordering of the subject matter of the former law. This has been described as "the most extensive, profound and generally more perfect means of renewing law."[109] It is this form of revocation that is the focus of this study. How integral reordering has been understood and applied since its inception in *CIC/17* and how it determines the *ius vigens* today will be examined.

1.4 — INTEGRAL REORDERING

Integral reordering is not to be understood merely as the revocation of a past law. Nor is it to be confused with substituting a law that is contrary to another. Rather, integral reordering as a means of abrogation indicates that an entire law or juridic institute is abrogated by a new one, even though the past norms are not expressly revoked nor is the new law necessarily contrary to the former one. The later law, both in its formal and juridical aspects, is considered to be a total reformulation. Therefore the former law, as well as those norms accessory to it, no longer have force because they are replaced by the new law.[110] Likewise, as will be demonstrated, a new law can bring about the derogation of a law or juridic institute by the integral reordering of its subject matter.[111]

---

[108] See OTADUY, "De las normas generales: título I," p. 403.

[109] CABREROS DE ANTA, *Vigencia y estado actual de la legislación canónica*, pp. 20-21: "Esta es la forma más amplia, profunda y generalmente más perfecta de la renovación del derecho...."

[110] See IBID., p. 21. See also ÖRSY, "General Norms," p. 38: "The subject of the later law is the same as that of the former one, but the later gives a wholly new structure, so that the two edifices, former and later, cannot coexist in any way." In other words, the matter of the law has been legislated all over again. See also ÖRSY, *Theology and Canon Law*, p. 42.

[111] A definition of integral reordering was proposed in the Introduction of this book (see p.. 4). That description is the result of the research that follows.

1.4.1 — Mind of the legislator

Integral reordering can occur even if the legislator treats only one aspect of the law or institute, provided that it determines a certain matter in its integrity. In this sense both abrogation and derogation accomplish the same end in regard to integral reordering. A derogation that is essential to the nature of law itself becomes, in fact, total abrogation in the context of integral reordering. According to G. Ghirlanda it is not necessary that all or even most of the properties of the former law be reordered. Even if it appears that the new law refers in part to some of the same matter as the previous law, the juridic force of the similarities is only realized through the newly reorganized law.[112] By integrally reordering some matter, the legislator manifests his complete intention and will in the new law. Therefore, there is no need to look elsewhere to ascertain its meaning.[113] Chiappetta states, "The reason for this is obvious: the legislator, who enforces *'ex nova'* all of a determined matter, shows clearly his intention to abrogate the old law, even if he does not say it expressly."[114] The new law, then, expresses and manifests the *integra mens et voluntas legislatoris*.[115]

Thus, the revocation of a law or of a juridic institute should not be sought by establishing a contrary principle between the new and the old. For this would entail revocation by reason of contrariety. Rather a new law, or in some cases, a decisive part of the law or a summary of various laws has intentionally been reordered and synthesized.

---

[112] See G. GHIRLANDA, *Il diritto nella Chiesa, mistero di communione, compendio di diritto ecclesiale*, Milano, Edizione Paoline, Editrice Pontificia Università Gregoriana, 1990, p. 444.

[113] See VAN HOVE, *De legibus*, p. 355.

[114] CHIAPPETTA, *Il Codice di diritto canonico*, p. 72: "La ragione è ovvia: il legislatore che disciplina 'ex nova' tutta una determinata materia, manifesta chiaramente la sua intenzione di abrogare la vecchia legge, anche se non lo dice espressamente."

[115] See OJETTI, *Commentarium in Codicem iuris canonici*, pp. 158-159. Also ABBO and HANNAN, *The Sacred Canons*, p. 46 substantiate this: "A subsequent law abrogates a former law if the entire subject matter of the older law is freshly dealt with in the new, the same issues and cases being involved. In this case not only are the provisions in the old law incompatible with the new one repealed, but also by legitimate presumption, the unaltered or unmentioned sections of the former."

While the new law may sustain some of the values of the former law, entirely or partially, identically or in diverse ways, it nonetheless forms a new entity, objective and complete in itself. Thus it automatically revokes the previous law.[116] The integrally reordered law is *velut si esset prima eiusdem legislatio*. The legislator treats the whole matter of the previous law from scratch, as if the new law were the first law dealing with that subject.[117]

1.4.2 — Extent of integrity

There is no doubt that the new law must reorder the whole matter of the previous law. Commentators caution, however, that it is not easy to determine what constitutes the "whole matter" of a law. The authors do not dispute the meaning of integral reordering, yet they all remark on the ambiguity and difficulty of applying it. All agree that integral reordering must be radical and substantial rather than accessory and general; however, disagreement has centered on the *extent* of the integrity, or the completeness required for revocation.[118]

> What is the *whole matter* is not easy to determine; whole in one respect is partial in another. Thus a matrimonial impediment can be considered *total* in regard to the impediment, yet is part of the matrimonial matter. It is not required that the total scope of some question be reordered, nor that all dispositions be new. From the tenor of the new law and the circumstances, one is to conclude whether the legislator intended to reorder the entire matter or to determine some point, keeping the force of the law for the other parts.[119]

---

[116] See MICHIELS, *Normae generales*, p.658.

[117] A. BLAT, *Commentarium textus Codicis iuris canonici*, vol. 1, Romae, Typographia Pontificia in Instituto Pii IX, 1921, p. 107.

[118] See OTADUY, "El derecho canónico postconciliar," p. 123.

[119] REGATILLO, *Institutiones iuris canonici*, p. 68: "Quid sit 'tota materia' non facile determinatur; totum sub uno respectu est pars sub alio. Sic impedimentum matrimoniale considerari potest 'totum' quid relate ad impedimenta, pars materiae matrimonialis. Non requiritur ut totus complexus alicuius quaestionis reordinetur, neque ut omnes dispositiones sint novae. Ex tenore legis novae et adjunctis coligendum est utrum legislator totam materiam intenderit ordinare, aut punctum aliquod determinare, servata caeteris vi legali."

As previously indicated, this ambiguity regarding *ex integro/ex parte* was a concern for the *coetus* on general norms in dealing with c. 6.[120] E. Regatillo offers a general guideline to resolve this ambiguity: one must examine "the tenor of the law and the circumstances" that give rise to it. This will be discussed below.

1.4.3 — Formal integral reordering

To this ambivalence regarding the *extent* of the reordering, Otaduy adds a second interpretative factor that he refers to as *formal* integral reordering. He admits that this theory is not treated conclusively by other commentators; however, he believes that the basis of it has been sufficiently established especially by those who have addressed integral reordering in *CIC/17*.

Otaduy posits that the reordering of a law can be understood from the perspective of *formal integrity*, in addition to the material reordering of the old law. In such cases the new law does not adequately embody every aspect of the former law. Rather, the integrally reordered law compiles the main juridic thrusts of the legal institute in question.[121] This occurs when the code contains only certain sections of the juridic matter of a postconciliar document. However, those sections are so strongly characteristic of the area regulated by the law that the presumption is in favor of abrogation of the norms contained in the document.[122]

---

[120] See above nn. 51, 53, 54 and 55.

[121] See OTADUY, "El derecho canónico postconciliar," p. 125-126. Otaduy posits that the existence of a number of postconciliar documents could cause practical problems in regard to determining juridic effects. These documents contain juridic elements that are not directly opposed to *CIC/83* nor have they been materially reordered, since it was not the purpose of the code to embody the totality of the law. However, there are elements of these documents that are found in *CIC/83*. Without a more open understanding of integral reordering, these documents and the *ius* they contain would be considered as having juridic effects.

[122] See OTADUY, "Introducción: cc. 1-6," p. 285. See also E. CORECCO, "Aspects of Reception of Vatican II in the *Code of Canon Law*," trans. by M. O'CONNELL, in G. ALBERIGO, J.P. JOSSUA and J. KOMONCHAK (eds.), *The Reception of Vatican II*, Washington, DC, Catholic University Press, 1987, p. 263. Corecco notes that "some conciliar contents were not received or were received only partially ... not all the contents materially received in the code have completely retained the formal value and dynamism that is theirs in the conciliar texts."

In support of his theory of formal integral reordering by means of the code, Otaduy cites three postconciliar documents whose contents were not dealt with directly nor thoroughly in *CIC/83*. Yet its canons touch on the content of these documents and, he submits, effectively reorder their juridic matter.[123]

1.4.3.1 — The Ecumenical Directory

One such example is the Ecumenical Directory published in two parts in 1967 and 1970. The document itself, proceeding from the Decree on Ecumenism *Unitatis redintegratio* of Vatican Council II, has been cited as an example of integrally reordered law. Otaduy, however, regards the Directory as integrally reordered by *CIC/83* in a formal way. Although the code does not extensively deal with ecumenism, he suggests that cc. 755 and 844 brought about critical changes to the contents of the Directory.[124] Canon 755 specifies precisely who is responsible for fostering and directing the ecumenical movement. It establishes a hierarchy of competencies which significantly impacted n. 2 of *Ad totam Ecclesiam*, the first part of the Directory, and nn. 65 and 66 of *Spiritus Domini*, its complement.[125] Likewise

---

[123] See OTADUY, "Introducción: cc. 1-6," pp. 284-285 and "El derecho canónico postconciliar," pp. 127-128, n. 27. The examples cited by Otaduy include the Ecumenical Directory, 1967, see SECRETARIAT FOR THE PROMOTION OF THE UNITY OF CHRISTIANS, Directory Concerning Ecumenical Matters: Part One, *Ad totam Ecclesiam*, 14 May 1967, in *AAS*, 59 (1967), pp. 574-592 (= Ecumenical Directory I, 1967); English translation in A. FLANNERY (gen. ed.), *Vatican Council II: vol. 1 The Conciliar and Post Conciliar Documents*, new rev. ed., Costello Publishing Company, Northport, New York, 1996 (= FLANNERY I), pp. 483-501; *Ratio fundamentalis institutionis sacerdotalis*, 6 January 1970, in *AAS*, 62 (1970), pp. 321-384; and *Dispensationis matrimonii*, in regard to the dispensation of ratified but non-consummated marriages, 7 March 1972, in *AAS*, 64 (1972), pp. 244-252. These were later reordered by *Directorium oecumenicum noviter compositum*, 25 March 1993, in *AAS*, 85 (1993), pp. 1039-1119 (= Ecumenical Directory II, 1993); English trans. in *Origins*, 23 (1993-1994), pp. 129-160; *Ratio fundamentalis institutionis sacerdotalis (editio approbata post Codicem iuris canonici promulgatum)*, Typis polyglottis Vaticanis Romanis, 1985, pp. 3-4; and the circular letter *De processu super matrimonio rato et non consummato*, 20 December 1986, in *Communicationes*, 20 (1988), p. 78.

[124] See OTADUY, "El derecho canónico postconciliar," p. 127, n. 27.

[125] See Ecumenical Directory I, 1967. See also SECRETARIAT FOR THE PROMOTION OF THE UNITY OF CHRISTIANS, Directory concerning Ecumenical Matters: Part Two, *Spiritus Domini*, 16 April 1970, in *AAS*, 62 (1970), pp. 705-724 (= Ecumenical Directory I, 1970). Canon 755, §1 places the responsibility for the overall direction of the ecumenical movement with the College of Bishops and the Apostolic See; §2 outlines the role of the conference of bishops in issuing norms in accord with this direction. Number 2 of *Ad totam Ecclesiam* lacked this specificity. The responsibilities put

c. 844 emended the provisions of n. 55 of the Ecumenical Directory which pertained to *communicatio in sacris*.[126]

Otaduy believes that such adaptation of key juridic components of the Ecumenical Directory by *CIC/83* could be considered a formal type of integral reordering of its juridic matter. He contends that this notion is corroborated by the fact that it was necessary to rework the entire Directory in light of the integral reordering of ecumenism brought about by the code. He maintains that this theory is in some way analogous to what commentators on *CIC/17* meant when they stated that only *"ex tenore legis novae et ex variis circumstantiis"* can a sure sign of integrity be experienced. The content or sense of the new law and its various circumstances indicate whether the legislator intended either to mandate some specific matter by the law or whether by determining a particular point he intended to reorder the law itself and discontinue the juridic force of other aspects of the same matter.[127]

---

forth in numbers 65 and 66 in *Spiritus domini* are also clarified by the stipulations set forth in *CIC/83*.

[126] Canon 844, §2 gives broader justification for the *christifidelis* to receive the sacraments of penance, eucharist and anointing of the sick from non-catholic ministers. It extends the requirement of "danger of death or other urgent need (during persecution, in prison)" put forth in the Directory to "whenever necessity requires or a genuine spiritual advantage commends it" and includes the physical as well as the moral impossibility to approach a catholic minister. See J. PROVOST, "Canon 844," in P.J. COGAN, (ed.), *CLSA Advisory Opinions 1984-1993*, Washington, DC, The Catholic University of America, 1995, p. 242. Provost concurs that c. 844 broadens the meaning of "grave necessity" as well as the discretionary power of the bishop in regard to exceptional cases in accord with the "Instruction Concerning Cases When Other Christians May Be Admitted to Eucharistic Communion in the Catholic Church," see SECRETARIAT FOR CHRISTIAN UNITY, Instruction, *In quibus rerum circumstantiis*,1 June 1972, in *AAS*, 64 (1972), 99, 518-525; English translation in *CLD*, 7, pp. 583-590. In regard to receiving sacraments because of lack of access to one's own minister, *CIC/83* integrally reorders the norms by giving no indication of time. Both the Ecumenical Directory and the subsequent Instruction indicated that inaccessibility must be for a notable period of time. In addition OTADUY, "El derecho canónico postconciliar," p. 127, n. 27, points out that the canon alters some of the expressions used in the Directory. While he does not list these changes it appears that the use of the term "not in full communion" for "separated brethren" is one such example. Moreover, c. 844 indicates a gradation of being "in communion" not apparent in n. 55.

[127] See OTADUY, "El derecho canónico postconciliar," pp. 125-126. See also VAN HOVE, *De legibus*, pp. 355 and 357. The basis of Van Hove's conviction is that the code has in fact integrally reordered the law *"non materialiter forsan, sed formaliter."*

There are tenable aspects to this reasoning: it is in accord with the purposes of codification of *CIC/83* which did not intend to preserve the existing legislation; and it necessitates that one look broadly at the understanding of integral reordering, as well as the totality and inter-connectivity of *ius* itself. Nevertheless, the theory itself is not totally plausible. It does not differentiate between norms within a document being integrally reordered and the reordering of the entire document. Other canonists do not concur that *CIC/83* integrally reordered the Ecumenical Directory. J. Provost, for example, holds that the Ecumenical Directory continued to be the *ius vigens* except in those areas where *CIC/83* entirely reorganized the provisions of the document. He agrees that c. 844 integrally reordered the norms on *communicatio in sacris* but notes that other areas remain in force.[128] Although *CIC*/83 effected derogations regarding ecumenism, it cannot be asserted that it has integrally reordered the Ecumenical Directory from a formal perspective.

1.4.3.2 — Tone of document

Otaduy suggests another, likewise precarious, argument for applying this formal principle of integral reordering and thus presuming the revocation of the law. In further developing this concept he acknowledges that his theory could be considered as stretching the limits of what it means to integrally reorder a law. He begins with the premise that certain juridic norms exist that would have been technically impossible for the code to include. This is understandable in light of the purpose of the revised code and the nature of the postconciliar Church. However, Otaduy contends that the silence of the code in regard to these norms need not necessarily be perceived as an argument in favor of their remaining in force.

He suggests that such juridic norms could be affirmed as having been integrally reordered by virtue of their lack of harmony with the juridic technique which the legislator manifests in the code. Otaduy describes such norms as those

---

[128] See PROVOST, "Canon 767, §1," in *CLSA Advisory Opinions, 1984-1993*, p. 220. Provost, writing in 1984, indicates the differences between the Directory and *CIC/83*. Yet he also indicates areas that have maintained their force.

having an explicit or direct tone, thus making it difficult to assess any reasonable insinuations or suggestions against the matter contained in the code.[129] He bases this supposition on the third principle of revision of *CIC/83* which described the exigencies of the juridic language used in the code. This criterion underscores that pastoral care, the hallmark of the code, is to be reflected in the character of the laws. It notes that laws should be marked by a spirit of charity, temperance, humaneness and moderation. The principle maintains that canonical norms should not be excessively rigid, but rather leave discretionary judgment in the hands of pastoral leaders. Laws, in the strict sense, should not be used if instructions, exhortations, recommendations or other means could be more effective in achieving the same purpose.[130] However, Otaduy admits that this approach to formal integral reordering, that is, contrasting the tone of the document with the tone of the code, is juridically risky. It could obscure the very notion of integral reordering. At the same time he believes that there is a certain measure of truth in this theory that might enable integral reordering to be applied in a more moderate way.[131]

While acknowledging that this approach is precarious, lacks juridical certitude and could be difficult to verify, a modified adaptation of this theory could be the genesis for another way that integral reordering could be demonstrated: by attentiveness to the tone of a document. A significant change in the tone of a law could integrally reorder the norm itself. For example, an obvious disparity between an earlier law issued as a command and a later norm on the same subject matter that takes the form of an exhortation could exemplify integral reordering in this fashion.

---

[129] See OTADUY, "El derecho canónico postconciliar," pp. 127-128.

[130] See ALESANDRO, "The Revision of the *Code of Canon Law*," p. 108. See also R. CUNNINGHAM, "The Principles Guiding the Revision of the *Code of Canon Law*," in *The Jurist*, 30 (1970), p. 448-449. For the complete original text of this principle, see *Communicationes*, 1 (1969), pp. 79-80.

[131] Otaduy suggested this interpretation in his articles published in 1984 and 1985. See "El derecho canónico postconciliar," pp. 127-128 and "Funciones del Código en la recepción de la legislación postconciliar," in *Ius canonicum*, 25 (1985), pp. 493-495, respectively. He does not allude to this in discussing integral reordering in his later writing on cc. 6, 20 and 21 in *Comentario exegético*.

What had previously been obliged by the legislator and now is recommended indicates that an integral reordering of the law has occurred.

1.4.4 — Doubt of revocation: canon 21

Canon 21 provides a rule of law directly related to the integral reordering of the subject matter of a law. It makes clear that if there is doubt concerning the revocation, the pre-existing law is not presumed revoked. Canon 21 states:

> In a case of doubt, the revocation of a pre-existing law is not presumed, but later laws must be related to the earlier ones and, insofar as possible, must be harmonized with them.[132]

Even though c. 20 attempts to clarify conflicts between former and later laws, c. 21 acknowledges the possibility that doubt regarding the status of a past law can still exist. "If a law is expressly abrogated or derogated from by a subsequent intervention of the legislator, there can be no doubt concerning its status: it is deprived of its force."[133] Likewise, if the revocation takes the form of a subsequent contrary law, this is usually obvious. Thus one of the chief functions of c. 21 is to provide a rule for those laws that might be considered to have integrally reordered prior ones.

Chiappetta states that "the abrogation or derogation of a law must be positively demonstrated and if this does not happen the law continues to be operative." When revocation is not conclusive, however, he believes that "the first [law] prevails, and it is with this one that the latter must be reconciled as much as possible."[134] This position does not seem to be supported by other commentators nor by the code itself.

---

[132] "In dubio revocatio legis praeexistentis non praesumitur, sed leges posteriores ad priores trahendae sunt et his, quantum fieri potest, conciliandae."

[133] See MENDONÇA, Book I: General Norms, Canons 1-95," p. 20.

[134] CHIAPPETTA, *Il Codice di diritto canonico*, p. 72: "... l'abrogazione o la deroga di una legge dev'essere dimostrata positivamente, e finché questo non avviene, la legge continua ad essere operante ... La prevalenza spetta alla prima, ed è con questa che la successiva dev'essere conciliata per quanto è possibile."

45

Canon 21 asserts that in a case of doubt the revocation of the former law should not be presumed; but it does not say that the pre-existing law should be considered primary or upheld at all cost.[135] The wording of this canon is consequential, for it does not imply that the former law is necessarily maintained. "It is not redacted in a positive and absolute way, but in a limited and negative manner. Ultimately, to say that the preceding law is not presumed revoked is not the same as saying, as has been asserted, that 'the preceding law is presumed not revoked'."[136]

Nevertheless as long as authentic doubt exists, one is obliged to reconcile the two laws. That the former law must be considered part of the *traditio canonica* is necessary; that it be the primary focus is not. Canon 21 provides an important rule relative to integral reordering: it cannot be presumed, but must be demonstrated. Otherwise the prior law must be assumed to exist.

In discussing integral reordering commentators usually present examples of reordered laws that are obvious.[137] Yet numerous postconciliar juridical documents have not been so clearly integrally reordered. Do these maintain their juridic force? Otaduy argues that if the only recourse in evaluating these documents is c. 21, their

---

[135] See ÖRSY, "General Norms," p. 38.

[136] OTADUY, "De las normas generales: título I," p. 409: "Debe tenerse en cuenta, sin embargo, que tampoco dice el canon positivamente que en el caso de duda la ley anterior se mantiene; no está redactado de modo positivo y absoluto, sino de modo negativo y limitativo. Efectivamente, decir, que la ley precedente no se presume revocado no es lo mismo que decir, como se ha afirmado, que 'la ley precedente se presume no revocada'." See also MICHIELS, *Normae generales*, p. 669. What both Örsy and Otaduy appear to be saying is that one cannot make presumptions either in favor of or against the prior law without reasoned arguments to support the fact of integral reordering. Such evidence must include and be based on the tenor and circumstances of the law.

[137] See CICOGNANI, *Canon Law*, p. 631. The Constitutions *Apostolicae Sedis* of Pope Pius IX regarding censures and *Officiorum munerum* of Leo XIII concerning the prohibition of books are given as examples of laws which were already integrally reordered. See also MIGUÉLEZ DOMINGUEZ, ALONSO MORÁN and CABREROS DE ANTA, *Código de derecho canónico y legislación complementaria*, p. 16. The Apostolic Constitution, *Paenitemini*, of Pope Paul VI, 23 February 1966, concerning fast and abstinence and the Constitution, *Regimini Ecclesiae*, 15 August 1967, concerning the reform of the Roman Curia are also cited as integrally reordered law. Today canonists cite *Pastor bonus* or the Ecumenical Directory II, 1993 as examples of integrally reordered law. Yet there are numerous postconciliar juridical documents that are not as clear, whose juridic force needs to be considered.

revocation may not be presumed. Rather, later laws would have to be reconciled with them. However, he contends that this would be an excessive application of c. 21.[138]

To substantiate this he refers to the possible existence of *formal* integral reordering described above. He asserts that many postconciliar documents have been subjected to integral reordering in virtue of the canons of the code. *CIC/83* assembles fundamental juridic rules and principles and brings together norms on various matters. In addition it is necessary to consider the integrity at the root of the very concept of the code. The code, in principle, by the intent of its purpose and structure has a normativity and completeness lacking in any other source of the *ius vigens*.[139] As discussed above, this was also supported by commentators on *CIC/17* who believed that the notion of codification itself included the integral reordering of the matter contained in it.[140]

1.4.5 — Verification

The verification of integral reordering, then, cannot always be readily determined. Whereas certain laws are immediately recognized as having integrally reordered past ones, other laws raise doubts. For these more nebulous cases, the *extent* of the integral reordering as well as the other possible ways of looking at integral reordering of the law will need to be applied in ways that are not considered subjective or tenuous. Otaduy believes that these criteria could, at times, point to the existence of qualified doubt. Thus the pre-existing norms would be considered revoked.[141]

---

[138] OTADUY, "El derecho canónico postconciliar," p. 126.

[139] J. OTADUY, "Funciones del Código," in *Ius canonicum*, 25 (1985), p. 493: "La presunción de integridad que hay que conceder a toda ordenación codicial, que, en principio, acomete las medidas normativas con cierta voluntad estructurante y totalizadora."

[140] See VAN HOVE, *De legibus*, p. 357.

[141] See OTADUY, "De las normas generales: título I," p. 410. Otaduy believes that a qualified doubt, that is, one that is more probable than not, in favor of integral reordering is sufficient to presume that the law is revoked. However, this research supports the position that unless the doubt can be overcome in comparing the two laws, the former law cannot be presumed revoked.

Thus, appropriately applied, these criteria could offer greater clarity in determining the status of a past law in light of the plethora of documents that characterize the juridical life of the postconciliar church. However, there is an area of Otaduy's thinking that needs to be addressed. While the appeal to qualified doubt might be conceivable, Otaduy sees this as substantiated by the Code Commission in its preparatory phase.[142]

At the October 1981 meeting of the Code Commission, the Secretary and the consultors reiterated that the provisions of c. 6 of the schema dealt only with disciplinary laws whose matter is integrally reordered in the code or is contrary to it. After this clarification it was stated that "instructions and laws, if there are any, given by the Sacred Congregations are abrogated by the new code and must be elaborated anew or promulgated again, which though laborious, is best for juridic security."[143] No further discussion was recorded and the Commission proceeded to review c. 7.

However, the opinion of this author is that the above assertion of the Code Commission is not in itself accurately interpreted. This conclusion is based on several reasons. First, the comment stands out as unique in light of other discussions on c. 6, §1, 4°.[144] The statement is, in a sense, in direct opposition to the principle of c. 6 which abrogates only those laws contrary to or integrally reordered by the code. Secondly, after the Second Vatican Council it was the responsibility of the Roman Curia, among others, to implement the renewal of the Church engendered by Vatican II. Thus many postconciliar documents, while emanating from a specific congregation, were in fact the *ius* of Vatican II. Thirdly, instructions, as will later be discussed, are

---

[142] See OTADUY, "El derecho canónico postconcilar," p. 128; "Funciones del Código," pp. 495-496; and "De las normas generales: título I," p. 410. Consistently Otaduy refers to the statement that follows in n. 144 below as supporting the abrogation of post conciliar legislation.

[143] *Communicationes*, 14 (1982), p. 131: "... instructiones et, si quae sint, leges datae a S. Congregationibus per novum Codicem abrogantur et debent denuo exarari aut promulgari, quod, etsi laboriosum, optimum est pro certitudine iuridica." See also OTADUY, "De las normas generales: título I," p. 410.

[144] This is supported by the references to the work of the *coetus* and the commission already noted in this work. These and other sessions recorded in *Communicationes* are clear in stating that postconciliar laws are not abrogated unless they are contrary to the provisions of the code or unless they have been integrally reordered.

addressed to the executors of the law. Thus if the law to which it refers is not abrogated or derogated, the instruction pertaining to it would still remain. Finally, in retrospect, it has not been the policy of the Church to abide by this suggestion. Rather those documents that are neither contrary to the code nor integrally reordered by it are presumed to be in force and have been altered as needed by later legislation.

Two inherent dangers must be avoided when determining whether a law has been integrally reordered. The first is to understand this concept only in a strict and limited sense and maintain the former law unless the integral reordering is glaringly obvious. On the other hand, it is equally erroneous to presume that all postconciliar documents have been integrally reordered by the code. The literal acceptance of the comment of the Code Commission could enable the latter, mistaken view.

Based on this information regarding integral reordering, principles will be developed in Chapter 2 that apply this concept to postconciliar documents whose force is questionable. However, in order to deal with integral reordering on a practical level, it is first necessary to consider the nature of the juridic matter affected by this means of abrogation.

1.5 — JURIDIC DOCUMENTS AND INTEGRAL REORDERING

As discussed above, the principle of integral reordering applies not only to *leges* in the strict sense, but also to other norms contained in documents published with executive, rather than legislative power. Thus it is important to ascertain what norms can be subjected to the criteria for integral reordering in order to verify their juridic value or authenticate their abrogation. In addition, a practical construct for dealing with these norms will be proposed.

1.5.1 — Complexity of juridic norms

The complexity resulting from a multiplicity of juridic documents and the norms within them has been a reality in the Church for many centuries.[145] As indicated above, this ambiguity created by these documents was a motivating cause for the initial codification of law. However, *CIC/17* did not resolve the dilemma. *CIC/83*, likewise, still leaves some questions unresolved in this regard.[146] Nevertheless, the revised code has provided a structure that brings some clarity to this situation in Title III of Book I, *De decretis generalibus et de instructionibus*. Above all, canons 29-34 provide clear rules that distinguish acts issued by legislative power from those disseminated by executive authority, that is, administrative norms that have a general rather than individual character.[147]

1.5.2 — Practical working model

Many commentators acclaim Title III as a valuable innovation in the revised code; however, they also recognize that it is not without limitations. Most common

---

[145] See E. LABANDEIRA, "Clasificación de las normas escritas canónicas," in *Ius canonicum*, 29 (1989), pp. 679-680. Labandeira points out that throughout the centuries canonical science has used various terms to designate the governing norms of the Church. See also F. SANTI, *Prælectiones iuris canonici*, 4th ed., vol. 1, Romæ, Sumptibus et typis Friderici Pustet, 1904, pp. 12-13. The second title of the *Decretalium Gregorii IX*, "De Constitutionibus" dealt with all the written *ius* of a general character that properly was called *lex*.

[146] See F.G. MORRISEY, *Papal and Curial Pronouncements: Their Canonical Significance in Light of the Code of Canon Law*, 2nd ed., rev. by M. THÉRIAULT, Faculty of Canon Law Saint Paul University, Ottawa, 1995, p. 9ff. Morrisey notes that since the promulgation of *CIC/83* there have been over 20 different types of pronouncements by John Paul II. After describing those that could have particular canonical significance, he proceeds to list the various documents of the Second Vatican Council, those issued by the Roman Curia, as well as sources of particular and proper legislation. He concludes by suggesting that legislative organisms of the Church might clarify the legal import of their pronouncements. He urges those who interpret these documents to examine carefully the mode of promulgation, and to distinguish what is official as opposed to what is an opinion of an authoritative editor by considering the source of the document. See also J.M. GONZÁLEZ DEL VALLE, "Los actos pontificios como fuente del derecho canónico," in *Ius canonicum*, 16, no. 2 (1976), pp. 258-260. González includes an alphabetical list of 66 pontifical acts that was formulated shortly after the close of Vatican II and then proceeds to list at least five different types of acts not included in the list. This complexity is evident in analyzing the nature of norms as well. See WÄCHTER, *Gesetz im kanonischen Recht*, pp. 13-35.

[147] See M.J. CIÁURRIZ, "Titulus III: De decretis generalibus et de instructionibus," in *Comentario exegético*, p. 471.

among the criticisms of these canons is the fact that they are not sufficiently inclusive of the multiplicity of norms and forms of ecclesiastical documents that exist in canon law.[148] While conceding this reality Huels believes that this title provides a hierarchical ranking of juridical value which can be applied to all general norms and documents emanating from the Holy See as well as lower-level authorities.[149] His treatment of this, building upon the work of other canonists, will be used as the basic framework in discussing the integral reordering of documents, and the norms within them, throughout this study.

Central to Huels' theory is the need to determine the nature and weight of an ecclesiastical document. This cannot be done merely by examining the form of a given text. It requires that the contents of a document be evaluated to see if it is juridical in nature, that is, if its subject matter pertains to the governing function of the Church.[150] For only such documents affect or are affected by integral reordering.

1.5.2.1 — A hierarchy of juridic documents

Once a document has been identified as juridical, its weight or value can be determined by using the schema implicit in canons 29-34. Huels suggests three levels of juridic documents: legislative, administrative for the community, and administrative

---

[148] See CHIAPPETTA, *Il Codice di diritto canonico*, p. 82. "Nel nuovo Codice il diritto amministrativo ... riceve per la prima volta una **sistemazione organica**, la quale, anche se non è perfetta ed esige una ulteriore elaborazione, presenta una notevole utilità." See also E. LABANDEIRA, "Clasificación de las normas escritas canónicas," p. 679. "Entre las muchos problemas que suscita la interpretación del Código del 83, no es el menor el referente al contenido de los cánones 29 a 35, que resultan no sólo oscuros sino también insuficientes para distinguir las diversas clases de normas escritas en Derecho canónico."

[149] See HUELS, "A Theory of Juridical Documents," p. 343. Juridical documents pertain to matters concerning discipline, procedures, structures, rights and obligations, etc.

[150] See ibid., pp. 339-340. Huels distinguishes juridical documents from those that are magisterial. The latter, theological in nature, pertain to the *munus docendi*, the teaching Church. While these are important for the life and mission of the Church, it is the juridical that are of interest here. See also LABANDEIRA, " Clasificación de las normas escritas canonicas," p. 680. Labandeira gives a further example of the use of the word "decree." This type of document can signify a general or particular precept, any singular decision taken by the Ordinary in regard to discipline, a decision of a judge, or a response sent by a Roman congregation or council. The term spans the legislative, executive and judicial powers of the Church. The focus here, however, is in the juridical uses of the term, especially general decrees of legislative and executive power.

binding the executors of the law.[151] These classes correspond to the three categories listed in the canons: legislative acts, general executory decrees, and instructions. To these he adds a fourth level not included in Title III: documents that deal with canonical issues but are not juridically binding in themselves. Before examining the first three of these categories, it should be noted that other canonists have presented similar hierarchies from the perspective of the norms themselves. Shortly after the promulgation of *CIC/83*, J. Gaudemet addressed the hierarchy of norms inherent in Book I. He stated that the code, without explicitly stating so, presents a concise hierarchy of norms.[152] Likewise, E. Labandeira has done much work on the ranking of juridic norms.[153] Their insights correspond to the theory presented here.

---

[151] See HUELS, "A Theory of Juridical Documents," pp. 339-346, especially pp. 343-344, n. 15. Huels distinguishes between the terms "juridically binding" and "legally binding." The latter applies only to a law (level one juridic document) or legal custom; "juridically binding" includes acts of executive and judicial power as well as laws and customs.

[152] See J. GAUDEMET, "La Hiérarchie des normes dans le nouveau Code de droit canonique," in H. Schambeck (ed.), *Pro fide et iustitia*, Berlin, Duncker & Humblot, 1984, p. 210: "Le livre I du Code de 1983 instaure, sans le dire explicitement, mais de façon très nette, une hiérarchie des normes." Gaudemet identifies these levels in descending order as laws, the majority of which are issued by the supreme legislator, but also include decrees of ecumenical councils, particular laws, customs and general decrees according to cc. 29 and 30; general executory norms which, while subordinate to laws and issued by one with executive power, determine in greater detail the condition or manner of the laws and are promulgated in the same manner; and instructions, which are issued by one with executive power and are directed to the executors of the law. See. pp. 210-213.

[153] See LABANDEIRA, "Clasificación de las normas escritas canonicas," pp. 683-692. While Huels categorizes the documents themselves, Labandeira classifies the norms within them. Focusing on written canonical norms, he enumerates six distinct groupings: laws, legislative decrees, decree-laws (*decretos-leyes*), executive decrees, executory decrees and instructions. Included in the category of *laws* are those acts described in Book I, Title I of *CIC/83* as well as the general decrees defined in Title III, c. 29. Labandeira argues that general decrees according to their definition are true laws, in that they contain all the requisites required in Title II and lack no essential element. As autonomous norms they have the force of law and can derogate a former law of the same type. *Legislative decrees* are delineated in c. 30. They are issued by an executive authority who enjoys delegated legislative power in an advance and express manner. Although not laws in the proper sense, they have the force of law and can derogate ordinary laws. Normally such legislative decrees would come from a Roman Congregation. The *decree-laws* originate from an executive authority and receive the force of law only when approved or ratified by the competent legislator. The approbation of such acts is not delegated but is acquired in individual cases when necessity requires. *Executive decrees* are norms issued by one possessing executive authority. The executive decree is not mentioned in Book I, Title III of *CIC/83*; however, its importance is affirmed in c. 94 which deals with the statutes or internal norms established for specific groups or organizations. According to c. 94, §3 these decrees constitute independent norms established by executive or legislative power. Labandeira also cites *Pastor bonus* as alluding to this type of independent norm when in article 14

1.5.2.1.1 — Level 1: Legislative documents

Legislative documents contain *leges* and possess the highest authority. They are issued in diverse forms such as apostolic constitutions, apostolic letters, decrees, etc. While these documents have the *vis legis*, the word "law" itself is not specifically applied to them in their titles. As *leges* they have the highest juridic value in the Church's legal system.[154] It is important to note that regardless of the type of document used to promulgate a law, all *leges* "have exactly the same force and all are subject to the general rules on ecclesiastical laws."[155]

Canon 29, in describing general decrees, likewise provides a definition of the norms contained in documents in this first category. Like general decrees, all *leges* are provisions given by a competent legislator to a community capable of receiving law. They are regulated by the provisions set forth in Title I, *De legibus ecclesiasticis*.[156] Laws are promulgated by a legislator: the Supreme Pontiff, a council, a diocesan bishop, a conference of bishops or exceptionally through decrees issued by a Roman

---

it gives dicasteries competency to issue singular acts or general norms within the scope of their competency. *Executory decrees* are referred to cc. 31-33. They are given by those who have executive power within their competency and determine in a more detailed way the manner in which a law is to be executed or observed. They require the same adherence as the laws to which they refer. They do not derogate from laws and any of their prescriptions contrary to laws lack the force of law. Labandeira cites c. 1253 as providing an example of when such executory decrees might be used. The Bishops' Conference is to determine more particular ways in which the laws of fast and abstinence are to be observed. *Instructions* outlined in c 34 are norms issued by one who has executive power. They are intended for those persons whose responsibility it is to enforce the law. These internal norms of administration are similar to executory decrees in that they are intended to clarify the law and determine ways and procedures for its execution. Labandeira believes any juridical norms of Church government can be classified in one of these six categories.

While this theory supports that suggested by Huels, the latter will be used in this research in that it presents a simpler yet equally inclusive format. See also E. LABANDEIRA, *Trattato di diritto amministrativo canonico*, 2nd ed., trans. by L. GRAZIANO, Milano, Guiffrè, 1994, pp. 242-244. To distinguish general administrative norms from legislative, it is not enough to use the criteria of author, function, matter or the form in which these appear. It is first necessary to categorize documents according to the requisites of cc. 29-34.

[154] See HUELS, "A Theory of Juridical Documents," pp. 346-347.

[155] Ibid., p. 347. Huels is referring to laws issued at the same level, i.e., all universal laws have the same force, but they are higher than laws of a conference of bishops, which in turn are higher than laws of the diocesan bishop. See c. 135, §2.

[156] See c. 29: " Decreta generalia quibus a legislatore competenti pro communitate legis recipiendæ capaci communia feruntur præscripta, proprie sunt leges et reguntur præscriptis canonum de legibus."

dicastery with delegated legislative authority or curial norms approved *in forma specifica* by the Pope.[157]

1.5.2.1.2 — Level 2: Administrative documents for the community

Administrative documents for the community comprise the second level of juridic documents. In light of cc. 31-33, the norms in these documents can be defined as "common provisions for a community capable of receiving a law made by a competent *authority with executive power*."[158] At times these norms may appear in the same form or have the same style as *leges*, yet they are nonetheless subordinate to the law. Administrative documents, unlike legislative ones, are issued with executive power and must be in accord with the laws to which they correspond. According to c. 33, general executory decrees and other such norms cannot derogate from the law. If the law to which they refer is revoked, the administrative norm ceases to have force *ex iure*. Any provisions of these documents contrary to the law have no juridic force. Many documents issued by the Roman Curia fall in this category, including directories, circular letters, notifications, declarations, etc.[159]

1.5.2.1.3 — Level 3: Administrative documents binding executors of the law

Administrative documents intended for those who must enforce the law are very similar to the administrative documents described above. They are issued by executive authority; are subordinate to the law; may not be contrary to the law; and they are revoked if the law on which they are based is revoked. The major difference is that documents at this level oblige only those who must enforce the law. The parameters for the norms in such documents are set forth in c. 34 which refers to them as "instructions." They directly bind only the administrators for whom they are given.

---

[157] Essentially Huels includes in this level the first three types of written norms described by Labandeira in his classification, that is, laws, legislative decrees and decree-laws. See above n. 153.

[158] HUELS, "A Theory of Juridical Documents," p. 348. Huels intentionally parallels this definition with that given for general decrees in c. 29, thus highlighting the source of authority as the key difference between the two levels.

[159] See ibid., pp. 348-349 and 354.

54

Huels believes that such documents can exemplify the principle of subsidiarity in operation. The leaders of particular Churches or the other administrators to whom they are addressed must carefully consider their contents and determine how they will be implemented in particular situations.[160]

1.5.2.2 — Practical implications of hierarchical model

This theory provides a practical working model for dealing with the integral reordering of laws. Only by identifying to whom the document is addressed, and examining its contents to determine its nature and weight, can the canonist ascertain its appropriate juridic value.[161]

Some overall parameters regarding integral reordering can be outlined from this theory and the context of Title III. In describing general executory decrees, c. 33, §2 asserts that "such decrees cease to have force by explicit or implicit revocation made by competent authority as well as by the cessation of the law for whose execution they were given ...."[162] Therefore such decrees are subject to tacit revocation through integral reordering. Instructions, likewise, are subject to the same means of revocation according to c. 34, §3.[163] In light of this it may be asserted that:

---

[160] See ibid., pp. 349-351. Huels also identifies a fourth level consisting of non-binding documents, but these are not a concern here since it is meaningless to speak of the integral reordering of a non-binding text. Documents at the fourth level, while not juridically binding, are nonetheless important. Often their contents are morally influential or significant in given areas. Frequently they are issued without any specified form; at other times they might be designated as guidelines, recommendations, directives, letters, etc. These non-binding documents, like the administrative documents that bind only the executors of the law, allow for the principle of subsidiarity to be operative within the local churches. See also pp. 351-352 and 355-356.

[161] It is important not to confuse the weight of individual norms, that is, their "intrinsic" juridical value, with the weight given them by the competent authority, which might be termed their "extrinsic" value.

[162] "Eadem vim habere desinunt revocatione explicita aut implicita ab auctoritate competenti facta, necnon cessante lege ad cuius exsecutionem data sunt...."

[163] Canon 134, §3 states: "Vim habere desinunt instructiones non tantum revocatione explicita aut implicita auctoritatis competentis, quae eas edidit, eiusve superioris, sed etiam cessante lege ad quam declarandam vel exsecutioni mandandam datae sunt."

1. Laws (*leges*) can integrally reorder other laws at the same level (universal, conference of bishops, diocese, etc.) and general administrative norms at the same level;
2. Norms in documents at level two can integrally reorder general administrative norms in documents at levels two and three;
3. Norms in documents at level three can only integrally reorder previous norms in a document at level three.

The hierarchy of documents presented above provides a framework in assessing whether postconciliar laws have been integrally reordered by the code or by a document that has been issued since the promulgation of *CIC/83*. It will serve as a practical construct both in categorizing and evaluating juridical norms.

Both before and after the promulgation of *CIC/83*, canonists expressed concern that the code would not provide the necessary flexibility to deal with ecclesiastical legislation in today's world.[164] Communication continues to be a key issue as society moves into the new millennium. This is echoed in the life of the Church. The multiplicity of documents emanating from the Holy See since the Second Vatican Council parallels the current trend of society.

Integral reordering provides the Church with a means of adjusting and adapting the law in the reality of rapidly changing times. Properly understood and applied, this concept enables canonists to assess the status of laws and to bring clarity to the *ius vigens*. The once restricted use of integral reordering as a means of revocation continues to be broadened as the concept is better understood and more frequently applied. This chapter has delineated the canonical basis for integral reordering as a means of revocation highlighting its importance and practicality as a common and efficient way of extrinsic cessation of law. At the same time it has been acknowledged that there are ambiguities inherent in this type of tacit revocation. In

---

[164] See L. ÖRSY, *From Vision to Legislation: From the Council to a Code of Laws*, The Père Marquette Theology Lecture, Milwaukee, WI, Marquette University Press, 1985, p. 43-45. See also CORECCO, "Aspects of Reception of Vatican II in the Code of Canon Law," p. 251. Corecco believes the choice of codification is problematic if not totally inadequate. In itself it expresses a societal view of the Church rather than Church as a sacramental mystery; and A. GARCIA Y GARCIA, "Las codificaciónes y su impacto en la iglesia a través de la historia," in *Temas fundamentales en el nuevo Código*, Bibliotheca Salmanticensis Estudios 65, Salamanca, Universidad Pontificia, 1984, p. 58.

order to deal effectively with integral reordering, a model of hierarchical ranking for juridic documents has been adopted.

Research reveals that canonists have done relatively little analysis on integral reordering.[165] Yet its importance particularly in regard to postconciliar laws and present day documents is paramount. The theoretical background presented in this chapter establishes the basis for the formulation of principles that will be proposed as determinants of integral reordering. These assumptions will be tested in light of postconciliar documents to ascertain their credibility. Through the blending of the theoretical and the practical aspects of integral reordering, its value for determining the *ius vigens* will be more precisely defined and clarified.

---

[165] Perhaps the reason for such omission has been the more practical and pastoral direction that canonists have pursued in regard to implementing *CIC/83*.

CHAPTER 2

PRINCIPLES OF INTEGRAL REORDERING

This chapter offers greater clarity into the concept of integral reordering by translating the theoretical input of the material previously presented into a practical perspective. Relatively little has been written on the specific topic of the integral reordering of law. Apart from commentaries on cc. 6 and 20, canonists have not focused on this topic in itself.[1] Given this reality, a deductive approach to the material presented in Chapter 1 will be employed in order to develop the concept of integral reordering of law in a more functional way.

This chapter first considers an explanation of integral reordering especially in regard to individual laws and general administrative norms. This provides an additional basis for the principles which follow as well as serving to clarify the revoking scope of integral reordering.

Following this, key principles are delineated for determining the use of this means of revocation of laws or general administrative norms.[2] These tenets, which

---

[1] In the books and periodicals surveyed for this research few articles, as is evident in the bibliography, were specifically centered on integral reordering as a means of revocation of law. Several canonists have made notable contributions in this area, apart from material found in commentaries, in particular J. Otaduy. However, they treat the concept of integral reordering from a broader perspective, for example, from that of postconciliar legislation, rather than focusing specifically on the integral reordering of law itself.

[2] Throughout this and the following chapter the word "law" will be used to refer to *lex* in the strict sense, that is, those norms that appear in level 1 documents as described in the hierarchy of documents proposed in Chapter 1. "General administrative norms" is employed for those norms that have juridic value and are found in documents at levels 2 and 3. The word "norms" is used generically in referring to laws and/or general administrative norms. However, phrases such as "ecclesiastical law" or "religious law" will incorporate the broader understanding of Church law, as *ius*, which includes *lex*.

provide a canonically based rationale for ascertaining whether integral reordering has taken place and protect against its arbitrary application, evolve from two sources. Some are contained within the code itself; others proceed from the *traditio canonica*, that is, the interpretation, praxis and development of those canons related to integral reordering in both *CIC/17* and *CIC/83* as well as the longer pre-code experience of the revocation of ecclesiastical law.[3]

Finally, a model of integrally reordered law is examined in order to demonstrate concretely the principles that have been proposed. This illustration, taken from liturgical law, tests and validates the assumptions put forth in this chapter. It also surfaces other aspects of integral reordering which may have been omitted or which complement the principles.

2.1 — INTEGRAL REORDERING OF NORMS

Before proposing the principles applicable to integral reordering which emerge from Chapter 1, a basic assumption of this study must be asserted. While most commentators on both *CIC/17* and *CIC/83* cite examples of integral reordering of a juridic institute or a specific juridic document or a complex law, this means of revocation is applicable to all individual norms, both laws and general administrative norms.[4] This assertion is based on several factors.

---

[3] Although the concept of integral reordering was first introduced into ecclesiastical law in *CIC/17*, this means of revocation was considered an iteration of what the Church had done in actual practice in its legal history. See CRNICA, *Commentarium theoretico*, p. 45: "Tali modo Pius IX const. 'Apostolicae Sedis' 12. X. 1869 de integro ordinavit disciplinam circa censuras latae sententiae, Leo XIII const. 'Officiorum et munerum' 25. I. 1897 reordinavit disciplinam de censura et prohibitione librorum." See also CICOGNANI, *Canon Law*, p. 631. Cicognani points out that in such instances of the integral reordering of law before *CIC/17* it was sufficiently clear, even without expressly declaring such, that the legislator had readjusted the subject matter of the former law. See also CABREROS DE ANTA, ALONSO LOBO and ALONSO MORAN, *Comentarios al Código de derecho canónico*, p. 171. The authors cite the decree, *Maxima cura*, of the S.C. Consistorial (a. 1910), concerning administrative removal of parish priests, as a pre-code example of integral reordering.

[4] In addition to the examples of integral reordering that are cited before the promulgation of *CIC/17*, those that were contained in or followed the initial codification, for the most part, referred to a juridic institute or document or a complex law. For example, see BERUTTI, *Institutiones iuris canonici*, pp. 95-96. Berutti cites c. 106 which effectively reordered the law regarding precedence

First, and most important among these, is the law itself contained in both Codes. Canon 22 of *CIC/17* and c. 20 of *CIC/83* speak of the integral reordering of the subject matter of *leges*. Neither canon singles out juridic institutes or documents; rather the focus of both is on the content of the law. Likewise c. 6 of *CIC/83* abrogates universal disciplinary *laws* which deal with matters which the code has wholly reordered. Although entire documents and juridic institutes can be subjected to integral reordering, the canon speaks of laws. As indicated in Chapter 1, the *coetus* that worked on general norms did not interpret *leges* in the strict sense of the word, but understood this term more broadly as referring to norms.[5]

That integral reordering can be applied to all norms is further supported by c. 33, § 2 that states:

> [General executory] decrees cease to have force by explicit or implicit revocation made by competent authority as well as by cessation of the law for whose execution they were given ....[6]

and c. 34, §3 that reads:

> Instructions cease to have force not only by explicit or implicit revocation of the competent authority who issued them or of the superior of that authority but also by the cessation of the law for whose clarification or execution they were given.[7]

Implicit revocation in these canons denotes the concept of norms being revoked by later norms that run counter to those in the general executory decree or in the

---

of persons. See also M. CABREROS DE ANTA, *Derecho canónico fundamental*, Madrid, Editorial y Libería Co., Cul. S.A., 1960, p. 302. Cabreros alludes to the Apostolic Constitution *Provida Mater* of Pius XII which organized the secular institutes and the Instruction of the Sacred Congregation of Religious *Inter ceteras* of 1956 which reordered *Nuper editio* of 1924, concerning the cloister of nuns.

[5] See *Communicationes*, 23 (1991), p. 120 and 14 (1982), p. 131.

[6] "[Decreta generalia exsecutoria] vim habere desinunt revocatione explicita aut implicita ab auctoritate competenti facta, necnon cessante lege ad cuius exsecutionem data sunt...."

[7] "Vim habere desinunt instructiones non tantum revocatione explicita aut implicita auctoritatis competentis, quae eas edidit, eiusve superioris, sed etiam cessante lege ad quam declarandam vel exsecutioni mandandam datae sunt."

instruction.[8] This would occur either by direct contrariety or through the integral reordering of the subject matter of the earlier norm.[9]

Second, commentators on *CIC/17* were quite logical in citing broad and obvious examples of instances in which integral reordering had occurred in the legal history of the Church. Introduced by the legislator as a new concept into ecclesiastical law in c. 22 of *CIC/17*, integral reordering would be applied more over the course of time. It was and is important to demonstrate this type of revocation by unmistakable examples in order to convey its capacity to revoke. In addition, the stability in canon law, which the initial codification of law brought about, resulted in a less extensive use of integral reordering as a means of revocation. This situation would change as a result of the Second Vatican Council.

Third, integral reordering as a means of revocation of past law was not present in c. 6 of *CIC/17*. Its absence was due in part to the purpose of codification, affecting a formal rather than a material change of the law, as well as to the novelty of the concept of integral reordering in canon law. However, its insertion into c. 6 of *CIC/83* is indicative of its value in clarifying the *ius vigens* especially in light of the changes engendered by Vatican II. Thus the *coetus* that dealt with general norms included this means of revocation for juridic certitude in respect to the many postconciliar documents that could not be taken into account by the code itself.[10] There are no

---

[8] See A. MENDONÇA, "Book I: General Norms, Canons 1-95," p. 27. See also CIÁURRIZ, "Titulus III: De decretis generalibus et de instructionibus," p. 494: "La revocacíon implícita se produce cuando se promulgan normas – tanto legales como reglamentarias – que sustituyen al decreto o lo contradicen."

[9] It could also be posited that due to the absence of rules governing general administrative norms that those specified for *leges* in title I are to be used in accord with c. 19. By analogy of law, what is said about *leges* could be applied to general administrative norms.

[10] See *Communicationes*, 14 (1982), pp. 130-131. It was during the final review of general norms that the Commission, after some discussion, reinserted the words *ex integro* into c. 6, §1, 4°. Even though integral reordering was stated as a general principle of revocation of law in c. 20, it was agreed to include it in c. 6 for juridic certitude. See also *Communicationes*, 3 (1971), p. 83. Early in the revision process the members of the Code Commission recognized the need for defining the efficacy of the *ius vetus* in regard to the revised code. While the revision of the preliminary canons of *CIC/17* was not an immediate concern at that time, the commission acknowledged that such norms would be needed to deal with *CIC/17* and the *ius* presently in force. They saw this as eventually being taken into consideration in cc. 5 and 6.

indications from the *coetus* that the extent of integral reordering was in any way restrictive, but rather that it was applicable to all norms.

Finally, while most canonists have referred to integral reordering only in regard to juridic institutes or documents, the concept has been applied by some commentators to individual laws and general administrative norms. This was true in a limited way even in regard to *CIC/17*. Cicognani pointed out, for example, that c. 1427, §4 reordered the law governing the dependence of a new parish on its mother church.[11]

In his commentary on c. 20, Otaduy states that what is reordered must have a certain character of unity; it must be an institution or *argumentum iuridicum* with a degree of autonomy and organization.[12] In regard to the term, *argumentum iuridicum*, he cites Michiels in a footnote. In the particular passage referenced, Michiels enumerates the various ways in which integral reordering can occur; among these possibilities he refers to individual laws as well as juridic institutes.[13] In speaking of c. 6 and integral reordering in light of postconciliar laws, Otaduy asserts that there are prior *norms* clearly subjected to integral reordering. However, he acknowledges that there are other *norms* whose integral reordering is less certain

---

[11] See CICOGNANI, *Canon Law*, p. 631. There were instances where individual laws or norms were referred to as integrally reordered in light of *CIC/17*; for example, see REGATILLO, *Institutiones iuris canonici*, p. 68. He cites c. 97 as having integrally reordered the law concerning affinity. However, most commentators used examples of juridic institutes.

[12] See OTADUY, "De las normas generales: título I," p. 401: "La materia debe tener cierto carácter de unidad, debe ser una institución o un 'argumentum iuridicum'con cierto grado de autonomía y organicidad ...."

[13] See MICHIELS, *Normae generales*, p. 658: "Quod ut verificetur, constare debet *legem novam*, seu in quibusdam casibus partialem legis dispositionem variarumve legum summam, ad hoc praecise fuisse conditam, *ut de integro ordinet*, id est ordinatim et synthetice, per modum verae cujusdam codificationis unificationem intendentis, etsi forsan partialiter reassumendo legem antiquam, proponat *totam materiam*, id est totum quoddam juris institutum, totum negotium totumve argumentum juridicum ..., vel saltem partem instituti, negotii argumentum in se et objective aliquid completi efformantem ..., per legem anteriorem vel respective varias leges anteriores, sive complete sive incomplete, sive indentice sive diversimode, ordinatam."

because *CIC/83* deals only with determined parts of the juridic matter of these norms.[14]

Örsy, discussing c. 20, refers neither to juridic institutes nor to documents in speaking of integral reordering. He simply states that "the subject matter of the later law is the same as that of the former one, but the later gives a wholly new structure so that the two edifices, former and later, cannot coexist in any way."[15] A. Mendonça also refers to integral reordering in terms of *laws* "substantially changed in the matter of discipline, not merely altered in detail."[16] Thus, while integral reordering is applied to entire documents and juridic institutes, it also serves as a means of revocation for individual norms, whether *leges* or general administrative norms.

2.2 — PRINCIPLES REGARDING INTEGRAL REORDERING

With this understanding of the scope of integral reordering in regard to ecclesiastical law, essential principles will be proposed to assist in determining whether or not a given juridic document, institute or norm has been integrally reordered. The first five principles presented below are more basic and significant in that they are explicit in the canons of the code itself. An identification and explanation of these will provide the framework for the sixth and seventh principles that proceed from them. The last principle serves as a summary statement of the effect of integral reordering. Together these principles present an overall guide that helps to clarify and determine the integral reordering of law. Canon 20, which provides the focal point for

---

[14] See OTADUY, "Introducción: cc.1-6," p. 284: "Existen normas anteriores sujectas con claridad a la 'ordinatio ex integro.' Hay otras cuyo sometimiento a reordenación integral es más dudoso, ya que el CIC recoge tan sólo determinados sectores de la materia jurídica sobre la que aquellas normas operaban."

[15] ÖRSY, "General Norms," p. 38.

[16] MENDONÇA, "Book I: General Norms, Canons 1-95," p. 6.

dealing with integral reordering, is pivotal and thus is the point of reference in establishing the principles.[17]

2.2.1. — Principle 1: Abrogation/derogation

Integral reordering results in abrogation or derogation; thus, it is necessary to determine the extent of the reordering. Canon 20 states that "a later law abrogates, or derogates from, an earlier law if it completely reorders the entire matter of the earlier law ...."[18] Integral reordering can result in either the abrogation of or the derogation from a former norm. *CIC/83* speaks of abrogation when the revocation is total, that is, when the new law completely replaces the earlier law, and it speaks of derogation when the revocation of a law is partial.[19] However, in the context of integral reordering, abrogation and derogation are not as neatly distinguished. For integral reordering does not require that the entire law be altered; it can occur even if only one segment of the law is affected, provided it brings about a definite change in the law itself.[20]

Accordingly, in cases of integral reordering, abrogation is the complete revocation of a juridic document, a juridic institute or an entire law. Derogation, however, can be understood as the reordering of norms which are part of a juridic document, or the reordering of a key component of a law itself. The derogation of norms of a juridic document or of a juridic institute might not necessarily impact its totality, yet given norms can be totally reordered in themselves.

It should also be noted that derogation is understood more broadly in light of the simplification of terms in *CIC/83*. Derogation implies not only changing the law in the material sense; it may also involve changing the meaning the law previously had.

---

[17] While c. 6, §1, 4° also speaks of integral reordering, it is c. 20 that places this concept in its context as a means of revocation of ecclesiastical law. The importance of c. 6 lies in the application of integral reordering specifically to the *ius vetus*, as will be demonstrated in Chapter 3.

[18] "Lex posterior abrogat priorem aut eidem derogat, si id ... totam de integro ordinet legis prioris materiam." As indicated in Chapter 1, the term "law" in this canon is used in the broad sense, inclusive of general administrative norms.

[19] See OTADUY, "De las normas generales: título I," p. 401.

[20] See OJETTI, *Commentarium in Codicem iuris canonici*, p. 158.

Thus derogation can be accomplished in various ways: by eliminating part of the law, by adding to the norm itself, by altering significant concepts or words, by changing the tone of the law, etc.[21]

The notion of the *extent* of integral reordering has been a concern among those who have interpreted the law since the formal institution of this means of revocation into ecclesiastical law in *CIC/17*. As previously noted, commentators on the initial code, while affirming integral reordering in terms of juridic institutes, appeared reluctant to attribute this means of revocation to part of a document or an institute or to part of a law. Perhaps this was due to their concern for the ambiguity it might have caused. Canonists concurred that distinguishing what was *whole* from that which was *partial* was relative to the perspective taken.[22]

This concern regarding the *extent* of integral reordering was also voiced by the *coetus* that worked with general norms in the revision process of the code. The more extensive use of integral reordering, particularly in light of the documents of the Second Vatican Council and the postconciliar period, made it a more common and effective means of revoking law.[23] Yet the *coetus* and even canonists today have referred to the ambiguity regarding total or partial reordering.[24]

Therefore this first principle of integral reordering establishes the importance of determining whether the entire law or juridic document or institute has been

---

[21] Before the simplification of terms in *CIC/83*, canonists referred to abrogation, derogation, obrogation and subrogation in regard to a change in the law. However, these terms have been subsumed into the terms abrogation and derogation as the means by which a law is altered.

[22] See REGATILLO, *Institutiones iuris canonici*, p. 68: "Quid sit 'tota materia' non facile determinatur; totum sub uno respectu est pars sub alio." See also MICHIELS, *Normae generales*, p. 658.

[23] Numerous canons of *CIC/17* and other legislative texts had already been integrally reordered by the documents of Vatican II and those documents that followed them in the postconciliar period. The revised code would, in turn, integrally reorder some of these postconciliar documents.

[24] See *Communicationes*, 23 (1991), p. 120: "Ill.mus sextus Consultor timet ne vacuum in legislatione creetur si per novum Codicem omnis legislatio anterior abrogetur. Et quaerit ut expressio 'ex integro', n. 4, tollatur ne difficultates stabiliendi quod ex integro est vel ex parte oriantur (Placet)." See also OTADUY, "De las normas generales: título I," p. 403: "No es siempre fácil; determinar en la práctica cuándo se verifica verdaderamente la ordenación integral de la materia. El problema consiste precisamente en determinar la extensión de la integridad."

integrally reordered (abrogation) or whether individual norms of a given juridic document or a segment of a more complex law have been reordered (derogation). Because both bring about revocation of their respective matter, the extent of what has been integrally reordered must be clearly ascertained. Several of the assumptions that follow are corollary to and interdependent with this initial principle.

2.2.2 — Principle 2: Distinct from direct contrariety

Integral reordering is distinct from revocation of law by means of direct contrariety. Both direct contrariety and integral reordering are specified as means of revocation in cc. 6 and 20. Canon 6 deals with the status of the *ius vetus* in regard to the *ius vigens*. Paragraph 1, 2° speaks of the abrogation of "universal or particular laws contrary to the prescripts" of the code; §1, 4° refers to "*universal disciplinary laws regarding matter which this code completely reorders.*" Likewise, c. 20 dealing with future law provides two possibilities for tacit revocation: if a former law is directly contrary to a later law; or if the later law entirely reorders the subject matter of the former law. The general principle of law is specified in c. 20; c. 6, while based on this principle, also creates an exception to c. 20.[25]

As indicated in the previous chapter, the distinction between these modes of revocation is not undisputed. Both direct contrariety and integral reordering result in an incompatibility with the former law. In the case of direct contrariety the disparity is more polar, and oftentimes more obvious. If the two laws are diametrically opposed, so that one excludes the possibility of the other, revocation occurs by means of direct contrariety. Other incompatibility, then, would be the result of integral reordering. This could take place in the form of abrogation or derogation as discussed above. With both direct contrariety and integral reordering the new law cannot coexist with the former.[26]

---

[25] Canon 6, §1, 2° revokes particular law contrary to the code unless otherwise provided for. This is an example of the express revocation spoken of in c. 20.

[26] From one perspective direct contrariety can be seen as a type of integral reordering. Both direct contrariety and integral reordering bring about an incompatibility with the past law, thereby

Norms within juridic documents may be revoked by later norms either by direct contrariety or by integral reordering. However, an entire juridic document or institute can be abrogated tacitly only through revocation by integral reordering; direct contrariety occurs only when individual norms are directly opposed to each other. The more extensive abrogating power of integral reordering is likewise indicated in the principle that follows.

2.2.3 — Principle 3: Reordering of entire document/juridic institute

An entire document on a given juridic matter can integrally reorder a previous document on that same subject; likewise an entire juridic institute can be integrally reordered by a later document or law. This principle reiterates the most obvious examples of integral reordering, that is, an entire juridic document or institute can integrally reorder a prior juridic document or institute on the same subject.[27] In regard to documents themselves, without explicitly revoking the previous document, the new law completely reworks the subject matter of the earlier one so that there is no doubt that the legislator is bringing about an entirely new treatment of the matter, thus abrogating the former law. Examples of such integral reordering have been cited in the previous chapter, particularly in reference to the pre-code existence of integral reordering and in light of the promulgation of *CIC/17*.[28] Likewise, the documents of the Second Vatican Council, and the many laws necessitated for the implementation of these conciliar documents, integrally reordered not only major sections of the *Code of Canon Law* of 1917, but also ecclesiastical law not contained in the code.

---

revoking the former norm(s). Direct contrariety is one way of wholly reordering the meaning of a law or of a general administrative norm. From this perspective tacit revocation could be equated with integral reordering of law. Yet at the time of the promulgation of *CIC/83* integral reordering as a means of revocation was, relatively speaking, still a new concept in ecclesiastical law. Therefore, the legislator wisely included both means of implicit revocation in cc. 6 and 20. Perhaps in the future integral reordering could be the sole means of tacit revocation.

[27] In addition to juridic documents, this principle is also applicable to specific sections of *CIC/83* which have integrally reordered postconciliar juridic documents. Likewise commentators cite *CIC/17* as having integrally reordered earlier juridic institutes. See, for example, BERUTTI, *Institutiones iuris canonici*, pp. 96-97.

[28] See, for example, Chapter 1, p. 28, n. 78 and p. 45, n. 137 and Chapter 2, pp. 58-59, nn. 3 and 4.

The Ecumenical Directory, published in two parts in 1967 and 1970, which stemmed from the Decree on Ecumenism, *Unitatis redintegratio*, wholly reordered the Church's discipline on ecumenism.[29] Yet this document itself was later integrally reordered in 1993 by the *Directorium oecumenicum noviter compositum*.[30] Likewise, *Pastor bonus* revised the organization of the Roman Curia which had been regulated by *Regimini Ecclesiae universae*.[31] Although some norms of the former and later documents might be similar or even identical, the earlier documents were significantly revised and replaced their predecessors. Consequently these earlier documents were revoked in their entirety. In such cases, although many norms from the earlier document are repeated in the later, the *ius vigens* is found only in the later document.

In addition to the reordering of entire documents, there are numerous examples of the integral reordering of juridic institutes.[32] In Chapter 1, for example, reference was made to the integral reordering of the discipline on *communicatio in sacris* by c. 844, which deals with participation in the sacraments by members of Christian denominations not in full communion with the Catholic Church. By broadening the meaning of "grave necessity" as well as the discretionary power of the bishop in regard to exceptional cases, *CIC/83* revoked some of the previous norms contained in the 1967 Ecumenical Directory.[33]

2.2.4 — Principle 4: Hierarchy of juridic documents

Some norms in a juridic document can integrally reorder, and thereby revoke, some of the norms in a previous document while leaving others intact. This

---

[29] See Ecumenical Directory I, 1967 in FLANNERY I, pp. 483-501 and Ecumenical Directory I, 1970, in FLANNERY I, pp. 515-532.
[30] See Ecumenical Directory II, 1993, in *Origins* 23 (1993-1994), pp. 129-160.
[31] See JOHN PAUL II, Apostolic Constitution, *Pastor bonus*, 28 June 1988, in *AAS*, 80 (1988), pp. 841-924; English translation in the *Code of Canon Law Annotated*, pp. 1167-1279; and PAUL VI, Apostolic Constitution, *Regimini Ecclesiae universae*, 15 August 1967, in *AAS*, 59 (1967), pp. 885-928.
[32] See OTADUY, "Introducción: cc.1-6," p. 284, n. 14.
[33] See Chapter 1, pp. 40-42.

occurs in various ways according to the hierarchy of juridical documents and the norms within them:

    a.   <u>Level one documents</u>
           Laws (*leges*) in legislative documents can integrally reorder
           i)   other laws of the same legislator (universal, conference of bishops, diocesan bishop, etc.); and
           ii)   general administrative norms issued by an executive authority of that legislator (e.g., a Roman congregation).
    b.   <u>Level two documents</u>
           General administrative norms contained in documents issued for the community can reorder other such norms as well as the norms in documents issued for the executors of the law.
    c.   <u>Level three documents</u>
           General administrative norms in documents issued for the executors of the law can only reorder other such norms.

Book I, Title III of *CIC/83*, which comprises cc. 29-34, underpins this principle, which deals with integral reordering in terms of derogation as well as abrogation. This tenet accentuates the need for identifying the juridic nature and value of the norms in question in order to provide a framework in which integral reordering can be assessed. A norm in a later document must deal with the same subject matter as the former norm, yet treat it in a substantially new manner. There must also be a parity between the norms in question according to the hierarchy of juridical documents as outlined in this principle.

2.2.4.1 — Level one documents: *leges*

Laws (*leges*), contained in level one documents in the proposed hierarchy, are issued in diverse forms by legislative power, and can integrally reorder earlier laws at their respective level. A universal *lex*, in whatever form it is promulgated, can integrally reorder another universal *lex*. Likewise, a law of a particular legislator can integrally reorder prior laws of that same legislator or his predecessor.[34]

---

[34] See HUELS, "A Theory of Juridical Documents," p. 347. Universal laws, whether they be "a decree of Vatican II, ... in a liturgical book, ... given by means of a general decree issued by a Roman dicastery with delegated power from the pope ... in a curial document approved *in forma specifica* by the pope, ... in an apostolic letter by the pope, or ... in the Code, all have exactly the

The integral reordering of an earlier law by a later one revokes the previous law. While the norms in level two and three documents might be affected by the later law, they are in fact revoked because the law to which they were subordinate no longer exists.[35] It is likewise possible for part of a law to be integrally reordered by a later law that derogates from the former. This could, in turn, bring about abrogation or derogation of norms in inferior documents.

2.2.4.2 — Level two documents: administrative norms for the community

Norms in documents at level two can integrally reorder general administrative norms in documents at levels two and three. Level two documents are administrative. Subordinate to *leges*, they are issued by executive authority for the community for which they are intended.[36] The norms in these documents sometimes "more precisely determine the methods to be observed in applying the law" or "urge the observance of laws."[37] Although level two documents do not have the *vis legis* they are juridically binding for the community to which they are given. Most of the documents of a general character[38] issued by the Roman Curia contain such norms, including many of the documents issued after the Second Vatican Council whose intent it was to apply the decrees of the council.[39]

Canon 33, §2 states that general executory decrees cease to have force in two ways: "by explicit or implicit revocation made by the competent authority" and by the

---

same force and all are subject to the general rules on ecclesiastical laws ...." This is also true in regard to particular *lex*, for instance, at the level of the conference of bishops or diocese.

[35] See cc. 33, §2 and 34, §3.

[36] See HUELS, "A Theory of Juridical Documents," p. 349. Huels notes that oftentimes level two documents appear little different than *leges*. They may have the same form and style and deal with the same subject matter. While they are juridically binding on the community for whom they were intended, they are subordinate to the law they must be in accord with it. Therefore, the norms of such a document could not integrally reorder *leges*.

[37] Canon 31: "Decreta generalia exsecutoria, quibus nempe pressius determinantur modi in lege applicanda servandi aut legum observantia urgetur ...."

[38] Documents of a general character are distinguished from singular administrative acts.

[39] See HUELS, "A Theory of Juridical Documents," p. 348.

cessation of the law on which they are dependent.[40] Thus norms within level two documents can be integrally reordered by subsequent norms within documents at this same level. However, whereas general executory decrees cannot integrally reorder level one documents (*leges*), they can integrally reorder level three documents, as will be discussed below.[41]

2.2.4.3 — Level three documents: administrative norms for the executors of the law

As level two documents appear similar to level one documents, while differing in their source of authority and in the fact that they are subordinate to *leges*, so too, level three documents bear a striking resemblance to level two documents. Both are issued by executive authority; both are dependent upon the law. However, level three documents are directed only to those who must enforce the law. The "instructions" of c. 34, §1 provide the paradigm for all norms in documents of this level, no matter what they may be called. Instructions "clarify the prescripts of laws and elaborate on and determine the methods to be observed in fulfilling them. They are given for the use of those whose duty it is to see that laws are executed and oblige them in the execution of the laws."[42]

Level three documents can only integrally reorder other level three documents or the norms within them. Like other general administrative norms, instructions cease when the law upon which they are dependent is revoked, or by explicit or implicit revocation by the competent authority or the competent authority's superior.[43] However, norms in level three documents can be integrally reordered by those in level

---

[40] "[Decreta generalia exsecutoria] vim habere desinunt revocatione explicita aut implicita ab auctoritate competenti facta, necnon cessante lege ad cuius exsecutionem data sunt ...."

[41] As will be discussed later, norms in level two or level three documents that are incompatible with those in level one documents are invalid.

[42] "Instructiones, quae nempe legum praescripta declarant atque rationes in iisdem exsequendis servandas evolvunt et determinant, ad usum eorum dantur quorum est curare ut leges exsecutioni mandentur, eosque in legum exsecutione obligant ...."

[43] See c. 34, §3: "Vim habere desinunt instructiones non tantum revocatione explicita aut implicita auctoritatis competentis, quae eas edidit, eiusve superioris, sed etiam cessante lege ad quam declarandam vel exsecutioni mandandam datae sunt."

71

two documents. For norms in a document directed specifically to an intended community have a higher juridic value than those given to the executor of the law for implementation.

2.2.4.4 — Further implications of principle

This fourth principle is based on Book I, Title III, "General Decrees and Instructions," which is new to the Code. This section provides a framework that can be used for assessing the juridic value of documents and the norms within them.[44] Postconciliar documents issued before 1983, however, are not subject to this schema.[45] The time between the council and the code marks a unique period in the history of ecclesiastical legislation. However, the juridic nature of the material promulgated during this interim helped provide the impetus for the development of this section of the code. Thus, the proposed hierarchy put forth in this principle can at times be applied to documents issued before the promulgation of *CIC/83*.

The assessment, then, of a published document becomes critical in the application of integral reordering as a means of revocation. A norm in a level two document cannot integrally reorder a similar norm in a level one document. Similarly norms in a level three document, such as an instruction, cannot integrally reorder norms in level one or two documents even if the complete reworking of the norms in question is obvious.[46] For such norms cannot contradict the law or higher norm to

---

[44] Generally canonists agree that this title is a valuable contribution to *CIC/83* in distinguishing the legislative and executive functions of governance in the Church. However, they also acknowledge its shortcomings. For example, some believe that c. 29, which deals with general decrees, would better be placed in Title II, on ecclesiastical laws. In addition, the title lacks a systematic treatment of general administrative norms, in that it deals only with those norms that execute specific *leges* and does not mention autonomous norms. See, for example, E. LABANDEIRA, *Trattato di diritto amministrativo canonico*, 2nd ed., trans. by L. GRAZIANO, Milano, Guiffrè, 1994, pp. 252-254; *Code of Canon Law Annotated*, p. 97; and CIÁURRIZ, "Titulus III: De decretis generalibus et de instructionibus," pp. 471-483.

[45] See E. LABANDEIRA, "Clasificación de las normas escritas canónicas," p. 692.Even some documents published after the promulgation of *CIC/83* do not always fit neatly into the schema established by Title III.

[46] A concrete example of the inability of a level three document to derogate from a level two document was evident in the publication of *Dopo le publicazione* (see SECRETARIAT FOR THE PROMOTION OF CHRISTIAN UNITY, 17 October 1973, in *AAS*, 55 (1973), pp. 616-619; English

which they are subordinate. General administrative norms may never contradict *leges* given by a legislator. This principle, regarding the juridic value of documents and the norms within them, is helpful in determining whether revocation in the form of integral reordering has taken place.

2.2.5 — Principle 5: Proof required

Integral reordering cannot be presumed; it must be proven. Canon 21 provides a basic rule relative to integral reordering: it can never be presumed; it must be proven. Without such proof, revocation does not occur and the later law must be reconciled with the former.

Otaduy alludes to the theory underlying this principle, dealing with it from the perspective of entire documents being integrally reordered. He notes that in some documents the integral reordering of the subject matter is manifest.[47] In others it is adequately substantive, that is, the later document covers essentially the normative matter of the former document.[48] However, he points out that doubts arise when the integral reordering of the subject matter of a document takes place by means of the code. This occurs in cases where the code touches on diverse matters of a given document but not in an adequate way. He believes that in these cases the data points to a qualified doubt and therefore the earlier document should be considered revoked.[49]

---

translation in FLANNERY I, pp. 560-563), a note which was published to interpret the Instruction, *In quibus rerum circumstantiis*. The instruction had given rise to broader and inaccurate interpretations of the Ecumenical Directory, I, 1967, n. 55, which dealt with admitting other Christians to eucharistic communion in the Catholic Church. Thus the Secretariat published the note to assure that the instruction (a level three document) was in line with the Directory (a level two document), on which it depended.

[47] See OTADUY, "De las normas generales: título I," p. 409. Otaduy cites the classic examples of integrally reordered documents: the Constitutions *Apostolicae Sedis* of Pius IX concerning *latae sententiae* censures and *Officiorum et munerum* of Leo XII regarding the discipline in regard to the prohibition of books; the Decree, *Maxima cura,* of Pius X in regard to the removal of pastors; and the Constitution, *Poenitemini,* of Paul VI concerning penitential discipline.

[48] See ibid., p. 409. Otaduy gives the example of *Pastor bonus* totally reordering, and thereby revoking, the Apostolic Constitution, *Regimini Ecclesiae universae.*

[49] See ibid., p. 410: "Todos los datos apuntan, sin embargo, a que en estos casos la duda es cualificada, es decir, que los documentos legislativos preexistentes deben considerarse revocados.

However, one needs to look to the norms in such documents that are neither obviously nor substantially reordered as a whole by the code. Those norms that are not directly contrary to nor clearly reordered by the canons of *CIC*/83 are not revoked. If there is a doubt concerning the integral reordering of earlier norms by the code, then the canon is to be harmonized with the earlier norm as far as possible.

By examining the norms in this fashion, one can ascertain whether the legislator has reordered the entire matter of the document itself or some of the norms within it. The integral reordering of some norms, even a majority of the norms, does not necessarily indicate that the entire document has been reordered. This would only be the case if the reordered norms are central to the contents of the subject matter of the entire document.

Determining that a juridical document has been integrally reordered by another document is a process that requires careful consideration. As alluded to in Chapter 1, the purpose of *CIC/83* was not to codify the entirety of the law. Furthermore, law, while maintaining a stable character, needs to develop to be of service to the community.[50] While the canons of the code often derogate from postconciliar documents and reorder norms within them, at times only a post-code document accomplishes the total reordering of a document. Such was the case with the 1993 Ecumenical Directory which completely reordered the previous Ecumenical Directory of 1967 and 1970.

Han sido muy significativas a este respecto las tomas de postura por parte de la potestad eclesiástica en torno a la revocacíon (por reordenacíon integral) de algunos documentos, como también lo fue la indicación de la Secretaría de la reforma del Código durante los trabajos preparatorios: 'las leyes dadas por elaboradas de nuevo o vueltas a promulgar, lo cual, aunque laborioso, es lo mejor para la seguridad jurídica.'Se trata sin duda de aquellas leyes que contienen múltiples prescripciones compatibles con la nueva ley, pero que han visto reordenados sus núcleos fundamentales, aunque esto no suponga más que una pequeña parte del texto normativo total." Otaduy refers to the *Ratio fundamentalis institutionis sacerdotalis* of 1985 and the circular letter *De processu super matrimonio rato et non consummato* of 1986 as examples of where the Code had sufficiently reordered the material of the prior documents. As discussed in Chapter 1 the position of this author differs from Otaduy regarding the need to repromulgate post-Vatican II documents that were issued by the Roman Curia. The documents to which Otaduy refers were not clearly reordered by the code. They existed as the *ius vigens* after the promulgation of the code, until they were integrally reordered.

[50] See ÖRSY, *From Vision to Legislation,* pp. 43-44.

2.2.6 — Principle 6: Tenor, circumstances of law; mind of legislator

It is necessary to consider the tenor and circumstances of the norms as well as the mind of the legislator to determine whether integral reordering has taken place. Canon 17 deals with the proper understanding of a law. The latter part of the canon, which concerns a doubtful or obscure law, states that such a law requires recourse "... to the purpose and circumstances of the law and to the mind of the legislator."[51] These are the same requisites that commentators cite as expedient in determining whether a law has been integrally reordered.[52] While such external factors must always be invoked with a certain caution in regard to a doubtful law,[53] they also need to be analyzed critically when determining whether or not integral reordering has taken place. If the tenor[54] of the new law is notably disparate from the earlier law or if the circumstances surrounding the new law prove significantly different, these could be indications that the legislator has intended something wholly different in the later law, thereby effecting an integral reordering of the prior law.[55]

---

[51] "... quae si dubia et obscura manserit, ad locos parallelos, si qui sint, ad legis finem ac circumstantias et ad mentem legislatoris est recurrendum."

[52] See, for example, MICHIELS, *Normae generales*, pp. 658-659.

[53] See ÖRSY, "General Norms," p. 36.

[54] The expression *tenor legis* has been used in discussing integral reordering both by commentators on *CIC/17* and *CIC/83*. See, for example, VAN HOVE, *De legibus ecclesiasticus*, pp. 355 and 357; MICHIELS, *Normae generales*, pp. 658-659; and OTADUY, "El derecho canónico postconciliar," pp. 125-126. In accord with these authors and *The Oxford Latin Dictionary* and the *Dictionary of Ecclesiastical Latin*, the word "tenor" as used here denotes the sense, the direction or the general drift of the law. It is not to be equated with the "tone" or the forcefulness of the law. Although these two terms are related, the latter is used in this work to indicate the forcefulness of a given law or norm.

[55] Regarding the purpose of the law, see OTADUY, "De las normas generales: título I," pp. 366-367. Otaduy describes the purpose of the law, the *ratio legis*, as the motivating cause of the law. It is not to be confused with the purpose of ecclesiastical law as a whole, that is, the *salus animarum*. Rather it is the specific external cause which impelled the legislator to give the norm. See also T.I. JIMÉNEZ URRESTI, "Libro I: cc. 1-123," in L. DE ECHEVERRIA (ed.), *Código de derecho canónico, edición bilingüe comentada por los professores de la Facultad de derecho canónico de la Universidad Pontificia de Salamanca*, 7th rev. ed., Madrid, Biblioteca de autores cristianos, 1986, p. 29. DeEcheverria notes that knowing the intrinsic, immediate and specific purpose of each law, and its ulterior end, helps to understand the scope of the obligation of the law.

Regarding the circumstances of the law, see ABBO and HANNAN, *The Sacred Canons*, p. 38. These authors describe the circumstances of the law as the accessory and extrinsic factors which accompany and surround a law. These encompass such factors as: the time the law was enacted; the

Otaduy notes that the mind of the legislator refers not to the physical person but rather the institutional figure of the legislator. In this sense, to appeal to the legislator is to connect with the system of laws and the reasons that support them.[56] The mind of the legislator is contingent upon the purpose and the circumstance of the law; it does not exist in isolation. It has to do with the motivating cause for a certain law being given at a specific time. In addition, the mind of the legislator encompasses the style or the concrete "political attitude" of the legislator in each law itself: for example, that of Pius XII or Paul VI; that of the Council of Trent or of the Second Vatican Council. Although *ratio legis non est lex*, the mind of the legislator is helpful in understanding and interpreting it.[57]

Whereas the mind of the legislator is a recourse in dealing with a doubtful law, it can also be an important component in determining integral reordering. For at times the legislator can integrally reorder a law without changing it materially. This is essentially what occurs when an authentic interpretation issued by the legislator or his delegate is either extensive or restrictive.[58] For the law as authentically interpreted is not directly contrary to the former law; yet there is a basic incompatibility that occurs between the former and present *understanding* of the subject matter of the law. The

---

persons involved; discussions which preceded the drafting as well as the preparatory drafts, etc. OTADUY, in "De las normas generales: título I," p. 369, speaks of the historical context of the law. He points out: "En este último sentido no podemos olvidar que la circunstancia histórica que ha ocasionado la legislación codicial – aunque por supuesto constituye más que una mera ocasión de la ley – ha sido el concilio Vaticano II."

[56] See OTADUY, "De las normas generales: título I," p. 371.

[57] See JIMÉNEZ URRESTI, "Libro I: cc. 1-123," p. 29: "En esa mente entra el estilo o *actitud politica* concreta del legislador en cada ley suya: p. ej., una fue la de Pio XII, otra la de Pablo VI; una fue la del Concilio de Trento y otra ha sido la del Vaticano II. Y aunque *ratio legis non est lex*, contribuye a entenderla e interpretarla."

[58] See c. 16, §§ 1 and 2. See also L. WRENN, *Authentic Interpretations on the 1983 Code*, Washington, DC, Canon Law Society of America, 1993, pp. 1-5. Wrenn holds that proper authentic interpretations are either declarative or explanatory in nature. A declarative interpretation is made when the meaning of the law is not in a true sense doubtful, at least objectively doubtful. The declarative interpretation merely clarifies or brings greater clarity to what is already certain. The explanatory interpretation, however, clarifies a law that is objectively doubtful or has been interpreted in various ways. Since an objectively doubtful law does not obligate, it has no binding force until the doubt is resolved. Once the explanatory interpretation is made it begins to bind in the interpreted sense. Its force is not retroactive. The explanatory interpretation can restrict or extend the meaning of the canon.

intention of the legislator is manifest in the interpretation given. Thus the objectively doubtful law becomes one that is objectively certain.[59]

Integral reordering also takes place without material change when a former law is incorporated into a new law. This was the case with many postconciliar norms that became part of the code. This is also the case when a norm in a level two or three document is later issued by the legislator as *lex*. The norm, though identical with the earlier one, is integrally reordered because it has now been given a higher juridic value.

2.2.7 — Principle 7: Change in tone or forcefulness

Integral reordering can occur through a change in the tone or forcefulness of a given law or general administrative norm. This principle is rooted in several of those previously mentioned.[60] It is based on the third principle of revision of *CIC/83* which treated the nature of the juridic language used in the code. This criterion emphasized that pastoral care, the hallmark of the code, was to be reflected in the character of its canons. Charity, temperance, humaneness and moderation were to mark the spirit of the law. Canonical norms were not to be excessively rigid, but rather were to leave discretionary judgment in the hands of pastoral leaders. Laws, in the strict sense, were not to be used if instructions, exhortations, recommendations or other means could be effective in achieving the same purpose.[61] In line with this,

---

[59] See WRENN, *Authentic Interpretations*, p. 4.

[60] This principle is a corollary to principles one, four, and six presented above, as well as number eight that will follow. The first principle deals with derogation as affecting integral reordering. The change in tone of a given norm can bring about abrogation or derogation of the respective law or norms by the change of meaning that it produces to the original law. In regard to principle four, integral reordering through a change in tone could take place in norms in levels one, two and three documents as described above. Oftentimes the change of tone reflects the tenor and circumstances of the law as well as the intent of the legislator as described in the sixth principle. As this principle flows from Otaduy's discussion of *formal* integral reordering, it is likewise related to principle eight. As such the reordering must be demonstrated in its substance, not only in its form.

[61] See ALESANDRO, "The Revision of the *Code of Canon Law*," p. 108. See also R. CUNNINGHAM, "The Principles Guiding the Revision of the *Code of Canon Law*," in *The Jurist*, 30 (1970), p. 448-449. For the complete original text of this principle of revision, see *Communicationes*, 1 (1969), pp. 79-80.

a significant change in the tone or forcefulness of a given norm could indicate integral reordering on the part of the legislator. Norms which are strengthened or relaxed or which are restricted or expanded are reflected through the tone of the norm itself. This could be exemplified by a command that becomes a recommendation or an exhortation that takes on an obligatory character. Similarly, those norms that are more open and flexible, promoting subsidiarity or allowing pastoral leaders to exercise prudent judgment in the implementation of a law, could indicate a reordering.

2.2.8 — Principle 8: Independence of new norm

A law that has integrally reordered an earlier law does not depend on the prior law for its juridic force or its meaning. This principle is based upon those that have already been presented and implicitly underlies each of them. However, it is important to highlight this tenet in itself as it reiterates the effect of integral reordering. This assumption accentuates the fact that, because the legislator has ordained something entirely new, the meaning of the law is to be found in its present configuration. The later law, both in its formal and juridical aspects, is a total reformulation. The former law, as well as those norms accessory to it, no longer have force because their purpose and meaning have changed.[62]

The Church has always valued stability and continuity in its law. The very use of a code for the compilation of ecclesiastical law substantiates this fact. A code also demonstrates the relativity of laws which exist, not autonomously, but in a complementary context with other laws. At the same time ecclesiastical law is directed to a people who live in a world of constant change. Within the Church this change is also obvious. One only need consider the rapid evolution of theology before and after the Second Vatican Council as well as the on-going interpretation of dogma within

---

[62] See CABREROS DE ANTA, *Vigencia y estado actual de la legislación canónica*, pp. 20-21. See also ÖRSY, "General Norms," p. 38: "The subject of the later law is the same as that of the former one, but the later gives a wholly new structure, so that the two edifices, former and later, cannot coexist in any way."

the Church today. Yet converting intellectual advancements into practical structures is a slow process and often meets with resistance.[63]

E. Correco, reflecting on the revised *Code of Canon Law*, states that it is impossible to avoid the question of why the Latin Church preferred the legislative technique of the code, instead of adopting a technique that would be less binding.[64] Likewise, M. Cabreros de Anta, citing juridic institutes that were integrally reordered by Vatican II, believes that such evolution must continue in the juridic life of the Church.[65]

Such is the possibility offered by integral reordering. While acknowledging continuity with the past, in light of contemporary needs and theological development, the legislator completely reworks the law so that it is serviceable for the community for whom it is intended. The *vis iuris* is found only in the reordered law.

2.3 — SUMMARY OF PRINCIPLES

The above principles provide a canonically based rationale for determining whether the subject matter of a given law has been integrally reordered. The principles, both challenging and cautionary, are themselves uneven. Some are general, applicable in nearly all cases and basic to the process of determining integral reordering. Principles one and five exemplify this description. The first asserts the necessity of identifying the extent of what is reordered. This is essential to each instance of integral reordering as is the proof of complete reordering demanded by principle five. Whether the evidence is obvious or whether it requires a more detailed explanation, integral reordering is not to be presumed.

Other principles assist in providing the proof that the subject matter of a given law has been integrally reordered. Principles four, six and seven fulfill this role. The

---

[63] See L. ÖRSY,"Quantity and Quality of Laws after Vatican II," in *The Jurist*, 27 (1967), pp. 385-412.

[64] See E. CORECCO, "Theological Justifications of the Codification," p. 69.

[65] See CABREROS DE ANTA, *Vigencia y estado*, pp. 22-23.

use of the hierarchy of documents and the norms within them, the consideration of the tenor and circumstances of the law as well as the mind of the legislator, and the determination of the tone of the document can lead one to conclude that a given law or general administrative norm has or has not been integrally reordered.

At times a single principle may serve to demonstrate that a law has been integrally reordered. Generally, however, several principles employed together will provide the confirmation that is required. In light of the postconciliar documents and their relation with *CIC/83*, as well as the many documents that continue to be issued in the Church today, it is necessary to have a more open understanding of integral reordering.[66] However, this understanding must be rooted in a correct interpretation of ecclesiastical law, primarily that contained in the code itself. Properly applied, these principles provide such a base for demonstrating the integral reordering of juridic documents and institutes, laws and norms. Properly implemented, they can enable one to achieve clarity regarding the status of the *ius vigens*.

2.4 — MODEL OF INTEGRALLY REORDERED NORMS

Before applying these principles to religious law in the following chapter, it is helpful to look at laws that have been integrally reordered to see, in fact, if these principles are borne out in them and if any other aspects of integral reordering might be disclosed through these integrally reordered laws. The examples of completely reordered law used throughout this study have referred, for the most part, to juridic documents or institutes. However, a model of integrally reordered law that treats individual norms will be examined in order to exemplify the principles which underlie it.

---

[66] See OTADUY, "El derecho canónico postconciliar," p. 125.

Such an illustration of integrally reordered law is found in the "Emendations in the Liturgical Books following upon the New *Code of Canon Law*."[67] Published during the *vacatio* of *CIC/83*, these emendations are, in actuality, express revocations of liturgical laws.[68] However, it is the *preparation* of these adaptations that provides insight into the concept of integral reordering and allows them to be cited as an appropriate model as will be explained below. These emendations provide an authentic example, in that they were undertaken by the Holy See itself; thus they offer an authoritative verification of the principles in operation.

Canon 2 acknowledges that the majority of liturgical law is found outside the code. It states:

> For the most part the Code does not define the rites which must be observed in celebrating liturgical actions. Therefore liturgical laws in force until now retain their force unless one of them is contrary to the canons of the Code.[69]

Liturgical law, for the most part, remained unaffected by the promulgation of *CIC/83*; however, with the promulgation of the revised code there were some liturgical norms that required modification in order to conform to the canons.

Unlike the liturgical emendations necessary at the time of *CIC/17*, which were issued some eight years after its promulgation, the Congregation for the Sacraments

---

[67] See SACRED CONGREGATION FOR THE SACRAMENTS AND DIVINE WORSHIP, "Variationes in novas editiones librorum liturgicorum ad normam Codicis iuris canonici nuper promulgati introducendae," 12 September 1983, in *Notitiae*, 19 (1983), pp. 540-555. English translation in INTERNATIONAL COMMISSION ON ENGLISH IN THE LITURGY (= ICEL), "Emendations in the Liturgical Books following upon the New Code of Canon Law" (= "Emendations"), Washington, DC, 1984. In this publication the emendations are compared with the ICEL translation of the introductions to the ritual books in *Documents on the Liturgy, 1963-1979: Conciliar, Papal, and Curial Texts*, The Liturgical Press, Collegeville, Minnesota, 1982. All examples used in this chapter will be taken from this translation and referred to by the appropriate title and number. Latin excerpts of the Pre-Code norm are taken from R. KACZYNSKI (ed.), *Enchiridion documentorum instaurationis liturgicae*, vol. 1, Torino, Marietti, 1963.

[68] According to c. 20 of *CIC/83* express revocation and revocation by direct contrariety and integral reordering are the means of extrinsic cessation of law. Technically a law that is expressly revoked ceases by that very fact. However, as will be demonstrated, the process leading to the express revocation in the "Emendations" first necessitated determining those liturgical laws that were in opposition to the code, either by way of direct contrariety or by means of integral reordering.

[69] "Codex plerumque non definit ritus, qui in actionibus liturgicis celebrandis sunt servandi; quare liturgicae hucusque vigentes vim suam retinet, nisi earum aliqua Codicis canonibus sit contraria."

and Divine Worship appointed a group of liturgists and canonists to undertake the task of emending liturgical norms at the time the code was promulgated. The revised liturgical law would then be effective at the same time that *CIC/83* became the *ius vigens*.[70] It was the responsibility of this committee to modify those liturgical norms that were not compatible with the code and thus harmonize liturgical law with the canonical discipline. The introductory note to the "Emendations" reveals that the members of the work group relied in particular on cc. 20 and 21 in accomplishing the project. It states:

> The principles at work in such emendations are chiefly those found in the general norms of the Code itself, dealing with the abrogation or derogation of existing law by subsequent legislation (CIC, canon 20) and the presumption that favors continuity in the ecclesiastical law: "In doubt the revocation of a previous law is not presumed, but later laws are to be related to earlier ones and, as far as possible, harmonized with them" (CIC, c. 21).[71]

In order to enable the legislator to promulgate the changes expressly, the committee evaluated the existing norms in light of whether they were directly contrary to the code or whether the canons of *CIC/83* had integrally reordered them.[72] Those norms which presented a doubt of revocation were not included in the emendations in accord with c. 21. Where such a doubt between the norms existed, the *praenotanda*

---

[70] See P. GY, "Commentarium: les changements dans les praenotanda des livres liturgiques à la suite du Code de droit canonique," in *Notitiae*, 19 (1983), p. 557. For a list of those appointed to the committee entrusted with this task, see P. MARINI, "Codice di diritto canonico e legislazione liturgica," in *Notitiae*, 19 (1983), pp. 280-281.

[71] ICEL, "Emendations," p. 3.

[72] It is interesting to note that c. 2 speaks of liturgical norms "retaining their force unless a given norm is contrary" to the code. Yet, the group appointed to prepare the emendations for express revocation by the legislator used the principles of c. 20 in dealing with the abrogation/derogation of existing laws by subsequent legislation, not merely c. 2 itself. The principles of c. 20 include both direct contrariety and integral reordering. As previously noted, both means of revocation imply an incompatibility with the former norms. As already suggested, from one perspective direct contrariety can be considered a form of integral reordering (see n. 26 above). On the other hand, it is possible that another might argue that integral reordering is a form of direct contrariety by understanding "contrariety" in a broad sense. However, as indicated previously, the fact that commentators on *CIC/83* no longer speak of direct and indirect contrariety does not support this possibility. Also the greater revoking power of integral reordering in regard to entire juridic documents or complex laws appears to make integral reordering the more inclusive of the two terms. What is apparent is that the distinction between these two forms of revocation is not universally agreed upon.

were retained and thus the later norms were to be related to and harmonized with them.[73] Thus, the "Emendations," undertaken by the Apostolic See itself, provide an authoritative verification of the principles in operation.

The emendations affected, to some degree, "seventy-six articles, or numbers, of the *Institutio Generalis* of the Roman Missal and the *Praenotanda* of various sacramental and other liturgical rites, but many of them, indeed the majority of them, do not represent really significant modifications of liturgical law."[74] Nearly one-third of the adaptations were redactional, that is, the textual adaptations were merely updated references to sources or they incorporated terminological changes.[75] Some of the variations were made in light of the indirect impact of other areas of the law. For example, in a number of the *praenotanda* the term "local ordinary" was replaced

---

[73] See R. PAGÉ, "'Variationes': Réflexions d'un canoniste," in *Bulletin national de liturgie*, 18 (1984), p. 58. While it is not the purpose of this study to analyze the emendations in depth, it should be noted that Pagé identifies other canons that significantly changed liturgical norms which are not included in the "Emendations." For example, he points out that although the "Emendations" cite the change in regard to the homily in concurrence with c. 767, §2, they do not take into consideration the change in that same canon, §1 which speaks of the homily being reserved to the priest or deacon. Number 24 of the *praenotanda* of the "Lectionary for the Mass," which does not appear in the emendations, is much broader in stating that as a rule the homily is given by the one who is presiding. Pagé also cites similar examples in regard to extraordinary ministers of baptism and marriage witnessed by the laity. It could be that the group which prepared the emendations overlooked them at the time or believed that there was a qualified doubt as to whether or not these norms were tacitly revoked in light of *CIC/83*. This is mentioned in order to point out that one could argue that the code has indeed integrally reordered liturgical norms apart from the "Emendations" which are in actuality the express revocation of prior norms.

[74] A. TEGELS, "Chronicle," in *Worship*, 58 (1984), p. 55.

[75] See GY, "Les changements dans les praenotanda," p. 557. Many of the references were amended to include citations of the canons of *CIC/83*. See, for example, nn. 56, 153 and 277 of the *General Instruction of the Roman Missal*, which now include references to cc. 917, 902 and 938, respectively. Some examples of changes in terminology include: the word "dedicate" is used for churches, cathedrals and altars rather than the word "consecrate;" the bishop is identified as the "ordinary" minister rather than the "primary" minister of confirmation; the words "churches and oratories" have replaced the three-fold distinction of "churches, oratories and private oratories."

with "diocesan bishop."[76] Others, however, exemplified a decisive reworking of liturgical law.[77] These are of particular interest here.[78]

2.4.1 — Examples of emendations

A selection of the laws in the "Emendations" that are incompatible with the former norms by reason of integral reordering will be presented in the following sections. These provide a model of law which has been integrally reordered in accord with the theory discussed in Chapter 1 and the principles presented above.[79]

The emendations themselves support the initial assertion of this chapter: that integral reordering is applicable to individual norms as well as juridic documents and institutes, as opposed to many commentators who only cite entire juridic documents or institutes as examples of integral reordering. The "Emendations" demonstrate, as stated in the first principle above, that while the revised code derogated from liturgical law, the affected individual norms are abrogated or derogated by the emended norms.

The majority of the substantial emendations, that is, those not effected by a mere change in reference or terminology, but which evidence a basic incompatibility

---

[76] See GY, "Les changements dans les praenotanda," p. 558. Although Gy sees this change as having an indirect impact, the replacement of "local ordinary" with "diocesan bishop" integrally reorders a given law, as will be demonstrated below.

[77] See TEGELS, "Chronicle," pp. 55-56. See also GY, "Les changements dans les praenotanda," pp. 557-558.

[78] See GY, "Les changements dans les praenotanda," pp. 556-561. Gy presents the most comprehensive analysis of the "Emendations in the Liturgical Books Following upon the New Code of Canon Law." He has classified those norms that were significantly modified, i.e., those that were incompatible with the code, into four categories. The first group, relatively small in number, includes those changes in which *CIC/83* reverts to the former discipline from which the liturgical books themselves had been adapted. The second category contains emendations in which the code goes beyond the liturgical reform or simplifies its implementation. The third division, a unique class in itself, pertains to norms that treat general absolution without preliminary confession; while the fourth considers the insertion of canonical prescriptions which were not previously part of the liturgical books. This schema, however, will not be used in treating the emendations in this study.

[79] Not all the proposed principles will be modeled in the emendations. Principle three, for example, which deals with the reordering of an entire document, is not applicable. Likewise, there is no need to discern the hierarchical juridic value of the norms as outlined in principle four, since all are universal *leges*. The suppositions of principles five and six regarding necessary proof of integral reordering and consideration of the tenor and circumstances of the norms as well as the mind of the legislator, however, have already been applied by the preparatory work group. Insight will be provided into the working of these and other principles.

with the original norm, are the result of the former *praenotanda* having been integrally reordered by *CIC/83*.[80] Acknowledging the ambiguity between direct contrariety and integral reordering discussed in Chapter 1, and the understanding of it put forth in the second principle, examples of norms emended as a result of direct contrariety with the former norms will be considered first.

2.4.1.1 — Direct contrariety

It appears that omission is a principal way in which direct contrariety is evident in the emendations.[81] Number 86 of the *praenotanda* for *Holy Communion and Worship of the Eucharist outside Mass* provides such an example. The first part of this norm, identical in both the text in use in 1982 and the emended text, reads:

> In churches where the eucharist is regularly reserved, it is recommended that solemn exposition of the blessed sacrament for an extended period of time should take place once a year, even though this period is not strictly continuous. In this way the local community may meditate on this mystery more deeply and adore.

The second paragraph embodies the derogation wrought by c. 942 of *CIC/83*. The respective texts state:

Pre-Code Text	CIC/83	Emended Text
86. This kind of exposition, however, may take place, <u>with the consent of the local Ordinary</u>, only if there is assurance of the participation of a reasonable number of the faithful.	Canon 942. It is recommended that in these churches and oratories an annual solemn exposition of the Most Blessed Sacrament be held for an appropriate period of time, even if not continuous, so that the local community more	86. This kind of exposition, however, may take place only if there is assurance of the participation of a reasonable number of the faithful.

---

[80] Of the more than 40 emendations that are substantially altered, less than ten would be classified as the result of direct contrariety in light of the theory presented in chapter 1 and the further input provided in principle two above.

[81] As omission often indicates direct contrariety, it will be demonstrated later that a substantive addition to a given norm usually reorders the norms itself.

> profoundly meditates on and adores the eucharistic mystery. Such an exposition is to be held, however, only if a suitable gathering of the faithful is foreseen and the established norms are observed.

The omission of "with the consent of the local Ordinary" in the code can be considered directly contrary to the previous norm. Thus, the emended norm does not require such approval. What was obligatory is no longer necessary in light of c. 942. In this respect the latter parts of the two norms are diametrically opposed; accordingly the former was considered revoked by the code.[82]

Another more significant example of direct contrariety by reason of omission is found in the *Rite of Religious Profession*. The entire section on the "Rite of Religious Promise" has been suppressed as well as other norms related to it. In light of c. 654 religious profession requires the observance of a public vow to observe the three evangelical counsels. Thus, the emendation to n. 5 of the *Rite of Religious Profession* has omitted the section which read:

> Where a promise or some other kind of bond takes the place of profession, the proper setting for the rite is some suitable liturgical service, such as a liturgy of the word, a part of the liturgy of the hours, especially morning prayer or evening prayer, or, if circumstances require, the eucharistic sacrifice itself.

The new law, which does not allow other bonds but only vows, can be considered in opposition to the former that did permit this.

---

[82] Other examples of direct contrariety in this fashion include the following *praenotanda*: n. 24 of *Holy Communion and Worship of the Eucharist Outside Mass*, which eliminates the communion fast for the elderly and the infirm as well as those who care for them; n. 40 of the *Rite of Penance* which, in accord with c. 961, §2, no longer allows priests to decide to give general absolution when a grave need arises and recourse to the diocesan bishop is not possible; n. 31 of the *Pastoral Care of the Sick: Rites of Anointing and Viaticum*, which corresponds to c. 883, 3°, in which the law gives the priest the faculty to confirm, thus eliminating the hierarchy of those who might do this if the bishop were impeded; and n. 164 of the same title, in light of c. 918, in which the permission of the local ordinary is no longer required for viaticum to be given within the full eucharistic celebration.

However, the intent of this study is to focus on integral reordering. Several patterns emerge in the "Emendations" regarding ways in which laws are integrally reordered. Highlighting some of these will shed light on the difference between direct contrariety and integral reordering as well as demonstrate various ways in which the law is integrally reordered. Examples of this will be examined under four separate headings. These will include emendations that change the source of authority, those norms that reflect a substantive addition, norms that are significantly changed in tone and juridic institutes or complex laws that have been integrally reordered.

2.4.1.2 — Change of the competent authority

There are several emendations that have shifted responsibility from the local ordinary to the diocesan bishop or vice versa. For example, in nn. 101 and 102 of *Holy Communion and Worship of the Eucharist outside Mass* the term "local ordinary" was replaced, in accord with c. 944, §2 of *CIC/83*,[83] by "diocesan bishop" in regard to decisions concerning eucharistic processions.[84] On the other hand, the emendation to n. 11 of the *Rite of Baptism for Children*, corresponding to canon 858, §2, states that the local ordinary, rather than the diocesan bishop, may permit a baptismal font to be placed in another church or public oratory within parish boundaries.

Such changes derogate from the earlier norm because the code has integrally reordered the norms by changing the authority who is responsible for such actions. While the emendations are the result of the change in the role of the diocesan bishop,

---

[83] Canon 944, "§2: It is for the diocesan bishop to establish regulations which provide for the participation in and the dignity of the processions."

[84] Responsibility also shifted from the local ordinary to diocesan bishop in n. 32 of the *Rite of Penance* in regard to judging whether conditions are verified for giving general absolution in specific instances, in accord with c. 961, §2; n. 17 of the *Pastoral Care of the Sick: Rites of Anointing and Viaticum*, regarding the responsibility for supervising celebrations of communal anointing; and n. 108 regarding decisions concerning the rites of anointing outside Mass in accord with c. 1002.

which indirectly impinges upon liturgical law,[85] nonetheless, the norm has been completely reformulated in its juridical aspect. This is not an example of direct contrariety in that permission for such actions is still required but has been redirected.[86] The change affected a key component of the norm, thus bringing about a complete reordering of it.

2.4.1.3 — Norms integrally reordered by substantive addition

A common way that integral reordering occurs is through the addition of a phrase or clause to a given norm.[87] There are numerous examples of this occurring throughout the liturgical books that were emended. Two emendations of the *General Instruction of the Roman Missal* will serve to illustrate this.[88]

Pre-Code Text	CIC/83	Emended Text
42. There must be a homily on Sundays and holy days of obligation at all Masses that are celebrated with a congregation.	Canon 767, §2. A homily must be given at all Masses on a Sunday and holy days of obligation which are celebrated with a congregation, it cannot be omitted without a grave cause (*gravi de causa*).	42. There must be a homily on Sundays and holy days of obligation at all Masses that are celebrated with a congregation; it may not be omitted without a serious reason (*gravi de causa*).

---

[85] See GY, "Les changements dans les praenotanda," p. 558.

[86] From another perspective one might argue that such a change is the result of direct contrariety, that the nature of the authority of the diocesan bishop and that of the local ordinary are different. However, this author supports the reasoning that there is an incompatibility between the sources of authority in that they are not directly contrary.

[87] The addition of a phrase or clause to a given norm is rooted in principles one and six. As indicated in discussing the initial principle, derogation is understood more broadly in light of the simplification of terms in *CIC/83*. The addendum can reorder the meaning of the norm, thus bringing about an abrogation of the earlier norm. Principle six deals with the tenor and circumstances of the norm and the mind of the legislator that can be evident in the additional phrase or clause.

[88] Additional phrases or specific changes necessitated by *CIC/83* are underlined in the respective texts.

Pre-Code Text	CIC/83	Emended Text
211. The eucharist is to be reserved in a single, solid, unbreakable tabernacle.	Canon 938, §3. The tabernacle in which the Most Holy Eucharist is reserved habitually is to be immovable, made of solid and opaque material, and locked in such a way so that the danger of profanation is avoided as much as possible.	211. The eucharist is to be reserved in a single, solid immovable tabernacle that is opaque and is locked in such a way as to provide every possible security against the danger of desecration. (9)

In both cases the code is incompatible with the pre-code text in that the additional words have reordered its meaning. In the first example concerning the homily, the addition of the clause "it may not be omitted except for a grave cause," creates an exception, thus relaxing the rigor of the law. The two norms are not directly contrary, for both affirm the necessity of the homily on Sundays and holydays. The incompatibility between the two norms exists in that the addendum integrally reorders the law by establishing grounds for an exception.[89]

A similar reordering through an additional phrase occurs in the second example concerning the tabernacle. In this case, however, the law is strengthened through the change wrought by c. 938, §3. The later norm is more detailed in its demands. Because the emended norm includes the former in its revision and is not opposed to the earlier, it cannot be said to be directly contrary. Yet the addendum reorders the requirements to assure the security of the reserved eucharist.[90]

---

[89] It could possibly be argued that this is an example of direct contrariety in that the earlier norm had no exception whereas the later one did. However, the incompatibility between the norms does not result in direct opposition. It is the relaxation of the norm by *CIC/83* that integrally reorders the former norm.

[90] Similar examples can be found in the norms of other liturgical books, as well. See, for example, *praenotanda* nn.10 and 14 of *Holy Communion and Worship of the Eucharist Outside Mass*; nn. 8 and 11 of *Rite of Baptism for Children*; nn. 44 and 66 of "Christian Initiation of Adults;" n. 15 and 21of *Pastoral Care of the Sick: Rites of Anointing and Viaticum*; and n. 14 of the *Rite of Funerals*.

2.4.1.4 — Norms integrally reordered through change in tone

A number of the *praenotanda* which were integrally reordered by the Code reflect a decisive shift in their tone or forcefulness.[91] As presented in principle seven, such a change in tone can indicate that a norm has been integrally reordered. What was urged can become obligatory; what was mandated can become a recommendation. An example of this is found in n. 255 of *The General Instruction of the Roman Missal*.

Pre-Code	CIC/83	Emended Text
255. It <u>is preferable</u> (*praestat*) that churches be <u>solemnly consecrated</u> (*consecrari*).	Canon 1217, §1 – After construction has been completed properly, a new church <u>is to be dedicated or at least blessed</u> (*dedicetur ... benedicatur*) as soon as possible; the laws of the sacred liturgy are to be observed. §2 – Churches, especially cathedrals and parochial churches, <u>are to be</u>	255. All churches <u>are to be solemnly dedicated or blessed</u> (*dedicentur aut ... benedicantur*). But the cathedral and parish churches <u>are always to be dedicated</u> (*dedicentur*).

---

[91] See J. HUELS, "Liturgical Law: An Introduction," in E. FOLEY, *American Essays in Liturgy*, n. 4, The Pastoral Press, Washington, DC, 1987. Huels categorizes juridic norms used in liturgical law into four groups: preceptive norms, which are obligatory; recommendations, which do not impose any legal obligation; discretionary norms, which are quite common in liturgical law and provide the possibility of option(s); and statements of rights and capabilities, which do not necessarily need to be fulfilled. It appears that a norm that changes from one of these categories to another would demonstrate integral reordering. Furthermore Huels notes that preceptive laws themselves encompass varying degrees of obligatory strength. The most forceful norms use words such as "is bound by obligation" (*obligatione tenetur*), "is necessary" (*oportet*), "must" (*debet*), "is required" (*requiritur*), etc. Likewise the present indicative is also used preceptively to command what *must* be done. Subjunctive commands, another form of the preceptive norms, usually indicate what should be done as the general rule. It is a milder command, often indicated by the words "should" or "is to do." Such norms do not possess the same weight as those which use "must" but they are still binding. Negative commands, that specifically exclude a definite specific act, are generally more forceful than positive commands and use words such as "it is absolutely prohibited" (*nefas est*) or "must not" (*non debet*). Finally, exhortations are preceptive norms used to describe general obligations and traits of a specific function or office. Exhortations usually present the ideal as a value for which to strive. Thus, a preceptive law could be integrally reordered by another preceptive norm, depending on the tone employed in the later norm.

dedicated (*dedicentur*) by
the solemn rite.

It is obvious that the tone of the emended norm reorders the meaning of the earlier norm in light of c. 1217, §1. The change in the verb as well as the additional sentence serve to heighten the force of the norm from that of a recommendation to that of a precept. According to the second principle above, this would not be considered direct contrariety since both norms uphold consecration/dedication.[92] Due to its obligatory nature, c. 1217, §1 integrally reorders and thereby revokes the former norm as is reflected in the emended text.

Other such examples are obvious in *Pastoral Care of the Sick: Rites of Anointing and Viaticum*. CIC/83 integrally reordered the liturgical law pertaining to the sacrament of the anointing of the sick by a change in tone, making obligatory what had been optional. Several *praenotanda* exemplify this:

Pre-Code Text	CIC/83	Emended Text
12. Sick children may be anointed (*ministrari potest*) if they have sufficient use of reason to be strengthened by this sacrament.	Canon 1005. The sacrament is to be administered in a case of doubt whether the sick person has attained the use of reason, is dangerously ill, or is dead.	12. Sick children are to be anointed (*ministretur*) if they have sufficient use of reason to be strengthened by this sacrament. In a case of doubt whether a child has reached the use of reason, the sacrament is to be conferred (*conferatur*).
14. The sacrament of anointing may be conferred (*praeberi potest*) on sick people who, although they have lost consciousness or the	Canon 1006. This sacrament is to be conferred (*conferatur*) on the sick who at least implicitly requested it	14. The sacrament of anointing is to be conferred (*conferatur*) on sick people who, although they have lost consciousness or the use of reason, would, as

---

[92] As noted earlier, the word "dedicated" is simply a terminological change and does not affect the revocation of the pre-code text. See GY, "Les changements dans les praenotanda," p. 557.

use of reason, would, as Christian believers, probably have asked for it were they in control of their faculties.	when they were in control of their faculties.	Christian believers, have at least implicitly asked for it when they were in control of their faculties.
15. When a priest has been called to attend those who are already dead, he should not administer the sacrament of anointing. Instead, he should pray for them, asking that God forgive their sins and graciously receive them into the kingdom. But if the priest is doubtful whether the sick person is dead, <u>he may give</u> (*potest praebere*) the sacrament conditionally.	Canon 1005. See above.	15. When a priest has been called to attend to those who are already dead, he should not administer the sacrament of anointing. Instead, he should pray for them, asking that God forgive their sins and graciously receive them into the kingdom. But if the priest is doubtful whether the sick person is dead, <u>he is to confer</u> (*ministret*) the sacrament using the rite given in no. 269.

In each of these *praenotanda* the change in tone is significant. It affects the very essence of the norm itself. What was optional or permitted is now required. While n. 12 also contains additions in light of the respective canon, it is the tone of the canon that is central in bringing about a reordering of each of the norms above.[93]

The "Emendations" also reflect the integral reordering of the earlier norm in light of the canons of *CIC/83* where the tone of the later norm relaxes the previous discipline. Number 11 of *Holy Communion and Worship of the Eucharist Outside Mass* provides such an example:

Pre-Code Text	CIC/83	Emended Text
11. ... According to traditional usage, <u>an oil lamp or lamp with a wax candle is to burn</u>	Canon 940 – <u>A special lamp</u> (*pecularis ... lampas*) which indicates and honors the presence	11. ... As an indication of Christ's presence and as a mark of reverence, <u>a special lamp</u> (*pecularis*

---

[93] Number 12 expands the obligation to confer the sacrament even in the case of doubt; n. 14 does likewise in changing the "probable" asking for the sacrament to "implicitly" requesting it.

(*lampas, oleo vel cera nutrienda ... ardeat*) constantly near the tabernacle as a sign of the honor shown to the Lord.	of Christ is to shine continuously before a tabernacle in which the Most Holy Eucharist is reserved.	... *lampas*) should burn continuously before a tabernacle in which the eucharist is reserved. According to traditional usage, <u>the lamp should, if at all possible, be an oil lamp or a lamp with a wax candle</u> (*quantum fieri potest lampas oleo vel cera nutriatur*).

While number 11 of the emended text alludes to the fact that the custom regarding the oil lamp or wax candle should be maintained where possible, it is nonetheless no longer required, as in the former norm, but recommended. Through a relaxation in *CIC/83* the earlier norm was revoked in that it was integrally reordered by c. 940.

2.4.1.5 — Complex norms; juridic institutes

Other changes in norms of the *praenotanda* have a more complex nature than those presented thus far. Examining some of these will provide further insight into the nature and working of integral reordering. Number 153 of the *General Instruction of the Roman Missal*, which treats concelebration, is one such example.

Pre-Code Text	*CIC/83*	Emended text
153. Concelebration effectively brings out the unity of the priesthood, of the sacrifice, and of the whole people of God. In addition to the times when the rite itself prescribes it, concelebration is also permitted at: 1. a. the chrism Mass and the evening Mass on Holy Thursday;	Canon 902 – <u>Unless the welfare of the Christian faithful requires or suggests otherwise,</u> priests can concelebrate the Eucharist. They are completely free to celebrate the Eucharist individually, however, but not while a concelebration is taking place in the same church or oratory.	153. Concelebration effectively brings out the unity of the priesthood, of the sacrifice, and of the whole people of God. The rite itself prescribes concelebration at the ordination of bishops and of priests and at the chrism Mass. <u>Unless the good of the faithful requires or suggests otherwise,</u> concelebration is also recommended at:

b. the Mass for councils, meetings of bishops, and synods;
　　c. the Mass for the blessing of an abbot.
2. In addition, *with the permission of the Ordinary, who has the right to decide on the advisability of concelebration*, at:
　　a. the conventual Mass and the principal Mass in churches and oratories when the needs of the people do not require that all priests celebrate individually;
　　b. the Mass for any kind of meeting of priests, either secular or religious.

　　a. the evening Mass on Holy Thursday;
　　b. the Mass for councils, meetings of bishops, and synods;
　　c. the Mass for the blessing of an abbot;
　　d. the conventual Mass and the principal Mass in churches and oratories;
　　e. the Mass for any kind of meeting of priests, either secular or religious.

This norm has been reordered by the code which imposed an exception to the right of concelebration, namely, the welfare of the Christian faithful. The pre-code norm only considered the needs of the faithful in regard to the conventual Mass and the principal Mass in churches and oratories (see 2.a). Now, however, the welfare of the Christian faithful is an overarching determinant of the times when priests may concelebrate. Although all other components of the earlier norm are included in the emended text, the change initiated by c. 902 gives the later norm a completely distinct thrust.

It should be noted that the permission of the ordinary, who formerly had the right to decide on the advisability of concelebration, is no longer required. This is an example of direct contrariety between the two norms since the earlier norm required permission whereas the later does not. However, in this case the contrariety is itself subsumed in the integral reordering of the law. For the direct contrariety only results in a derogation from the second part of the norm. It is the integral reordering in regard to the exception for concelebration which revokes the norm in its entirety.

Another example of the reordering of a juridic institute appears in n. 10 of "Christian Initiation: General Introduction," which deals with godparents.[94] Unlike the previous example, it is reordered by a number of specifications to components of the norm itself brought about by *CIC/83*.

Pre-Code Text	CIC/83	Emended Text
10. Therefore the godparent, chosen by the catechumen or the family, must, in the judgment of the pastor, be qualified to carry out the proper liturgical functions mentioned in no. 9, that is: 1. Be mature enough to undertake the responsibility; 2. Be initiated with the three sacraments of initiation, baptism, confirmation, and eucharist; 3. be a member of the Catholic Church, canonically free to carry out this office. A baptized and believing Christian from a separated Church or Community may act as a godparent or Christian witness along with a Catholic godparent, at the request of the parents and in accordance with the norms laid down for various ecumenical cases.	Canon 873 – There is to be only one male sponsor or one female sponsor or one of each. Canon 874 – §1. To be permitted to take on the function of sponsor, a person must: 1° be designated by the one to be baptized, by the parents or the person who takes their place or, in their absence, by the pastor or minister and have the aptitude and intention of fulfilling this function; 2° have completed the sixteenth year of age, unless the diocesan bishop has established another age, or the pastor or minister has granted an exception for a just cause; 3° be a Catholic who has been confirmed and has already received the most holy sacrament of the Eucharist and who leads a life of faith in keeping	10. Therefore the godparent, chosen by the catechumen or the family, must, in the judgment of the pastor, be qualified to carry out the proper liturgical functions mentioned in no. 9, that is: 1. be designated by the candidate or the candidate's parents or whoever stands in their place or, in the absence of these, by the pastor or the minister of baptism and have the ability and the intention to carry out the responsibility of a godparent; 2. be mature enough to fulfill this responsibility; a person sixteen years old is presumed to have the requisite maturity, but the diocesan bishop may have stipulated another age or the pastor or minister may decide that there is a legitimate reason for allowing an exception;

---

[94] See ICEL, "Emendations," p. 12: "The text of this General Introduction appears in the "Rite of Baptism for Children" and is found both in the *Rite of Baptism for Children* and in *Christian Initiation for Adults*.

with the function to be taken on;
4° not be bound by any canonical penalty legitimately imposed or declared;
5° not be the father or mother of the one to be baptized;
§2. A baptized person who belongs to a non-Catholic ecclesial community is not to participate except together with a Catholic sponsor and then only as a witness of the baptism.

3. be initiated with the three sacraments of initiation, baptism, confirmation, and eucharist, and be living a life consistent with faith and the responsibility of a godparent.
4. be neither the father nor the mother of the candidate;
5. be chosen as godfather or godmother; but the candidate may have both a godfather and a godmother;
6. be a member of the Catholic Church, canonically free to carry out this office. A baptized and believing Christian not belonging to the Catholic Church may act as a Christian witness along with a Catholic godparent, at the request of the parents. In the case of separated Eastern Christians, the special discipline for the Eastern Churches is to be respected.

The institute has been integrally reordered in virtue of the additional stipulations added to it in light of cc. 873 and 874. In a way similar to that in which a juridic document would integrally reorder another document on the same issue, it appears obvious that the legislator intended something new; thus earlier law is abrogated.[95] The emended norm reflects the fact that the legislator through *CIC/83* has determined more comprehensive requirements and a more formidable role for the godparent(s). This is obvious through significant, specific additions to each of the

---

[95] See principle two above.

three qualifications of the pre-code text that serve to make the emended norm more restrictive as well as the fact that the canons have necessitated adding still other stipulations to the role of godparent.[96]

2.4.2 — Significance of examples

As previously acknowledged, the examples taken from the *praenotanda* were in actuality the express revocation of liturgical law. It was the *preparation* of these norms by the work group appointed by the Congregation for the Sacraments and Divine Worship that enables them to be used as examples of tacit or implicit revocation. For the introduction to the "Emendations" clarifies that they were made in accord with the principles of c. 20.[97]

Consequently, these emendations, made on the authority of the supreme legislator, are a valid model that supports the principles of integral reordering enumerated in this chapter. A survey of these assumptions indicates that the "Emendations" both affirm and concretize them.

In accord with principle 1, the "Emendations" demonstrate that while *CIC/83* derogated from the liturgical law in force, some of the individual *praenotanda* were integrally reordered and thereby abrogated by the later norms put forth in the code. Others norms were derogated, in that only a part of the norm was reordered. The "Emendations" also provide examples of the difference between revocation brought about by direct contrariety and integral reordering as specified in principle 2. As demonstrated in the particular *praenotanda* given as examples, direct contrariety often results when what was previously required is omitted in the later norm.[98]

---

[96] Number 6 of the emended text adds: "In the case of separated Eastern Christians, the special discipline for the Eastern Churches is to be respected." This was included in the pre-code text which alluded to "in accordance with the norms laid down for various ecumenical cases." This referred to nn. 48 and 57 of the 1967 Ecumenical Directory. Its inclusion here shows that, had the legislator not stated this, there would have been a doubt regarding the Orthodox as godparents due to the code's integral reordering of the norm.

[97] See ICEL, "Emendations," p. 3.

[98] See pp. 84-86 above.

Although the model employed does not demonstrate the integral reordering of an entire document set forth in principle 3, the "Emendations" do afford examples of the integral reordering of juridic institutes.[99] They also provide an example, albeit a limited one, of revocation of norms within the hierarchy of juridic documents as illustrated in principle 4. The liturgical *praenotanda* are *leges*. Therefore, they can be integrally reordered by *leges* contained in the code.

While the model used does not provide examples of doubt of revocation, in that such norms would not have been included as emendations by the committee who prepared them, in light of principle 5, the examples selected have illustrated how integral reordering can be proven. This has been done by the application of principles 6 and 7, which deal with the tenor and circumstances of the norms and the change in the tone or forcefulness of the norm, respectively.[100] Thus principle 8 has been validated in that the meaning of the law is found only in the reordered norm, not in the earlier law, even if similarities exist between the two. Overall, the brief summary of the "Emendations" and the examples cited illustrated the common and efficient use of integral reordering as a means of revocation.[101]

Although the emendations themselves suggest no additional principles, the illustrations indicate patterns that could denote that a given norm has been integrally reordered in accord with one of the principles above. These patterns, in turn, further explicate the proposed principles. As has been demonstrated, for example, integral reordering can occur through a change in the competent authority required to perform a certain act. Likewise, a substantive addition to a norm is an indication that it has been integrally reordered. This occurs when the addendum creates an incompatibility with the earlier norm which renders a key change its meaning. The additional phrase,

---

[99] See, for example, pp. 92-96 above. This section provides examples of the integral reordering of concelebration and of the role of godparent in the sacrament of baptism.

[100] See pp. 87-92 above.

[101] See CABREROS DE ANTA, *Vigencia y estado actual de la legislación canónica*, pp. 20-21. See also OTADUY, "Normas y actos jurídicos," p. 254. Both Cabreros and Otaduy refer to integral reordering as the more perfect and efficient way of renewing the law. Perhaps this serves to offer an explanation of why the work group used the criteria of c. 20 rather than the more limited scope of c. 2 in their preparation of the emendations.

as exhibited in the emendations cited, does not render the later law directly contrary to the first. Both the former and the later law both treat the same matter, but the substantive addition to the later renders the two norms incompatible. Likewise, the strengthening or relaxing of the forcefulness of a given norm indicates that the norm has been reordered. The later norm reflects a different tone or a more precise indication of the mind of the legislator in accord with the surrounding circumstances of the law.

The "Emendations" provide a working model supportive of the principles regarding the integral reordering of law proposed in this chapter. In addition they offer further insight into these same principles by demonstrating certain patterns or signs that indicate that an integral reordering of a law has occurred.

The preface to the 1983 *Code of Canon Law*, in speaking of this most recent codification of ecclesiastical law, states:

> But, if due to the dynamics which affect our human society, certain imperfections in the law arise which necessitate a new revision, the Church possesses such resources that, no less than in past centuries, it will be able to undertake the mission of revising the laws of its life.[102]

In line with this, R. Potz, writing on the concept and development of law according to *CIC/83*, holds that a basic pattern emerges once law has been codified. He states that the first stage is the exegesis of the law itself. This is followed in time by the need for the law to be interpreted, with the support of jurisprudence, in order to meet new problems which emerge. In this second phase, the interpreters of the law become more and more involved in actually creating new law.[103] Integral reordering can allow the legislator to reflect this development in ecclesiastical law.

---

[102] *Codex iuris canonici, auctoritate Ioannis Pauli PP. II promulgatus*, Vatican City, Libreria editrice Vaticana, 1983 in *AAS*, 75 (1983), p. xxx: "Quod si ob nimis celeres hodiernae humanae societatis immutationes, quaedam iam tempore iuris condendi minus perfecta evaserunt ac deinceps nova recogitione indigebunt, tanta virium ubertate Ecclesia pollet ut, haud secus ac praeteritis saeculis, valeat viam renovandi leges vitae suae rursus capessere." English translation *Code of Canon Law Annotated*, p. 79.

[103] R. Potz, "The Concept and Development of Law According to 1983 CIC," in *Concilium*, 185 (1986), p. 15.

The principles of integral reordering afford the canonist an important tool to clarify and interpret the *ius vigens*. The tenets that have been developed and exemplified through the "Emendations" function as a guide in such interpretation. As has been demonstrated, these principles apply to individual norms as well as juridic documents and institutes. Without the explicit revocation of a determined law by the legislator, the application of the principles of integral reordering allows one to recognize that a given norm has been tacitly revoked by the legislator and thus to interpret the *ius vigens* with accuracy.

In this chapter, building upon the theory of integral reordering presented in chapter 1, principles regarding the integral reordering of law have been developed and demonstrated. These provide a practical tool for canonists that can be used to evaluate juridic documents and the norms within them, thus arriving at a clear understanding of the *ius vigens*. This will be further substantiated by the application of these principles to religious law in the chapter that follows.

CHAPTER 3
THE APPLICATION OF THE PRINCIPLES
OF INTEGRAL REORDERING TO RELIGIOUS LAW

Having investigated a model of expressly abrogated law that included illustrations of integral reordering, the principles will now be used to determine the *ius vigens* for religious. Taking the Second Vatican Council as the starting point, those universal and potentially juridically binding documents that have impacted religious life over the past four decades will be examined.

Although the legal institute of religious life was not integrally reordered by the Second Vatican Council, religious life itself was significantly affected and altered by the *aggiornamento* that characterized the conciliar period.[1] In particular, *Perfectae caritatis* and *Lumen gentium* provided the impetus for the extensive renewal and adaptations in religious life that were reflected in its revised law.[2] However, some

---

[1] See OTADUY, "De las normas generales: título I," p. 403. In referring to institutes that have been integrally reordered Otaduy gives examples of the parish, indulgences, the episcopal ministry, impediments to marriage and ecumenism. While specific institutes within religious life and numerous norms pertaining to religious life were integrally reordered by the Second Vatican Council, the law on religious life in its entirety was not.

[2] See SECOND VATICAN COUNCIL, Decree on the Up-to-date Renewal of Religious Life *Perfectae caritatis*, 28 October 1965 (= *PC*), in *AAS*, 58 (1966), pp. 637-696; English translation in A. FLANNERY (gen.ed.), *Vatican Council II: The Basic Sixteen Documents* (= FLANNERY), completely rev. ed. in inclusive language, Costello Publishing Company, Northport, New York, 1966, pp. 385-401; and Dogmatic Constitution on the Church *Lumen gentium*, 21 November 1964, in *AAS*, 57 (1965), pp. 5-67. English translation in FLANNERY, pp. 1-96. Other conciliar documents that have particular bearing on religious life include the Decree on the Church's Missionary Activity, *Ad gentes divinitus*, 7 December 1965, in *AAS*, 58 (1966), pp. 947-990; English translation in FLANNERY, pp. 443-497; and Decree on the Pastoral Office of Bishops in the Church, *Christus Dominus*, 28 October 1965, in *AAS*, 58 (1966), pp. 673-701; English translation in FLANNERY, pp. 283-315.

juridic institutes within religious life, as well as individual norms pertaining to other juridic institutes or areas of religious life, were abrogated or derogated.[3]

The cornerstone of religious law is found in the code, which transcribed into canonical norms "the rich conciliar and postconciliar teaching of the church on religious life."[4] Together with the documents of the Second Vatican Council and the pronouncements of the successive popes, the code provides the basis on which current church law regarding religious life is founded.[5] Thus, the universal *ius vigens* embraces more than the code itself.

A definition of "religious law" and an explanation of the scope of this study preface this chapter, which is divided into two main sections. The first part includes an examination of those documents of the universal Church that could be considered to contain juridic matter pertaining to religious life, which were issued either by the supreme legislator or by the Congregation for Consecrated Life and Societies of Apostolic Life (= CICLSAL).[6] The documents and the norms within them will be analyzed in order to determine whether their subject matter forms part of the *ius vigens* for religious or whether they have been abrogated or derogated by the code or by later documents. Based on this survey a summary listing of the documents, which together with *CIC/83* form the universal *ius vigens* for religious, will be compiled.

---

[3] Institutes within religious life that were integrally reordered include formation, departure of a member from the institute, the cloister, etc. These and other examples will be addressed in the context of this chapter.

[4] VATICAN CONGREGATION FOR RELIGIOUS AND FOR SECULAR INSTITUTES (= SCRIS), "Essential Elements in Church Teaching on Religious Life," 31 May 1983, in *Origins*, 13 (1983), p. 140. The document further notes that the revised *Code of Canon Law* and the current praxis do not exhaust the provisions for religious life within the church. See p. 142.

[5] See ibid., p. 140.

[6] This congregation has undergone several name changes since the Second Vatican Council. At the time of Vatican II, it was referred to as the Sacred Congregation for Religious (= SCR). Paul VI renamed it the Sacred Congregation for Religious and Secular Institutes (= SCRIS). The word "Sacred" was dropped with the enactment of *CIC/83* (= CRIS). The congregation received its present name with the promulgation of *Pastor bonus* in 1988. Throughout this chapter the congregation will be referred to by the title in use at the time a particular document was issued.

The second part of this chapter summarizes each of the principles of integral reordering in light of the documents discussed in the first section. While many of the principles will be evident in their application to the specific document, the summation affords a more focused presentation of the principles and their effectiveness.

3.1 — SCOPE OF THE STUDY

The term "religious law" as used in this chapter includes cc. 607-709, which deal specifically with religious institutes, as well as those norms applicable to all institutes of consecrated life, cc. 573-606, with the exclusion of cc. 603 and 604, which treat hermits and virgins, respectively. In its broadest sense "religious law" embraces the *ius religionis,* including all those documents which complement these canons. However, in the context of this work it does not include laws pertaining to religious that are found in other books of the Code.[7] Nor does the term "religious law" as understood here deal with the *ius proprium* pertaining to each institute.

Likewise, the documents that were the fruit of the Second Vatican Council are not part of the corpus to be analyzed. As a result this chapter does not deal with the changes regarding religious life that the council effected. Neither does this work reference the 1917 *Code of Canon Law.*[8] Rather the scope of this study embraces the period of years spanning the time of the Council to the present. The analysis that follows seeks to clarify which of the juridic documents issued during this period, together with *CIC/83,* wholly or partially serve as the *ius vigens* for religious.[9]

---

[7] Religious are specifically mentioned in each of the other six books of the code, as well as other parts of Book II, in numerous canons, not including those that refer to Ordinaries. These canons will not be used in the context of this study, with the exception of canons in Book I that might be needed for the proper interpretation of religious law.

[8] While the documents of the Second Vatican Council extensively integrally reordered *CIC/17,* the starting point of this analysis, which is based on cc. 6 and 20 of *CIC/83,* is the documents that were issued to implement the basic documents of Vatican II. Two documents that were issued during the council itself are also part of the corpus to be analyzed. The reasons for their inclusion will be noted when they are discussed.

[9] Postconciliar documents that have not been integrally reordered by the code, as well as norms within these documents that are not contrary to or have not been integrally reordered by the canons of *CIC/83* or a later document on the same subject matter, remain part of the *ius vigens.*

Within these parameters, the survey encompasses some 22 documents,[10] listed here in chronological order:

> Paul VI, Motu proprio *Pastorale munus*, 30 November 1963
> Secretary of State, Rescript, *Cum admotae*, 6 November 1964
> SCR, Decree, *Religionum laicalium*, 31 May 1966
> Paul VI, Motu proprio, *Ecclesiae sanctae*, 6 August 1966
> SCRIS, Instruction, *Renovationis causam*, 6 January 1969
> SCRIS, Instruction, *Venite seorsum*, 15 August 1969
> SCRIS, Decree, *Clericalia instituta*, 27 November 1969
> SCRIS, Decree, *Cum superiores generales*, 27 November 1969
> SCRIS, Decree, *Ad instituenda*, 4 June 1970
> SCRIS, Declaration, *Clausuram papalem*, 4 June 1970
> SCRIS, Decree, *Dum canonicarum legum*, 8 December 1970
> SCRIS, Decree, *Processus judicialis*, 2 March 1974
> SCRIS and SC Bishops, Directives, *Mutuae relationes*, 14 May 1978
> SCRIS, "Religious and Human Promotion," 12 August 1980
> SCRIS, "The Contemplative Dimension of Religious Life," 12 August 1980
> SCRIS, "Essential Elements in Church Teaching on Religious Life," 31 May 1983
> CRIS, Decree, *Iuris canonici Codice*, 2 February 1984
> CRIS, Decree, *Praescriptis canonum*, 2 February 1984
> CRIS, "Procedures for the Separation of Members from Their Institute," June 1984
> CICLSAL, Directives, *Potissimum institutione*, 12 February 1990
> CICLSAL, "Fraternal Life in Community," 2 February 1994
> CICLSAL, Instruction, *Verbi sponsa*, 13 May 1999

Other documents that deal totally or in part with religious have been published by various congregations, such as the Congregation for Divine Worship and the Discipline of the Sacraments and the Congregation for the Evangelization of Peoples.[11] These are not included here in that they touch on areas of law involving religious that are treated in canons other than cc. 573-606 or matters outside the

---

[10] These documents were compiled from *AAS*, vols. 56-91; *Enchiridion Vaticanum*, vols.1-14; *The Pope Speaks*, vols. 9-43; *Origins*, vols. 1-29; *CLD*, vols. 6-11; and M. J. DINN (ed.) *Canonical Documentation on Consecrated Life (1963-1976)*, Ottawa, Faculty of Canon Law, Saint Paul University, 1977. Decrees, letters, addresses, etc. issued to a specific group of religious are not included in this survey, which is limited to documents of the Apostolic See with a general application. The appropriate reference for each of the documents listed will be cited at the time the document is discussed in the text.

[11] A number of liturgical documents were issued by the Congregation for Divine Worship and the Discipline of the Sacraments in regard to the rituals for entering the novitiate and for profession of vows. Likewise, the Congregation for the Evangelization of Peoples issued norms applicable to religious ministering in missionary territory.

code. Also excluded are those universal documents pertaining directly to religious that are not juridic in nature. Accordingly, the three apostolic exhortations issued during this period, though making reference to and reinforcing principles of council documents and the norms of the revised *Code of Canon Law*, are not treated here since they are magisterial rather than juridic documents.[12]

3.2 — EXPRESSLY ABROGATED DOCUMENTS

Among the juridic documents listed above, a specific group can be summarily excluded from this study. This category consists of those documents that were published explicitly as interim measures after the council until the revised *Code of Canon Law* would take effect. They include: the motu proprio *Ecclesiae sanctae* of Paul VI, issued in 1966, and four decrees and the instruction, *Renovationis causam*, issued by the Sacred Congregation for Religious.

3.2.1 — *Ecclesiae sanctae*

Ecclesiae sanctae, which provided disciplinary norms that served to implement *Perfectae caritatis* and other conciliar documents, did so on an interim and experimental basis.[13] The motu proprio contained within it provision for the express abrogation of its norms once the revised *Code of Canon Law* was promulgated. The introduction of *ES* ordained that the norms be observed "by way of experiment ... until the new *Code of Canon Law* is promulgated ...."[14] Even though *CIC/83*

---

[12] See PAUL VI, *Evangelica testificatio*, 29 June 1971, in *AAS*, 63 (1971), pp. 497-526; English translation in *CLD*, 7, pp. 425-449, JOHN PAUL II, *Redemptionis donum*, 25 March 1984, in *AAS*, 76 (1984), pp. 513-546, English translation in *Origins*, 13 (1984), pp. 721-731, and JOHN PAUL II, *Vita consecrata*, 25 March 1996, in *AAS*, 88 (1996), pp. 377-486; English translation in *The Pope Speaks*, 41 (1996), pp. 257-338. Magisterial documents proceed from the *munus docendi*, the teaching office of the Church. See HUELS, "A Theory of Juridic Documents," in *Studia canonica*, 32 (1998), pp. 339-341.

[13] See PAUL VI, Motu proprio, *Ecclesiae sanctae*, 6 August 1966 (=*ES*), in *AAS*, 58 (1966), pp. 264-298. English translation in *CLD*, 6, pp. 264-298. *ES* contained norms implementing the decrees of *Christus Dominus*, *Presbyterorum ordinis* and *Ad gentes divinitus* in addition to those pertaining to *PC*.

[14] *ES*, introduction.

completely reworked many of the norms set out in *ES*, the motu proprio was revoked expressly by the supreme legislator. Revocation occurred not because the subject matter of *ES* had been integrally reordered by *CIC/83*, but due to its expressly stated interim nature.

This position, however, is not held by all canonists. Otaduy, for example, cites *ES* among the documents that have been integrally reordered by *CIC/83*. In his writings, both after the promulgation of the revised code and more recently, he uses *ES* as an example of a document that was integrally reordered by *CIC/83*.[15] While it is true that the code presents *ES* in a completely reordered fashion, in the strict sense integral reordering as a means of revocation does not apply to this document. Although it can be argued that *CIC/83* integrally reordered the subject matter of *ES*, the express statement within the document is the source of its revocation.

3.2.2 — SCRIS decrees

Similarly, four decrees issued by the Sacred Congregation for Religious and Secular Institutes were expressly revoked at the time the revised code took effect. *Ad instituenda*, issued by SCRIS in 1970, granted dispensations from the common law to religious institutes in order that they might initiate experiments in accord with *ES*.[16] In ceding these faculties the decree made it clear that they would "be valid until the revised *Code of Canon Law* takes effect."[17] *Dum canonicarum legum*, a decree issued by SCRIS in 1970, contained norms regarding the use and administration of the sacrament of penance especially for religious women.[18] These norms, likewise, were

---

[15] See OTADUY, "El derecho canónico postconciliar," pp. 122-123, n. 14 and "Introducción: cc. 1-6," p. 284, n. 14. In the earlier work Otaduy classified postconciliar documents into seven categories, listing *ES* among the integrally reordered documents. He likewise used *ES* as an example of an integrally reordered document in his later commentary on c. 6.

[16] SCRIS, Decree, *Ad instituenda*, 4 June 1970 (= *AI*), in *AAS*, 62 (1970), pp. 549-550. English translation in *CLD*, 7, pp. 80-82. The term "common law" is used here in the context of universal law.

[17] *AI*, n. 8.

[18] See SCRIS, Decree, *Dum canonicarum legum*, 8 December 1970 (= *DCL*), in *AAS*, 63 (1971), pp. 318-319. English translation in *CLD*, 7, pp. 531-533.

to be put into practice "until the revised *Code of Canon Law* shall take effect."[19] Two shorter decrees were published by SCRIS in 1972 and 1974, respectively. *Experimenta circa regiminis rationem*, which dealt with the ordinary form of government and the eligibility of secularized men for ecclesiastical offices, and *Processus judicialis*, which considered the dismissal of perpetually professed religious in clerical exempt institutes, contained interim norms.[20] The provisional nature of both documents is clear: they are valid until the new code takes force.[21] A commonality exists among these four decrees in that all of them stipulate the revised *Code of Canon Law* as their point of termination.

3.2.3 — *Renovationis causam*

The instruction, *Renovationis causam*, issued by SCRIS in 1969, focused on the renewal and adaptation of formation for living the religious life.[22] The norms in *RC* broadened the canon law in force at the time in order to permit greater experimentation in accord with *ES*.[23] However, the instruction states that its "norms are issued by way of experiment."[24] In light of the fact that *CIC/83* ended the period of experimentation which followed the Council, *RC* was abrogated when the revised code took effect.[25] Although certain norms contained in *RC* underwent a complete reworking in *CIC/83* and in the subsequent post-code document, *Potissimum*

---

[19] *DCL*, Part II.

[20] See SCRIS, Decrees, *Experimenta circa regiminis rationem*, 2 February 1972, in *AAS*, 64 (1972), pp. 393-394; English translation in *CLD*, 7, pp. 484-485; and *Processus judicialis*, 2 March 1974, in *AAS*, 66 (1974), pp. 215-216; English translation in *CLD*, Supplement 1974, pp. 2-3.

[21] See ibid.

[22] See SCRIS, Instruction, *Renovationis causam*, 6 January 1969 (= *RC*), in *AAS*, 61 (1969), pp. 103-120. English translation in *CLD*, 7, pp. 489-508.

[23] See *RC*, introduction.

[24] Ibid., Part III, n. VII.

[25] The period of experimentation following the Second Vatican Council ended when *CIC/83*, the final document of the council, came into force. See, for example, CRIS document, "Essential Elements in Church Teaching on Religious Life," n. 2: "Now with the ending of the period of special experimentation mandated by *ES II*, many religious institutes dedicated to works of the apostolate are reviewing their experience. With the approval of their revised constitutions and the coming into effect of the newly formulated *Code of Canon Law*, they are moving into a new phase of their history."

institutione, the instruction was expressly revoked by its explicit claim to be only experimental. The juridic force of *RC* ceased when *CIC/83* took effect.

It can be concluded, then, that the six documents cited above, having been expressly revoked with the promulgation of *CIC/83*, are not part of the *ius vigens* in regard to religious. Although they were implementations of Vatican II and an important part of the *ius religionis* during the postconciliar/pre-code period, as well as a rich source of material for *CIC/83*, their significance today is principally historical as part of canonical tradition.

3.3 — JURIDIC DOCUMENTS NOT EXPRESSLY REVOKED

It remains, then, to examine those documents that were not expressly revoked, as well as the norms within those documents, to determine whether they have been abrogated or derogated and what, if any, juridic force they have today. For the most part the documents will be considered in chronological order. However, those that integrally reorder an earlier document or whose contents are explanatory of or supplementary to an earlier document will be discussed in relation to the earlier text.

The code is the starting point for ascertaining the status of postconciliar documents published before it entered into force in 1983. *CIC/83* tacitly revokes postconciliar laws either by direct contrariety or by integral reordering. As previously noted, direct contrariety applies merely to *norms* that are in direct opposition with the canons. It is only through integral reordering that the code tacitly revokes an *entire document* or an *entire institute* by treating anew the complete subject matter of that document or institute.

Likewise, the code can integrally reorder *norms within the document*, without revoking the entire document, in several ways. First, integral reordering occurs when certain norms of the earlier document are incorporated into the canons, while not touching other norms. In this case the subject matter of the earlier norm is not materially changed; it is revoked simply by its being restated substantially in the code. Second, integral reordering takes place when the entire subject matter of a given norm is treated anew in the code. Third, integral reordering occurs as a result of a derogation from an individual norm by the code, leaving the other part of the norm intact. Each of these bring about a derogation in the postconciliar document.

Finally it must be noted that the code, since its promulgation, has been augmented by new discipline, including several juridic documents affecting the discipline of religious life. These later documents must also be examined to see whether they revoke any previous documents, or whether any norms within them have revoked pre-code norms not touched by the code. Thus will the *ius vigens* be clarified.

3.3.1 — *Pastorale munus*

Pastorale munus, an Apostolic Letter issued motu proprio by Paul VI in 1963, which dealt with faculties and privileges granted to local ordinaries, was actually promulgated two years before the end of the council.[26] It granted diocesan bishops substantial new powers and gave all bishops several privileges.[27] The episcopacy itself was more comprehensively addressed in the Decree on the Pastoral Office of Bishops in the Church, *Christus Dominus*, and the subsequent documents which implemented this decree.[28] While it is not within the scope of this work to study the entire document, those norms that have a bearing on religious life will be considered.

Articles 33-39 of *PM* specifically pertain to religious law as defined in this chapter. *CIC/83* is the starting point in determining whether these norms are still in force or whether they have been abrogated.[29]

---

[26] See PAUL VI, Motu proprio, *Pastorale Munus*, 30 November 1963 (= *PM*), in *AAS*, 56 (1964), pp. 5-12. English translation in *CLD*, 6, 370-378. Even though this document was issued before the end of the Council it is usually listed among postconciliar documents in that some of its norms were the source of the *ius vigens* until *CIC/83* came into force.

[27] For the faculties given to residential bishops, see *PM*, I, nn. 1-40; for the privileges given to all bishops, see *PM* II, nn. 1-8.

[28] See, for example, PAUL VI, Motu proprio, *De episcoporum muneribus*, 15 June 1966 in *AAS*, 58 (1966), pp. 467-472. English translation in *CLD*, 6, pp. 394-400. See also JOHN PAUL II, *De episcoporum muneribus* and *ES*. These documents implemented what was set forth in *CD* and served as the *ius vigens* until *CIC/83* took effect.

[29] In actuality *PM*, nn. 35 and 36 were integrally reordered originally by n. 7 of the pontifical rescript *Cum admotae* which granted these same faculties to the Superiors General of pontifical clerical religious institutes and Abbots President of monastic congregations. Number 35

PM, nn. 35 and 36 were integrally reordered by *CIC/83*. These articles granted the diocesan bishop the faculty to dispense, at the request of the competent superior, from two impediments to religious life – adherence to a non-Catholic sect and illegitimacy, respectively. Neither of these is included in c. 643 that lists the five impediments that constitute an invalid entrance into the novitiate.[30] Likewise, n. 37, which granted the diocesan bishop the faculty to dispense, at the request of the competent superior, from the dowry required of postulants, was revoked in that the code states that life in a religious institute begins with the novitiate and does not deal with pre-novitiate.[31] In each of these norms what was previously required no longer obliges.

PM, n. 39 granted diocesan bishops the faculty to dismiss a religious from the diocese for an urgent and very serious reason if the major superior after having been notified failed to take proper measures. It stipulated that such action must be immediately referred to the Apostolic See. This norm was integrally reordered through its incorporation into c. 679:

Pastorale munus	*CIC/83*
[It is for the diocesan bishop:] 39. To dismiss from the diocese for an urgent, very serious reason, individual religious if the major superior, after having been notified, fails to take proper measures. However, the matter must be immediately referred to the Apostolic See.	Canon 679 — When a most grave cause demands it, a diocesan bishop can prohibit a member of a religious institute from residing in the diocese if his or her major superior, after having been informed, has neglected to make provision; moreover, the matter is to be referred immediately to the Holy See.

Thus, it is the later law embodied in the code that is the *ius vigens*.

---

was likewise integrally reordered by n. 7 of the decree *Religionem laicalium*, which granted the Superiors General of pontifical lay institutes the faculty to dispense from the impediment of illegitimacy. *CIC/83* then integrally reordered them again.

[30] These impediments include: one not having completed the seventeenth year of age; one bound by marriage; one who is bound to another institute of consecrated life or society of apostolic life; one who enters under or who is accepted under the influence of force, fear or deceit; and one who has concealed her or his incorporation into an institute of consecrated life or society of apostolic life.

[31] See c. 646.

The subject matter of articles 33, 34 and 38 of *PM* was integrally reordered by *CIC/83*. A comparison of these faculties with the corresponding canons readily indicates this.

Pastorale Munus	*CIC/83*
[It is for the diocesan bishop:] 33. To appoint for as many as five terms the ordinary confessor of religious women if other provision cannot be made because of a dearth of priests suitable for this office or if the majority of the religious, including even those who in other matters have no right to vote, petition by secret voting for the reappointment of the same confessor. For those who dissent, it must, however, if they so desire, be otherwise provided for.	Canon 630, §1 — Superiors are to recognize the due freedom of their members regarding the sacrament of penance and direction of conscience, without prejudice, however, to the discipline of the institute. §2 — According to the norm of proper law <u>superiors are to be concerned that suitable confessors are available to the members, to whom the members can frequently confess.</u>
34. To enter for a just reason within the papal enclosure of nuns' monasteries which are located in his diocese and to permit, for a just and serious reason, that others may be admitted within the enclosure and that the nuns may leave it. The permission is only for the amount of time truly necessary.	667, §4 — For a just cause the diocesan bishop has the faculty of entering the cloister of monasteries of nuns which are in his diocese, and, for a grave reason <u>and with the consent of the superior,</u> of permitting others to be admitted to the cloister and nuns to leave it for a truly necessary period of time.
38. To permit religious to transfer from one religious institute of diocesan law to another institute of diocesan law.	684, §1 — A member in perpetual vows cannot transfer from one religious institute to another <u>except by a grant of the supreme moderator of each institute and with the consent of their respective councils.</u>

Article 33, the first example given above, was integrally reordered by c. 630 which, while still providing for the opportunity of the sacrament of reconciliation for members of the religious institute, now places that responsibility on the superior. A key element of the norm was reordered. The second example, n. 34, was integrally reordered and changed by c. 667, §4 by the addition of the phrase "and with the consent of the superior," thus bringing about a decisive limitation on the bishop's power. The final article cited, n. 38, is similar to n. 33. The authority who can permit power. The final article cited, n. 38, is similar to n. 33. The authority who can permit a transfer was changed in c. 684, §1, which integrally reordered the previous norm.

Therefore, the norms in *Pastorale munus* pertaining to bishops and religious life are clearly abrogated. The revocation of these norms by *CIC/83*, however, does not provide grounds for the abrogation of *PM* itself. This would entail a study of the document in its entirety.[32]

3.3.2 — *Cum admotae*

Cum admotae was also published before the termination of Vatican Council II.[33] Through this pontifical rescript the Apostolic See delegated certain faculties to superiors general of clerical religious institutes of pontifical law and to abbots presidents of monastic congregations.[34] Several of these faculties, some of which are related specifically to clerical responsibilities, are not treated in the section of the code dealing with religious institutes themselves.[35] Of interest here are the faculties granted in nn. 7, 9, and 13-19 which treat matters within the parameters of this study.

Article 7 granted superiors general of clerical religious institutes the faculty to dispense from the impediment that bars those who have adhered to a non-Catholic sect from entering religious life. This norm was integrally reordered as this impediment was not included in those put forth in *CIC/83*. Article 14, which permitted the superior general with the consent of his council "to restore temporarily

---

[32] Commentators concur that *PM* is an example of a document that has been integrally reordered. See, for example, OTADUY, "El derecho canónico postconciliar," p. 122, n. 14 and "Introducción: cc. 1-6," p. 284, n. 14. While this author agrees with this assessment, this study approaches the document only from the perspective of those faculties which touch directly on religious law.

[33] SECRETARY OF STATE, Pontifical Rescript, *Cum Admotae*, 6 November 1964 (= *CA*), in *AAS*, 59 (1967), pp. 374-378. English translation in *CLD*, 6, pp. 147-152. Like *PM*, *CA* is usually listed with the postconciliar documents because some of its norms served as the *ius vigens* until the promulgation of *CIC/83*.

[34] This rescript makes clear that the Supreme Pontiff, Paul VI, acceded to the request of the Secretary of State, H. J. Cardinal Cicognani, and decreed that the superiors general of clerical religious institutes be empowered to enjoy certain faculties that could facilitate their role in the internal government of their institutes.

[35] Articles 1-6, 8, and 10-12 of *CA* deal with laws pertaining to religious that are dispersed throughout other sections of the code.

113

professed subjects to the condition of seculars," was integrally reordered by its incorporation into c. 688, §2.[36] Accordingly, the supreme moderator of an institute of pontifical right, with the consent of his council, could grant an indult to those who asked to leave during temporary profession.[37] Likewise, n. 16, which allowed simply professed religious who so requested the right to cede their patrimony, was incorporated into c. 668, §4.[38]

However, each of the other norms of *CA* was changed when they were integrally reordered by *CIC/83*. Article 13, which granted the superior general the faculty to perform acts of jurisdiction for government and internal discipline, now extends to major superiors of the institutes in light of c. 134, §1. This canon states that major superiors of clerical religious institutes of pontifical right are ordinaries for their own subjects.[39] This is also the case with *CA*, nn. 15 and 17. Article 15 allowed the superior general, with the consent of his council, to subdelegate to other major superiors the permission for subjects to be absent from their religious house for a year for a just cause. Canon 665, §2 grants this authority to the major superior with the consent of the council. Likewise, n. 17, which granted the faculty to allow simply professed subjects to change their last will and testament, was changed by c. 668, §2.

---

[36] See *CIC, fontium annotatione*. Canon 688, §2: "During the time of temporary profession, a person who asks to leave the institute for a grave cause can obtain an indult of departure from the supreme moderator in an institute of pontifical right. In institutes of diocesan right and in monasteries mentioned in can. 615, however, the bishop of the house of assignment must confirm the indult for it to be valid."

[37] This faculty has undergone a terminological change. It is stated more positively in *CIC/83* as an indult to leave during temporary profession rather than a restoration to the condition of seculars.

[38] Canon 668, §4: "A professed religious who has renounced his or her goods fully due to the nature of the institute loses the capacity of acquiring and possessing and therefore invalidly places acts contrary to the vow of poverty. Moreover, whatever accrues to the professed after renunciation belongs to the institute according to the norm of proper law."

[39] Canon 134, §1: "In addition to the Roman Pontiff, by the title of ordinary are understood in the law diocesan bishops and others who, even if only temporarily, are placed over some particular church or a community equivalent to it according to the norm of can. 368, as well as those who possess general ordinary executive power in them; namely vicars general and episcopal vicars; likewise, for their own members, major superiors of clerical religious institutes of pontifical right and of clerical societies of apostolic life of pontifical right who at least possess ordinary executive power."

This canon is located in Book I. The nature of general norms necessitates its consideration here, in that these norms are applicable to all books throughout the code.

According to the code this authority now belongs to "the superior who is competent according to the norm of proper law."

Canon 638, §3 integrally reordered *CA*, n. 9:

Cum admotae	*CIC/83*
9. [The superior general:] With the consent of the council, to allow for a just cause that property belonging to the religious institute may be alienated, pledged, mortgaged, rented out or perpetually leased and that moral persons belonging to the religious institute may contract debts to the sum of money determined by the National or Regional conference of Bishops and approved by the Apostolic See.	638, §3 — For the validity of alienation and of any other affair in which the patrimonial condition of the juridical person can worsen, <u>the written permission of the competent superior</u> with the consent of the council is required. Nevertheless, if it concerns an affair which exceeds the amount defined by the Holy See for each reason, or <u>things given to the Church by a vow, or things precious for artistic reasons, the permission of the Holy See is also required.</u>

In this example *CA*, n. 9 was both broadened and restricted by c. 638, §3. According to *CIC/83* the competent superior, rather than the superior general, may alienate property with the consent of his council. However, the canon also restricts in that the permission for such alienation must now be in writing. In addition, the canon is more detailed regarding that which needs the approval of the Apostolic See than was the earlier norm.

Article 18, which permitted the superior general to transfer the location of the novitiate, was integrally reordered by its further simplification in c. 647, §1.[40] The earlier norm carried the stipulation, "provided that notice has been given to the Ordinary of the place where the novitiate was located." This is not required by the code. Now the erection, transfer or suppression of a novitiate house takes place through a written decree of the supreme moderator of the institute with the consent of his or her council.

---

[40] Canon 647, §1: "The erection, transfer and suppression of a novitiate house are to be done through written decree of the supreme moderator of the institute with the consent of the council."

Article 19, which granted the diocesan bishop the faculty to confirm local superiors for a third three year term, was integrally reordered by c. 624, §§1 and 2.[41] The canon states that "superiors are to be constituted for a certain and appropriate amount of time according to the nature and needs of the institute." It further stipulates that "proper law is to provide suitable norms that superiors constituted for a definite time do not remain too long in offices of governance without interruption."

It can be concluded that the rescript, *Cum admotae*, was integrally reordered by *CIC/83* in its application to religious law. The entire matter of its norms on religious was taken up anew in the code, and many of these norms were significantly changed in the process. The document has no bearing on the *ius vigens* for religious.

3.3.3 — *Religionum laicalium*

Religionum laicalium, a decree issued by the Sacred Congregation for Religious in 1966, granted nine faculties to superiors general of lay religious institutes.[42] For the most part, these faculties corresponded to those that specifically concerned religious life which had already been granted to clerical religious institutes in *Cum admotae*.[43] However, the faculty that dealt with dispensing a member from temporary vows, *RL*, n. 3, required the superior general to obtain the dispensation from the local ordinary of the house to which the petitioner was assigned.[44] In

---

[41] Canon 624: "§1. Superiors are to be constituted for a certain and appropriate period of time according to the nature and need of the institute, unless the constitutions determine otherwise for the supreme moderator and for superiors of an autonomous house. §2. Proper law is to provide suitable norms so that superiors, constituted for a definite time, do not remain too long in offices of governance without interruption."

[42] See SACRED CONGREGATION FOR RELIGIOUS, Decree, *Religionum laicalium*, 31 May 1966 (=*RL*), in *AAS*, 59 (1967), pp. 362-364. English translation in *CLD*, 6, pp. 153-156.

[43] Seven of the faculties granted in *RL* nn. 1-2 and 4-8 were based on those granted in *CA*. They included dispensing from the impediment of illegitimacy; the alienation of property and the contraction of debts; permitting leaves of absences up to one year; allowing simply professed to cede their patrimony; allowing subjects to change their wills; transferring the location of the novitiate; and confirming local superiors for a third three year term. These parallel nn. 7, 9, and 15-19 of *CA* respectively, which were determined to have been integrally reordered by the code.

[44] This was later integrally reordered by the Decree, *Cum superiores generales*. However, since *CIC/83* is used as a starting point in this study for determining the integral reordering of postconciliar documents issued before its promulgation, it can also be deduced from the Code itself

addition, the ninth faculty permitted superioresses general of orders of nuns and the superioresses of autonomous monasteries to dispense individual nuns from the obligation of reciting the divine office when they had been absent from choir or to commute this obligation into other prayers. This norm was integrally reordered by c. 663, §3 which states that religious institutes are to celebrate the liturgy of the hours in accordance with the provisions of their own law. Thus, it can be affirmed that the document, *RL*, was integrally reordered and abrogated by *CIC/83* because all of its provisions were treated anew by the code, and some of them were changed.

3.3.4 — *Cum superiores generales*

The Decree, *Cum superiores generales*,[45] at the time it was issued by SCRIS in 1969, integrally reordered n. 3 of *RL*.[46] *CSG* granted superiors general of lay religious institutes of men and women, with the consent of their council, the faculty to change to the secular status those in temporary vows who so requested. It no longer required that an indult for this be obtained from the local ordinary of the house where the petitioner resided. This decree was integrally reordered by its incorporation into *CIC/83* and further changed. Canon 688, §2 states that one in temporary profession who, for a grave reason, asks to leave the institute "can obtain an indult of departure." This indult is given by the supreme moderator with the consent of the council.

However, some maintain that the importance of *CSG* lies in the fact that the decree provides insight into the question regarding whether supreme moderators of lay religious communities, by having the faculty to grant the indult, also dispense the vows.[47] *CSG* makes clear that the faculty that is granted is to change the *status* of the individual. It states that it is the return to the secular state that causes the temporary

---

that the norm as it appeared in *RL* was reordered. This will be explored further in discussing *Cum superiores generales*.

[45] See SCRIS, Decree, *Cum superiores generales*, 27 November 1969 (= *CSG*), in *AAS*, 61 (1969), pp. 738-739. English translation in *CLD*, 7, p. 77.

[46] See n. 44 above.

[47] See *Code of Canon Law Annotated*, p. 469.

vows to cease *ipso facto*. Since this detail is omitted from c. 688, §2, it could also be argued that this indicates a change in the *mens legislatoris* on this point in that it leaves open the question whether the superior may dispense from the vows. In light of c. 6, §2, however, the former argument is stronger. From this perspective, *CSG*, while no longer part of the *ius vigens* on religious life, provides an insight into the *traditio canonica* of the canon, and the canon is to be assessed in light of it.[48]

3.3.5 — *Venite seorsum* and *Verbi sponsa*

The instruction, *Venite seorsum*, issued by SCRIS in 1969,[49] was not integrally reordered by *CIC/83*. As will be illustrated, however, this document has been abrogated through its integral reordering by the instruction, *Verbi sponsa*, issued by CICLSAL in 1999.[50] The first five sections of *Venite seorsum* present a theological description and defense of the contemplative life. Parts VI and VII of the document, which are of a juridic nature, are of interest to this study. Part VI speaks in general terms of the maturity required to live the contemplative life; the need for adequate testing of the monastic vocation before admitting postulants, as well as throughout the period before perpetual profession; and the living out of the uniqueness of the institute especially in regard to enclosure. This section also carries an affirmation that new forms of contemplative life are a possibility within the Church.[51] Part VII enumerates norms regulating the papal enclosure of nuns.

Many of the concepts of Section VI are reflected in *CIC/83*, though not specified for contemplative life, since the code speaks of religious institutes in general

---

[48] For additional insight that c. 688, §2 does not depend on the decree *Cum superiores generales* for its proper understanding, see E. MCDONOUGH, "The *Potestas* of Canon 596," in *Antonianum*, 63 (1988), pp. 568-573.

[49] See SCRIS, Instruction, *Venite seorsum*, 15 August 1969, in *AAS*, 61 (1969), pp. 674-690. English translation in *CLD*, 7, pp. 536-541.

[50] See CONGREGATION FOR INSTITUTES OF CONSECRATED LIFE AND SOCIETIES OF APOSTOLIC LIFE, Instruction, *Verbi sponsa*, 13 May 1999, at ‹http://www.vatican.va/romancuria/ congregations/ ccscrlife/ documents/rc_con_ccscrlife_doc_13051999_verbisponsa_lt.html›. English translation in *Origins*, 29 (1999-2000), pp. 155-164.

[51] See *Venite seorsum*, Section VI.

and makes appropriate applications to the contemplative life only when necessary.[52] For example, c. 642 treats the responsibility of the superior to be vigilant in admitting only those who have the necessary health, character and maturity to embrace the particular life of the institute. Canons 641-661 consider the importance of formation through perpetual vows and beyond. The emphasis on the spirit of the institute and reference to its proper law are hallmarks of the code in regard to religious life.[53] Likewise, c. 605 speaks of new forms of consecrated life.

However, Section VII of *Venite seorsum* retained its force even after the promulgation of the code.[54] Indeed, *CIC/83* makes reference to the norms that govern papal enclosure. Canon 667, §3 states: "Monasteries of nuns which are ordered entirely to contemplative life must observe *papal* cloister, that is, according to the norms given by the Apostolic See." These norms, then, were mandated by the Code.[55]

The publication of *Verbi sponsa* integrally reordered *Venite seorsum*. This later instruction on contemplative life and the enclosure of nuns, while not expressly revoking *Venite seorsum*, nonetheless implies as such when it reaffirms "the doctrinal foundations of enclosure set out by the instruction *Venite seorsum* (I-V) and the exhortation *Vita consecrata* (n. 59)."[56] *Verbi sponsa* makes clear that it "establishes the norms which are to regulate the papal enclosure of nuns who are dedicated to a wholly contemplative life."[57] Since the later instruction reaffirms only the doctrinal content of the earlier document and promulgates norms regulating the same juridic

---

[52] See, for example, cc. 609, §2; 614; 615; 616, §4; 628, §2, 1°; 630, §3; 637; 638, §4; 667, §§1-4; 684, §3; 686, §2; and 699, §2 that make specific reference to monasteries of nuns.

[53] See F.G. MORRISEY, "Introduction," in J. HITE, S. HOLLAND, and D. WARD (eds.), *A Handbook on Canons 573-746*, Collegeville, MN, The Liturgical Press, 1985, pp. 15-16.

[54] Number 16 of *Venite seorsum* was abrogated by *CIC/83*. This stated that penalties for violators of the cloister would be without force until the new code was promulgated. Since *CIC/83* eliminates such penalties in Book VI and c. 6, §1, 3° states that all penalties enacted by the Apostolic See are abrogated unless they are resumed in the code, this norm was revoked. However, this was simply a derogation from *Venite seorsum*; the rest of the norms remained the *ius vigens*.

[55] See J.F. HITE, "Book II, The People of God: Part III, Title II: Religious Institutes (cc. 607-709)," in *CLSA Commentary*, p. 501 and *Code of Canon Law Annotated*, p. 456.

[56] *Verbi sponsa*, n. 2.

[57] Ibid., n. 2.

subject matter as *Venite seorsum*, it appears obvious that the earlier instruction was integrally reordered by *Verbi sponsa*.

This is verified by comparing the contents of *Verbi sponsa* with the earlier instruction, *Venite seorsum*. The later document is broader in its scope, embodying norms for more areas of the contemplative life than the former document, which provided norms solely for papal enclosure.[58] The norms of the earlier instruction have been reordered by *Verbi sponsa*, nn. 14-21 in Part II, Enclosure of Nuns. While the later document repeats some of the former norms verbatim, the entire matter is integrally reordered so that juridic force is found only in the later instruction. The discipline on the extent of the enclosure and means of social communication exemplifies the reordering that occurred throughout the document. In regard to the extent of the enclosure the documents state:

Venite seorsum	*Verbi sponsa*
2. The law of papal enclosure applies to all of the house which the nuns inhabit as well as to the gardens and wooded areas reserved for access by the nuns. 3. The section of the monastery which is subject to the law of cloister must so be set up that it effects material separation which, that is, prevents entrance and exit (for example, by a wall or other effective means such as a wooden fence, an iron mesh, a thick strong hedge). Entrance and exit should be through doors which are locked with keys. 4. The mode of making this separation effective, especially as regards the choir and the parlor, should be defined in the constitutions and in supplementary legal documents, with attention given to the differences of the traditions of each institute and of conditions of time and place (e.g. grilles, latticework, stationary partition, etc.). In conformity with article 1, however, the above-mentioned mode of separation must be	14, §2 — The law of papal enclosure extends to the residence and to all areas indoor and outdoors reserved to nuns. The means by which the monastery building itself, the choir, the parlors and all areas reserved to the nuns are separated from the outside must be physical and effective, not just symbolic or "neutral." These means are to be defined in the constitutions and supplementary legislative documents, with due regard both for the places themselves and for the different traditions of individual institutes and monasteries. The participation of the faithful in the liturgy is not a reason for the nuns to leave the enclosure nor for the faithful to enter the nuns' choir. Guests cannot be allowed to enter the monastery enclosure.

---

[58] In addition to the papal enclosure of nuns, *Verbi sponsa* deals with the issues of formation, relations with institutes of men, and associations and federations.

submitted to the S. Congregation for Religious and Secular Institutes for prior approval.

Verbi sponsa deals with the physical enclosure in broader terms than did the earlier instruction. It omits the details and examples given in *Venite seorsum*. However, it also adds a specific example of a reason insufficient for not maintaining the cloister: participating in the liturgy with the faithful. Both documents contain norms that deal with entering and leaving the enclosure, but this directive regarding participating in liturgy with the faithful, which is new in *Verbi sponsa*, is placed within the context of the obligation of enclosure.

The use of social communications, likewise, is indicative of the later instruction integrally reordering the earlier discipline with substantive additions.

Venite seorsum	*Verbi sponsa*
10. The use of radio and television can be permitted in monasteries of nuns totally dedicated to the contemplative life only in special circumstances having a religious character. 11. Newspaper, periodicals and other communication media must neither be too numerous nor be indiscriminately admitted. For by those media the spirit of this world can pervade and disturb even the best communities.	20. Rules regarding the means of social communications in all their present forms are aimed at safeguarding the spirit of recollection; contemplative silence can in fact be undermined when noise, news and talk fill the cloister. The communications media should be used with moderation and discretion, not only with regard to the content but also the amount and the medium itself. It should be remembered that, inasmuch as contemplatives are accustomed to interior silence, the media have a more powerful impact on their sensitivity and emotions, making recollection more difficult. The use of radio and television can be permitted on particular occasions of a religious character. With prudent discernment and for everyone's benefit, in accordance with the decisions of the conventual chapter, the use of other modern means of communication such as fax machines, cellular telephones or the Internet may be permitted in the monastery for the exchange of information or for reason of work. Nuns should make efforts to be duly informed about the church and the world, not through the great volume of news, but by wise discernment of what is essential in the light of God in order to make this a part of their prayer, in union with the heart of Christ.

In the above example, *Verbi sponsa,* while including the content of *Venite seorsum,* also expands the norms regarding social communication in light of present day technology. In addition, the values of the cloister that the norms of *Venite seorsum* promote are stated in a more positive tone in the later instruction. The reason for restricting communications media is not to prevent the "spirit of the world" from pervading and disturbing the community, but rather to safeguard the spirit of recollection so essential to the contemplative life. However, the norms of *Verbi sponsa* call nuns to an informed stance regarding Church and world even with the restrictions imposed on the use of the means of social communications.

Thus, *Venite seorsum,* while part of canonical tradition, has no juridic force today. The document has been revoked by *Verbi sponsa,* which has integrally reordered the subject matter of the former instruction.

3.3.6 — *Clericalia instituta*

The decree *Clericalia instituta,* issued by SCRIS in 1969, focused on the degree to which lay members can participate in the government of clerical religious institutes.[59] It specifically addressed the offices that lay members of a clerical institute could assume. These were summarized in four norms:

1. That general chapters could decree that lay religious could exercise purely administrative offices that had no direct relation to the ministry that is properly priestly;
2. That general chapters could grant active and passive voice to lay members in regard to chapters on any level, according to the measures and conditions imposed or as stipulated by the general chapter;
3. That lay members could discharge the function of councillor on any level;
4. That non clerical members would not be able to assume the office of superior or of vicar on the general, provincial or local level.[60]

---

[59] See SCRIS, Decree, *Clericalia instituta,* 27 November 1969 (= *CI*), in *AAS,* 61 (1969), pp. 739-740. English translation in *CLD,* 7, pp. 468-471.

[60] See *CI,* nn.1-4.

The first norm, dealing with the exercise of purely administrative offices, was integrally reordered by cc. 150 and 626. Canon 150 incorporates the essence of this norm in stating that "an office that requires the full care of souls and for whose fulfillment the exercise of the priestly order is required cannot be validly conferred on one who is not yet a priest." Canon 626 further asserts that "superiors in the conferral of offices, and members in elections, are to observe the norms of the universal and proper law ..." Thus no restrictions are listed in universal law that preclude a lay member of a clerical institute from being elected to or having an administrative office conferred upon him, provided it does not involve the full care of souls.[61]

The second norm, concerning active and passive voice at chapters, has been integrally reordered by c. 631, §2 of *CIC/83* which states: "The constitutions are to define the composition and extent of the power of a chapter; proper law is to determine further the order to be observed in the celebration of the chapter, especially in what pertains to elections and the manner of handling affairs." Consequently, there is no restriction in the code concerning who may be elected to the general chapter or other chapters. This decision is dependent upon the *ius proprium* of the institute.

In the same way, article 3, which permitted lay members of clerical institutes to serve as councillors at any level, is relegated to the discretion of the institute. Canon 627, §1 asserts that "according to the norm of the constitutions, superiors are to have their own council ..." Accordingly, the composition and requirements for councillor are dictated by the *ius proprium*.

The fourth norm, regarding lay members as superiors, was also integrally reordered by its incorporation into the code. That non-clerical members cannot assume the office of superior general or provincial is evident in c. 134, §1, which confers the status of ordinary on major superiors of clerical religious institutes, thereby requiring one in sacred orders to hold this position. Likewise, c. 620 states

---

[61] Canon 274, §1 states: "Only clerics can obtain offices for whose exercise the power of orders or the power of ecclesiastical governance is required." However, this canon is not directly pertinent since it deals specifically with clerics. Canons 150 and 626, on the other hand, apply also to lay religious.

clearly that the vicar to a major superior is also considered a major superior.[62] According to c. 596, §2, local superiors are to be clerics in that they have ecclesiastical power of governance both for the external and internal forum. Therefore, it is evident that the norms of *CI* have been incorporated into and thereby integrally reordered by the code. Thus *CI* has been revoked. The *ius vigens* on these matters is found only in *CIC/83*.

3.3.7 — *Clausuram papalem*

The declaration, *Clausuram papalem,*[63] granted the superiors general of canons regular, mendicants and clerics regular the permission to relax their papal enclosure.[64] This declaration was integrally reordered by c. 667, §1 that states: "In all houses, cloister adapted to the character and mission of the institute is to be observed according to the determinations of proper law, with some part of the religious house always reserved to the members alone." The canon further specifies in §2 that a "stricter discipline of cloister must be observed in monasteries ordered to contemplative life." Papal enclosure is prescribed only for monasteries of nuns which are totally ordered to the contemplative life.[65] Other observance of the cloister is regulated by the *ius proprium* of each institute.

3.3.8 — *Mutuae relationes*

Mutuae relationes, a set of directives issued by SCRIS and the Sacred Congregation for Bishops in 1978, addresses the relations between religious and the

---

[62] Canon 620: "Those who govern an entire institute, a province of an institute, or part equivalent to a province, or an autonomous house, as well as their vicars are major superiors ...."

[63] SCRIS, Declaration, *Clausuram papalem*, 4 June 1970, in *AAS*, 62 (1970), pp. 548-549. English translation in *CLD*, 7, p. 536.

[64] This was to be done in accord with the common enclosure prescribed for those in simple vows as delineated in c. 604 of *CIC/17*.

[65] See c. 667, §3: "Monasteries of nuns which are ordered entirely to contemplative life must observe *papal* cloister, that is, cloister according to the norms given by the Apostolic See ...."

particular Church.[66] The purpose of the document was to continue to implement that which was put forth in *CD*, nn. 33-35.[67] *MR* is divided into two parts. Part I, which comprises the first four chapters, deals with doctrinal points while the second part, chapters 5-7, sets forth directives and norms that address practical aspects of the relations between bishops and religious.

Part I primarily proceeds from *LG* and *CD*. A number of the doctrinal sections that comprise this section are reflected in the canons that pertain to religious. For example, *MR*, nn. 8, 10 and 22 address the authority of the Supreme Pontiff and the episcopal college in regulating the practice of the evangelical counsels; religious life as a special way of participating in the sacramental nature of the People of God, not an intermediate way between the clerical and lay states; and the pastoral meaning of exemption, respectively. Accordingly, these directives are reflected in cc. 576, 588, 591.[68]

---

[66] SACRED CONGREGATION FOR RELIGIOUS AND FOR SECULAR INSTITUTES AND SACRED CONGREGATION FOR BISHOPS, Directives, *Mutuae relationes*, 14 May 1978 (=*MR*), in *AAS*, 70 (1978), pp. 473-506. English translation in *CLD*, 9, pp. 296-339.

[67] Numbers 33-35 are located at the end of Chapter 2 of *CD*, entitled "Bishops in Relation to Their Own Churches or Dioceses" in section III that includes those who cooperate with the diocesan bishop in his pastoral ministry. Number 33, while acknowledging the unique charism of each religious institute and the responsibilities inherent in religious life, calls religious to work for the building up of the body of Christ, especially in the context of the particular church; n. 34 speaks of religious priests being part of the diocesan clergy in their apostolic works under the authority of the bishops as well as how all religious women and men should collaborate with the hierarchy as part of the diocesan family; n. 35 in greater detail, lists principles for religious in order to ensure that the apostolate is carried out harmoniously in each diocese and that the unity of the particular church is assured. See also the *Code of Canon Law Annotated*, p. 460. *ES* likewise actualized the principles put forth in *CD*. However, this document, as has been noted above, was expressly revoked when the revised code took effect.

[68] Canon 576: "It is for the competent authority of the Church to interpret the evangelical counsels, to direct their practice by laws, and by canonical approbation to establish the stable forms of living deriving from them, and also, for its part, to take care that the institutes grow and flourish according to the spirit of the founders and sound traditions." Canon 588: "§1. By it very nature, the state of consecrated life is neither clerical nor lay. §2. That institute is called clerical which, by reason of the purpose or design intended by the founder or by virtue of legitimate tradition, is under the direction of clerics, assumes the exercise of orders, and is recognized as such by the authority of the Church. §3. That institute is called lay which, recognized as such by the authority of the Church, has by virtue of its nature, character, and purpose a proper function defined by the founder or by legitimate tradition, which does not include the exercise of sacred orders." Canon 591: "In order to provide better for the good of institutes and the needs of the apostolate, the Supreme Pontiff, by reason of his primacy in the universal Church and with a view to common advantage, can exempt

125

However, it is the norms in Part II of *MR* that are relevant to this chapter. This second section contains 44 directives (nn. 24 - 67, inclusive).[69] Yet, not all of these norms are within the parameters of this study. Some are directed primarily toward bishops while others have to do with law that pertains to religious found in other books of the code. For example, *MR*, n. 24 speaks of the responsibility of bishops, in accord with religious superiors, to promote among priests, laity and local religious an awareness and experience of the Church and of the indwelling of the Holy Spirit through seminars on spirituality as well as to promote an appreciation of public and personal prayer. This is primarily the responsibility of the bishop and as such would not come under the domain of religious law per se. Likewise, *MR*, n. 60, which deals with episcopal conferences and patriarchal synods, is directed toward bishops.

In addition, there are other norms that pertain to religious, but are addressed by other areas of the code. For example, n. 33 states:

> Religious have the special and dedicate [sic] obligation (*peculiare ac grave officium*) of being attentive and docile to the Magisterium of the Hierarchy and of facilitating for bishops the exercise of the ministry of *authentic teachers and witnesses of the divine and catholic truth* (cf. *LG*, 25) in the fulfillment of their responsibility for the doctrinal teaching of faith both in the centers where its study is promoted and in the use of means to transmit it.

The article then proceeds to delineate the responsibilities of religious in regard to books and other means of social communications that are proper to Book III, Title IV of *CIC/83*. Likewise, *MR*, n. 36 considers the role of religious in cooperating and planning in places where there is more than one rite; n. 43 deals with the role of religious in light of the bishops's responsibility to exercise vigilance over the liturgy.[70]

---

institutes of consecrated life from the governance of local ordinaries and subject them to himself alone or to another ecclesiastical authority."

[69] See the Appendix for a listing of the present status of the norms of Part II.

[70] In addition to *MR*, nn. 24, 60, 33, 36 and 43 cited above, other norms pertain to the role of bishops or deal with religious law interspersed throughout other books of the code. These include: n. 28, which speaks of the bishop's responsibility to be the guardian of fidelity to the religious vocation in the spirit of each institute; n. 30, b, which concerns the bishop's responsibility to educate diocesan clergy in understanding religious life; n. 31, which deals with collaboration of centers of study in meeting the requirements of formation; n. 32, which treats pastoral planning on the part of the bishop; n. 40, which regards the bishop's responsibility to discern new ways of apostolic presence while maintaining those ways that are properly traditional; n. 44, which details the activities in

It is the remaining 36 norms that are related to religious law as defined in this chapter that will be addressed here. Some of these norms have been integrally reordered and no longer have juridic force.[71] Other norms raise a doubt as to whether they have been reordered and need to be examined from this perspective. Those norms that are not incompatible with *CIC/83*, nor have been restated by it, remain part of the *ius vigens*. These categories will be examined in the sections that follow.

3.3.8.1 — Integrally reordered norms

CIC/83 integrally reordered several of the norms of *MR*. Number 53 a, which is taken directly from *ES*, 25, §1, was revoked by c. 678, §1.

MR	CIC/83
53. All religious, even exempt, are bound by the laws, decrees and ordinances laid down by the local ordinary affecting various works, in those matters which concern the exercise of the sacred apostolate as well as the pastoral and social activity prescribed or recommended by the local ordinary.	678, §1 — Religious are subject to the power of bishops, whom they are bound to follow with devoted submission and reverence in those matters which regard the care of souls, the public exercise of divine worship and other works of the apostolate.

According to the code, religious are subject to the authority of the bishops, not the local ordinary, in regard to the care of souls, liturgy and the apostolate. The areas of the bishops' authority are more clearly delineated in the canon. The *ius vigens* on this matter, then, is found only in the code, not in *MR*.

Another example of integral reordering is evident in *MR*, n. 57. The norm itself is presented in three sections. The first part, n. 57 a, was integrally reordered by *CIC/83*. It states that "the difference existing between the *distinctive works* of an

---

[71] The norms in the second part of *MR* are cited as a source for some eleven canons. The doctrinal norms of *MR* are likewise cited for a number of canons.

which religious are subject to the authority of the diocesan bishop; n 52 a, which speaks of the bishop's responsibility to cultivate sincere and familiar relations with religious superiors; n. 53 b, which states that religious are bound by laws of decrees and ordinances of local ordinaries and episcopal conferences; n. 55, which pertains to the bishop's obligation to exhort diocesan priests to recognize the contributions of religious and to approve the nomination of religious to positions of greater responsibility; n. 56, which speaks of religious in regard to priests' councils; and n. 67, which deals with the unique role of the Pope in fostering relations between bishops and religious superiors.

institute and the *works entrusted* to an institute should be kept in mind by the local ordinary. In fact, the former depend on the religious superiors according to their constitutions, even though in pastoral practice they are subject to the jurisdiction of the local ordinary according to law." This differentiation is incorporated into the Code and is presumed by several canons. For example, canon 677, §1 speaks of *opera instituti propria* and canon 681, §1 refers to *opera quae ab Episcopo dioecesano committuntur religiosis*. However, it is the bishop, not the local ordinary, who is pastorally responsible for works of the apostolate.[72]

Both *MR*, n. 57 b and c[73] have been integrally reordered by canon 681, §§1 and 2, and canon 682, §1 respectively.

MR	CIC/83
57. b) "Whenever a work of the apostolate is entrusted to any religious institute by a <u>local ordinary</u> in accordance with the prescriptions of law, a written agreement shall be made between the local ordinary and the competent superior of the institute which will, among other things, set down precisely all that concerns the work to be done, the members of the institute assigned to it and the finances."	681, §1 Works which a <u>diocesan bishop</u> entrusts to religious are subject to the authority and direction of the same bishop, <u>without prejudice to the right of religious superiors according to the norm of can. 678, §§2 and 3.</u>
c) "For works of this nature members of the religious institute who are really suitable should be selected by the religious superior after discussion with the <u>local Ordinary</u> and, where an ecclesiastical office is to be conferred on a member of the institute, the religious should be appointed by the <u>local Ordinary</u> himself upon presentation by, or at least, with the consent of, <u>his own superior,</u> for a <u>definite term</u> to be mutually agreed upon."	§2 — In these cases the <u>diocesan bishop</u> and the competent superior of the institute, are to draw up a written agreement which, among other things, is to define expressly and accurately those things which pertain to the work to be accomplished, the members to be devoted to it, and economic matters.

682, §1 — If it concerns conferring an ecclesiastical office in a diocese upon some religious, the <u>diocesan bishop</u> appoints the religious, with the <u>competent superior</u> making the presentation, or at least assenting to the appointment. |

---

[72] See c. 678, §1.
[73] *MR*, 57 b and c have been taken directly from *ES*.

Canon 681, §§1 and 2 integrally reordered *MR*, n. 57 b by treating anew its entire subject matter and making significant changes in it. This is borne out in several ways. First, according to the Code, it is the diocesan bishop, not the local ordinary, who both entrusts the work to religious and enters into the written agreement.[74] Secondly, canon 681 speaks of "the right of religious superiors" and references canon 678, §§2 and 3. Paragraph two of canon 678 clarifies that in the exercise of this work, religious are also subject to the their own superiors and are to remain faithful to the discipline of their institute; §3 reiterates the mutual consultation between the diocesan bishop and the religious superior. Thus the later more inclusive norm in the Code revokes the former.

Canon 682, §1 integrally reordered *MR*, n. 57 b. It also prescribes that the diocesan bishop, not the local ordinary, confer an ecclesiastical office upon the religious with at least the assent of the competent superior.

The second part of *MR*, n. 58, which deals with a religious being removed from an office entrusted to him, was integrally reordered by c. 682, §2. The norm in *MR*, quoting *ES*, 32, states that a religious "may <u>for a grave cause</u> (*gravi vero de causa*) be removed from an office entrusted to him either at the wish of the authority who entrusted him with the office ... or by the superior." Canon 682, §2 states that the religious can be removed at the discretion of the one who entrusted the office or of the religious superior, without specifying the nature of the cause.

3.3.8.2 — Doubt of revocation and the *ius vigens*

Some norms of *MR* raise doubt regarding their revocation in light of *CIC/83*. An example of this is n. 37, which is similar to c. 680, and is listed as one of the

---

[74] Although canon 198 of *CIC/17* applied the term "local ordinary" like the present code, before *CIC/83* the term was often used non-technically to refer to what is now the diocesan bishop or his equivalent. However, the difference in terminology indicates a change in the norms themselves. Pre-*CIC/83* norms that mention the "local ordinary" now must be understood as including the vicar general and episcopal vicar, unless *CIC/83* has changed them to "diocesan bishop."

sources of the canon.[75] However, it can be argued that there is a doubt regarding the revocation of n. 37 by the code.

MR	CIC/83
37. <u>Efforts should be made to renew the bonds of fraternity and cooperation between the diocesan clergy and communities of religious</u>. Great importance should, therefore, be placed on all those means, even though simple and informal, which serve to increase mutual trust, apostolic solidarity and *fraternal harmony*. This will indeed serve not only to strengthen genuine awareness of the local Church, but also to encourage each one to render and request help joyfully, to foster the desire for cooperation, and also to love the human and ecclesial community, in whose life each one finds himself a part, almost as if it were the fatherland of his own vocation.	Canon 680 — Among the various institutes and also between them and the secular clergy, there is to be fostered an ordered cooperation and a coordination under the direction of the diocesan bishop of all the works and apostolic activities, without prejudice to the character and purpose of individual institutes and the laws of the foundation.

Canon 680 captures the essential thrust of *MR*, n. 37 regarding the cooperation between and coordination of various institutes and also between them and the diocesan clergy. It further identifies that this is to be accomplished under the direction of the diocesan bishop. However, *MR*, n. 37 advocates a less formal approach in regard to the cooperation and coordination called for in the code. The emphasis placed on fraternity is not reflected in c. 680. Therefore, n. 37 is not revoked and in part it remains the *ius vigens* to be interpreted in light of c. 680.[76]

Similarly, *MR*, n. 59 speaks of associations of religious on the diocesan level. While this dimension of the norm is included in c. 680, n. 59 also lists the purposes for encouraging such organizations. These include aspects not present in the canon, such as the "promotion and renewal of religious life in fidelity to the directives of the

---

[75] See *CIC, fontium annotatione*, c. 680.

[76] Canon 21 states that if there is doubt of revocation the later laws are to be related to the earlier ones. This rule is applicable to level two and level three norms as well. However, in the case presented above, *MR*, a level three document, would be interpreted in light of c. 680 of *CIC/83*, a level one norm.

Magisterium" and "for coordinating the activities of religious families with the pastoral action of the diocese." This norm, then, is still in force but is to be interpreted in light of c. 680.

MR, n. 51 is another example of where doubt of revocation exists. This norm deals with discerning the authenticity of new religious institutes.[77] Canon 579 states that diocesan bishops can erect institutes of consecrated life in their own territory by formal decree after having consulted the Apostolic See.[78] Canon 605 asserts that while approving new forms of consecrated life is reserved to the Apostolic See alone, diocesan bishops should strive to discern the new gifts of the Holy Spirit and aid the promoters to express their proposals.[79] While these two canons delineate the responsibility for new institutes and for new forms of consecrated life that is stated

---

[77] *MR*, n. 51: "In some regions there is noticeable a certain overabundance of initiatives to found new religious institutes. Those who are responsible for discerning the authenticity of each foundation should weigh – with humility, of course, but also objectively, constantly, and seeking to foresee clearly the future possibilities – every indication of a credible presence of the Holy Spirit, both to receive His gifts 'with thanksgiving and consolation' and also to avoid that 'institutes may be imprudently brought into being which are useless or lacking in sufficient resources.' In fact, when judgment regarding the establishment of an institute is formulated only in view of its usefulness and suitability in the field of action, or simply on the basis of the comportment of some person who experiences devotional phenomena, in themselves ambiguous, then indeed it becomes evident that the genuine concept of religious life in the Church is in a certain manner distorted.

"To pronounce judgment on the authenticity of a charism, the following characteristics are required: a) its special origin from the Spirit, distinct, even though not separate, from special personal talents, which become apparent in the sphere of activity and organization; b) a profound ardor of love to be conformed to Christ in order to give witness to some aspect of His mystery; c) a constructive love of the Church, which absolutely shrinks from causing any discord in Her.

"Moreover, the genuine figure of the *Founders* entails men and women whose proven virtue demonstrates a real docility both to the sacred hierarchy and to the following of that inspiration, which exists in them as a gift of the Spirit.

"When there is a question, therefore, of new foundations, all who have a role to play in passing judgment must express their opinions with great prudence, patient appraisal and just demands. Above all, the bishops, successors of the apostles 'to whose authority the spirit himself subjects even those who are endowed with charisms,' and who, in communion with the Roman Pontiff, have the duty 'to give a right interpretation of the counsels, to regulate their practice and also to set up stable forms of living embodying them' should feel themselves responsible for this."

[78] Canon 579: "Diocesan bishops, each in his own territory, can erect institutes of consecrated life by formal decree, provided that the Apostolic See has been consulted."

[79] Canon 605: "The approval of new forms of consecrated life is reserved only to the Apostolic See. Diocesan bishops, however, are to strive to discern new gifts of consecrated life granted to the Church by the Holy Spirit and are to assist promoters so that these can express their proposals as well as possible and protect them by appropriate statutes; the general norms contained in this section are especially to be utilized."

more generically in *MR*, nonetheless, n. 51 provides directives and cautions not found in the canons. For example, it lists the characteristics required in judging the authenticity of a charism and it also addresses qualities of the founders. Thus, *MR*, 51 is derogated from by the code, but the norm is not abrogated by the canons. In its interpretation it is to be reconciled with the appropriate canon.

3.3.8.3 — Norms not incompatible with the code

Many of the norms of *MR* are not incompatible with *CIC/83*. One example of this is evident in comparing *MR*, nn. 61- 66 with cc. 708 and 709. The norms in *MR* deal with relations between bishops and religious on the national, regional and universal levels.[80] The canons, which deal with conferences of major superiors and of these conferences coordinating and cooperating with conferences of bishops, state:

> 708 — Major superiors can be associated usefully in conferences or councils so that by common efforts they can achieve more fully the purpose of the individual institutes, always without prejudice to their autonomy, character and proper spirit, or to transact common affairs, or to establish

---

[80] *MR*, 61: " In many countries or regions, through the medium of the Sacred Congregation for Religious and for Secular Institutes ... the Holy See has set up Councils or Conferences of Major Superiors ... Such councils must ... work to enhance common consecration and to channel the energies of all dedicated to apostolic work toward the pastoral coordination of the bishops.
62: "Relations between the council of major superiors ... and the episcopal conferences ... should be regulated according to criteria which determine the rapport between the individual institute and the local ordinary; therefore extra guidelines should also be set up according to the different needs of the region.
63: "Since it is of utmost importance that the council of major superiors collaborate diligently and in a spirit of trust with episcopal conferences, 'it is desirable that questions having reference to both bishops and religious should be dealt with by mixed commissions consisting of bishops and major religious superiors, men or women.' ...
64: "Participation of major superiors, or, according to the statutes, of their delegates, also in other various commissions of the episcopal conferences or inter-ritual assemblies of local ordinaries (as, for example, in the commissions on education, health, justice and peace, social communication, etc.) can be of great utility for the purposes of pastoral action.
65: "The mutual presence of delegates both of episcopal conferences and of the conferences or councils of major superiors in each of the unions or assemblies of one and the other is recommended. Evidently, the necessary norms must be established in advance whereby each conference would treat by itself alone the matters of its exclusive competency.
66: "Regarding the international, continental or intra-continental sphere among various countries united together, some form of coordination, both for bishops as well as for major religious superiors, can be created with the approval of the Holy See..."

appropriate coordination and cooperation with the conferences of bishops and also with individual bishops.[81]

709 — Conferences of major superiors are to have their own statutes approved by the Holy See, by which alone they can be erected even as a juridic person and under whose supreme direction they remain.[82]

The norms of *MR* are both more extensive and detailed than those of the code. Although components of *MR*, 61 and 63 are included in c. 708, the scope of the earlier norms is much broader. Thus, these norms remain in force.

It is obvious, then, that *Mutuae relationes* as a document has not been integrally reordered by the code. While some of its norms have been integrally reordered, these account only for derogations in the directives themselves. The nearly twenty remaining articles of *MR* that pertain to religious law, then, still serve as part of the *ius vigens* for religious.[83] While not having the force of *leges*, these norms provide juridic directives for religious in their relations with bishops on a variety of themes.[84]

3.3.9 — SCRIS plenary documents

Two additional documents issued by SCRIS preceded the promulgation of *CIC/83*. Both "Religious and Human Promotion" and "The Contemplative Dimension of Religious Life" were issued in August, 1980.[85] The former, the fruit of the 1978 plenary session of the Congregation for Religious and Secular Institutes, focused on the contribution of religious to the development of humankind through fidelity to the

---

[81] "Superiores maiores utiliter in conferentiis seu consiliis consociari possunt ut, collatis viribus, allaborent sive ad finem singulorum institutorum plenius assequendum, salvis semper eorum autonomia, indole proprioque spiritu, sive ad communia negotia pertractanda, sive ad congruam coordinationem cum Episcoporum conferentiis et etiam cum singulis Episcopis instaurandam."

[82] "Conferentia Superiorum maiorum sua habeant statuta a Sancta Sede approbata, a qua unice, etiam in personam iuridicam, erigi possunt et sub cuius supremo moderamine manent."

[83] These would include *MR*, nn. 25, 26, 27, 29, 30 a, 34, 35, 38, 39, 41, 42, 45, 46, 47, 48, 49, 50, 52 b, and 54.

[84] These norms touch on prayer, poverty, witness, formation, the particular role of religious women, etc.

[85] See SCRIS, "Religious and Human Promotion," 12 August 1980, in *EV*, 7 (1980-1981), pp. 414-468 and "The Contemplative Dimension of Religious Life," 12 August 1980, in *EV*, 7 (1980-1981), pp. 468-504. Both documents were written in and published in English.

Gospel and witness to the beatitudes. "Religious and Human Promotion" called religious to a new presence in both traditional and modern apostolic works, to direct participation in concrete undertakings for justice, and to a presence in the world of labor and labor unions.[86] "The Contemplative Dimension of Religious Life," the result of the plenary session of SCRIS held in 1980, complemented its predecessor, synthesizing the values and requirements of a contemplative life, for both active and contemplative religious.[87]

However, these two documents raise a question in regard to their juridic value and thus their ability to integrally reorder a former document or to be considered matter for future integral reordering. Even though they are described as reaffirming and defining the specific role of religious life in the Church that *Mutuae relationes* had "described and studied in depth,"[88] these documents do not have the juridic force of *MR*. This judgment is based on the following premises. First, *MR* was published in *Acta Apostolicae Sedis* with the title *"notae directivae."*[89] The second part of *MR* was entitled *"Ordinationes et normae."* The introduction to this latter section states that its purpose is to apply the principles set forth in the first part.[90] However, neither "Religious and Human Promotion" nor "The Contemplative Dimension of Religious Life" were published in *AAS*.[91] Neither document was said to contain directives or any binding norms.[92] It is only in the forward that precedes the two documents where they are described as "guidelines" given by the plenary meetings of the Sacred

---

[86] See SCRIS, "Religious Profession and Human Promotion," in *The Pope Speaks*, 26 (1980), p. 98.

[87] See ibid., pp. 98-99.

[88] See "Life and Mission of Religious in the Church" in *EV,* 7 (1980-1981), p. 414.

[89] See SCRIS, *MR,* in *AAS,* 70 (1978), p. 473: "Recentium annorum experientia, principiis hucusque expositis perspectis, ad nonnullas ordinationes et normas redigendas induxit ad praxim praecipue spectantes."

[90] See ibid., p. 489.

[91] Although c. 34 does not require the publication of an instruction in *AAS*, nonetheless, oftentimes this occurs, either in *AAS* or another publication chosen by the legislator.

[92] The fact that the documents themselves are not titled provides an indication that they are not deemed to be juridic.

Congregation for Religious and for Secular Institutes.[93] Both "Religious and Human Promotion" and "The Contemplative Dimension of Religious Life" are written in a descriptive rather than a normative style.

Second, while both *MR* and the two plenary documents were seen by the pope, there is a difference in the approval that they received. The conclusion of *MR* states: "the foregoing was submitted for the examination of the Holy Father, who ... benevolently approved it and mandated its publication."[94] The forward to the plenary documents states that "the holy father expressed his deep appreciation of their content and gave his consent for their publication, hoping that they would contribute to an ever more generous, consistent and persevering commitment on the part of consecrated persons ..."[95] Thus, it is obvious that "Religious and Human Promotion" and "The Contemplative Dimension of Religious Life" do not carry the juridic force of *MR*. The plenary documents, directed toward all religious, provide valuable direction and guidance for them. However, neither are part of the *ius vigens* pertaining to religious and never were, because they are not juridically binding.

3.3.10 — "Essential Elements in Church Teaching on Religious Life"

"Essential Elements in Church Teaching on Religious Life" was prepared by SCRIS during the *vacatio legis* of *CIC/83*.[96] However, before the actual release of the document by the Congregation it was sent with an accompanying letter to the bishops of the United States by Pope John Paul II.[97] From this perspective, "Essential Elements" might be seen as a particular, rather than a universal document, designed

---

[93] *ES*, 7 (1980-1981), p. 414.
[94] SCRIS, *MR*, in AAS, 70 (1978), p. 506: "Haec omnia et singula Summo Pontifici subiecta fuerunt, ... benigne approbavit ac decrevit ut publici iuris fierent." English translation in *CLD*, 9, p. 339.
[95] *EV*, 7, (1980-1981), p. 414.
[96] See SCRIS, "Essential Elements in Church Teaching on Religious Life" (= "Essential Elements"), in *Origins*, 13 (1983-1984), pp. 133-142. The *vacatio* was between 25 January and 27 November 1983.
[97] See ibid., p. 133.

"to assist the American bishops in their special pastoral service to religious."[98] However, it has also been acknowledged that the document represents more than a mere particular document.[99] Nevertheless, like the plenary documents discussed above, "Essential Elements" bears no juridic weight in itself. The papal letter that accompanied the document, as well as "Essential Elements," indicate that it is a summary of existing teaching and that its intent is not to introduce new doctrine or law.[100] Article 2 of "Essential Elements" states that its purpose "is to present a clear statement of the church's teaching regarding religious life at a moment which is particularly significant and opportune."[101] Like the plenary documents, "Essential Elements," while a valuable resource for both bishops and religious, is not a source of the *ius vigens* for religious, although many provisions within it are taken from the universal law.

3.3.11 — Transitional CRIS decrees

In February, 1984, shortly after the revised code came into force, CRIS issued two decrees that were intended to bring the *ius proprium* of religious institutes into conformity with *CIC/83*. The first, *Iuris canonici Codice*,[102] addressed the possibility that laws and norms proper to religious institutes might be contrary to the code.[103] The first three articles of this decree provided a process for the supreme moderator, working collegially with his or her council, to identify such norms and explain them to the congregation. It authorized the supreme moderator and the council to

---

[98] S.L. HOLLAND, "The Code and *Essential Elements*," in *The Jurist*, 44 (1984), p. 337. See also p. 306. Holland notes that the customary signatures from SCRIS are missing from the document because it was prepared specifically to be included with the papal letter to the bishops of the United States.

[99] See *EV*, 9 (1983-1985), pp. 164-165: "... tale è nella sostanza e rappresenta indubbiamente qualcosa di più di un semplice documento particolare."

[100] See HOLLAND, "The Code and *Essential Elements*," pp. 304-305.

[101] SCRIS, "Essential Elements," n. 2.

[102] See CONGREGATION FOR RELIGIOUS AND FOR SECULAR INSTITUTES, Decree, *Iuris canonici Codici*, 2 February 1984, in *AAS*, 76 (1984), pp. 498-499. English translation in *CLD*, 11, pp. 84-85.

[103] Because several documents were expressly revoked when the code came into force and other documents were integrally reordered by the code, it was quite possible that the *ius proprium* of a religious institute could be contrary to the provisions of *CIC/83*. See also c. 6, §1, nn. 2 and 4.

formulate norms that might be needed in light of the revocation of other norms. These provisions would be in force until dealt with by the next general chapter of the institute. The fourth article prescribed further specifications for monasteries of nuns.

The second decree, *Praescriptis canonum*, clarified that novices admitted to temporary profession in religious institutes were to profess public vows.[104] Those in temporary profession who had made another form of commitment were to profess vows once that commitment terminated. The time spent in religious life temporarily undertaken by a bond other than a vow would be computed in the time stipulated in the code and the constitutions of the institute prior to perpetual profession.

Both *Iuris canonici Codice* and *Praescriptum canonum* were transitory in nature. They applied and clarified laws that might cause doubt in light of the revised code. Both were issued for specific instances that were to occur in the near future. Thus, having served their purposes, neither remains part of the *ius vigens* for religious.

3.3.12 — "Procedures for the Separation of Members from Their Institute"

Several months later in 1984 CRIS published "Procedures for the Separation of Members from Their Institute."[105] Unlike the two CRIS decrees cited above, the nature of this document as a juridic text is not as clear. The "Procedures for the Separation of Members from Their Institute" outline the specific measures required for implementing cc. 691, 692 and 693. The document has the character of an instruction in that it sets forth provisions for the manner in which the law is to be executed and is directed to those who must execute the law, namely, major superiors and their councils.[106] Moreover, it was listed in the category of *"Decisioni e orientamenti"* by CRIS in its semi-annual bulletin. The document has been called an "authoritative explanation" of the code, but in reality it is more than this because it

---

[104] See SCRIS, Decree, *Praescriptis canonum*, 2 February 1984, in *AAS*, 76 (1984), p. 500. English translation in *CLD*, 11, pp. 91-92.

[105] SCRIS, "Procédure pour la séparation d'un membre de son institut," June 1984, in *EV*, 9 (1983-1985), pp.848-860. English translation in *CLD*, 11, pp. 92-98.

[106] See c. 34, §1.

details procedures not found in the code.[107] Given these facts, it is a binding, juridic document and is part of the *ius vigens* for religious.

3.3.13 — *Potissimum Institutione*

In 1990 the Congregation for Institutes of Consecrated Life and Societies of Apostolic Life issued *Potissimum institutione*, which was entitled *"Normae directivae de institutione in religiosis institutis."*[108] The document, "Directives on Formation in Religious Institutes," has the juridic value of an instruction, according to c. 34. Its directives and ordinances are intended to assist religious both by explaining the norms of the law already in force and in the application of those same norms.[109] Thus *PI* does not derogate from the law already in place. Like an instruction that is directed to the executors of the law, the document is addressed to "major superiors of religious institutes and to the brothers and sisters charged with formation, including monks and nuns."[110] Thus, it is evident that *PI* is included in the *ius vigens* for religious.

PI acknowledges that *Renovationis causam* and other documents published by the dicastery in the years following the Second Vatican Council also touch on religious formation. It lists "Mutual Relations," "Religious and Human Promotion," "The Contemplative Dimension of Religious Life" and "The Essential Elements of the Teaching of the Church on Religious Life" as useful references in placing religious

---

[107] See *EV*, 9 (1983-1985), pp. 848-849: "Questo documento potrebbe essere definito, per analogia, 'una istruzione'. D'altra parte, la rubrica sotto cui è stato pubblicato sul bollettino semestrale della SCRIS è "Decisioni e orientamenti;" e in effetti esso manca di promulgazione su *AAS*, come è richiesto per le "istruzioni" (*CIC* can. 34) in quanto "decreti generali esecutivi" (*CIC* can. 31, §2). Si deve comunque ritenere che il documento sia senz'altro una 'autorevole spiegazione' del codice stesso." However, it should be noted that instructions are not required to be published in the *AAS*.

[108] See CONGREGATION FOR INSTITUTES OF CONSECRATED LIFE AND SOCIETIES OF APOSTOLIC LIFE, Directives, *Potissimum institutione*, 2 February 1990 (= *PI*), in *AAS*, 82 (1990), pp. 470-532. English translation in *Origins*, 19 (1990), pp. 667-699.

[109] See CICLSAL, *PI*, in *AAS*, 82 (1990), p. 470, note: "Congregatio pro Institutis Vitae consecratae et Societatibus Vitae apostolicae publici iuris faciens hoc documentum, valorem instructionis ei tribuere intendit, iusta *CIC*, c. 34. Agitur enim de dispositionibus et orientationibus a summo pontifice adprobatis, quae proponuntur a dicasterio ad declaranda legum iuris praescripta et ad navandam operam ut eadem observentur; innituntur igitur iuris praescriptis vigentibus post Codicem iurus canonici, ad quae pro opportunitate spectant, nulla facta derogatione."

[110] *PI*, n. 4.

formation in harmonious context with the pastoral directions of the universal Church and with particular churches.[111] Since it has been determined in the context of this chapter that of these documents only *Mutuae relationes* still has juridic force, it is necessary to look at those norms relative to formation in *MR* to ascertain if they have been abrogated or derogated from by *PI*.

Several themes are concurrent in the two documents. Both, for example, address the evangelical counsels.[112] Both speak of the need to be versed in the council documents and papal pronouncements.[113] Both affirm the importance of a mature awareness and concern for the local church.[114] Yet this overlapping of themes does not result in any duplication of norms. Each document proceeds from its own perspective.[115]

Some norms of *PI* embody quotations taken directly from *MR*. While most of these are from the doctrinal section of the earlier document,[116] a few are from the practical norms in the second part of *MR*. For example, part of *MR*, n. 26 is quoted in *PI*, n. 65, which states:

> If, as is provided for in the law, young professed are sent to study by their superior, "such studies should not be programmed with a view to achieving personal goals as if they were a means of wrongly understood self-fulfillment, but with a view to responding to the requirements of the apostolic commitments of religious family itself, in harmony with the needs of the church." The course of these studies and the pursuit of degrees will be suitably harmonized with the rest of the program for this stage of formation, according to the judgment of major superiors and those responsible for formation.

However, this use of *MR*, 26 in the later document is not indicative of any reordering of the earlier norm. For *PI* is speaking in the context of the formation of those

---

[111] See *PI*, n. 3.
[112] See *PI*, nn. 11-15 and *MR*, n. 27.
[113] See *PI*, nn. 24 and 68 and *MR*, n. 29.
[114] See *PI*, nn. 21-23 and *MR*, n. 30a.
[115] For example, *PI* addresses the evangelical counsels at length in the framework of religious formation and consecration. *MR* approaches the renewal of the vows as a means of serving the needy and witnessing to fraternal love and unity in the apostolate.
[116] References are cited from *MR*, nn. 5, 6, 8, 10, 11, 12, 13, and 23, all of which are in the doctrinal first half of the document.

members in temporary profession while *MR* treats this same matter from the need for cultural updating and specialized studies which would assist religious in living out the apostolic mission of the institute.[117]

The final paragraph of *PI*, n. 109 cites *MR*, n. 57 as one of its references as well as c. 520, §2.[118] *PI*, 109 reads: "Normally (*plerumque*) the position of a religious priest or of an institute to which the bishop has entrusted a mission or a pastoral work within the particular church must be regulated by a written agreement." Canon 520, §2, which speaks only of assignment to a parish, states that it should be made by means of a written agreement (*fiat mediante conventione scripta*). However, *MR*, 57, which is taken in part from *ES*, 30, §1, states that, whenever a work is entrusted to a religious institute, "a written agreement shall be made (*ineatur conventio scripta*)." *PI* does not reference c. 681, §1 that states: "works which a diocesan bishop entrusts to religious are subject to the authority and direction of the same bishop;" nor §2 that reads, "in these cases, the diocesan bishop and the competent superior of the institute are to draw up a written agreement (*ineatur conventio scripta*) ..." Thus *PI*, n. 109, which relaxes the stipulation of a written agreement through the use of word *plerumque* cannot derogate from the code, which requires such a written agreement. With this exception noted, *PI* is part of the *ius vigens* pertaining to religious.

3.3.14 — "Fraternal Life in Community"

In 1994 CICLSAL released simultaneously in several languages, "Fraternal Life in Community."[119] The form of this document is not identified. Its purpose is

---

[117] See *MR*, n. 26.

[118] Canon 520, §2: "The entrusting of a parish mentioned in §1 can be made either permanently or for a specific, predetermined time. In either case the assignment is to be made by means of a written agreement between the diocesan bishop and the competent superior of the institute or society, which expressly and accurately defines, among other things, the work to be accomplished, the persons to be assigned to the parish, and the financial arrangements."

It should be noted that *PI* also cited *MR*, 58. The section of this norm that was referenced was not included in the above discussion on *MR* in that it referred to law for religious found in another area of the code, which was not in the scope of this research.

[119] See CICLSAL, "Fraternal Life in Community," 19 February 1994, in *Origins*, 23 (1994), pp. 693-712. The various versions were published by the Vatican in booklet form.

primarily "to support the efforts made by many communities of religious, both men and women, to improve the quality of their fraternal life." In light of this, "Fraternal Life in Community" offers criteria for discerning authentic gospel evangelical renewal. It further serves as a reflection for those for whom the ideal of community has become remote.[120] The subject matter of the document does just that: it addresses contemporary influences on community life. It is an exhortation to live what has already been set forth in the law. Of itself, "Fraternal Life in Community" is not binding juridically.

The most recent universal juridic document issued by CICLSAL is *Verbi sponsa*. This instruction has been addressed earlier in this study as having integrally reordered *Venite seorsum*.[121]

3.4 — RELIGIOUS LAW: THE *IUS VIGENS*

Having completed the survey of documents pertaining to religious law, the universal *ius vigens* becomes evident. In addition to *CIC/83* and the conciliar documents, in which light the code is always interpreted, the *ius vigens* includes the following: those norms of *Mutuae relationes* that have not been integrally reordered by *CIC/83*, "The Procedures for the Separation of Members from Their Institutes," and the instructions *Potissimum institutione* and *Verbi sponsa*. "Religious Profession and Human Progress," "The Contemplative Dimension of Religious Life," "Essential Elements in Church Teaching on Religious Life" and "Fraternal Life in Community" are valuable documents in both understanding and applying the law but are not part of the *ius vigens* because they are not binding.

---

[120] See CICLSAL, "Fraternal Life in Community," n. 6.
[121] See pp. 117-121 above.

3.5 — ANALYSIS OF PRINCIPLES AS APPLIED TO DOCUMENTS

It remains, then, to examine the principles of integral reordering that were proposed in the previous chapter to see how they have been employed in this overview of juridic documents pertaining to religious law. While, at times, the use of one of the principles was obvious in dealing with a particular document, a synthesis of each tenet individually will demonstrate more precisely its application.

According to principle 1, integral reordering results in abrogation or derogation. Thus there is a need to determine the extent of the reordering. Essentially this principle was applied in each instance. For example, in *Pastorale munus* several norms were demonstrated to have been abrogated by the integral reordering brought about by *CIC/83*, but these norms in themselves would not have brought about the integral reordering of the entire document.[122] Rather they account for a derogation from the document. The same is true in considering *Cum admotae*. Only the section of the rescript that pertained to religious law as defined in this chapter was determined to have been abrogated by the code.[123] Thus, it is individual norms in both these documents that are abrogated, bringing about a derogation from the document.[124]

Mutuae relationes provides a further example of the integral reordering of norms bringing about a derogation of a document. As has been demonstrated, *MR* in its derogated form remains part of the *ius vigens* for religious. Those norms that are not contrary to or that have not been integrally reordered by the code remain in force. *MR* further exemplifies the derogation of part of a norm by the integral reordering of its subject matter. This was the case, for example, with *MR*, n. 37. The norm itself was derogated by c. 680; however, it remains in effect in its derogated form.[125]

---

[122] See pp. 109-112 above. *PM*, nn. 33, 34 and 35 were integrally reordered by *CIC/83* and thus were abrogated. However, the abrogation of these norms derogated from the document as a whole.

[123] See pp. 112-115 above.

[124] As noted earlier of this chapter, these documents are considered to be integrally reordered in their entirety. This was not proven, however, within the parameters of this study.

[125] See pp. 129-132 above.

On the other hand, it was demonstrated that the entirety of *Religionum laicalium* was integrally reordered by the revised code. Some of its norms were not taken up by *CIC/83*; others were integrally reordered by incorporation into the code or by other means. Thus the document, *RL*, was abrogated by the code, losing its juridic force.[126]

The second principle highlights the fact that according to the code there is a distinction between direct contrariety and integral reordering. Examples of revocation of norms by means of direct contrariety were not found in any of the documents that were examined.[127] This finding corresponds to an observation concerning the use of direct contrariety that was observed in the "Emendations" in the previous chapter, that is, that this means of revocation is used with less frequency than integral reordering.

The third principle notes that an entire document on a given juridic matter can integrally reorder a previous document on that same subject; likewise, a juridic institute can be integrally reordered by a later document or law. An entire document integrally reordering another was exemplified by *Verbi sponsa*, the CICLSAL instruction that integrally reordered *Venite seorsum*. In fact, this proved to be the only such document that was reordered by a later document. The integral reordering of all other documents or the norms within them that were surveyed was brought about by *CIC/83*.

This third principle also includes the concept of the integral reordering of an entire juridic institute.[128] One such example presented above is that of enclosure. The

---

[126] Other documents that have been shown to be abrogated through integral reordering by *CIC/83* include SCRIS decrees *Cum superiores generales, Clericalia instituta*, and the declaration *Clausuram papalem*.

[127] Direct contrariety with the code is evident in the norms of some documents that were expressly revoked. However, this was not a result of tacit revocation.

[128] Many institutes within religious life were entirely reordered by *CIC/83*. Many of these were done after the Second Vatican Council by those documents that were expressly revoked when the code came into force. Although the institute was reordered, the document which served as a source for the Code was expressly revoked. Therefore, it cannot be attributed to integral reordering as defined in cc. 6 or 20 of *CIC/83*.

143

declaration, *Clausuram papalem*, which treated the institute of papal enclosure, was integrally reordered by the code. The regulation of this institute was retained in the universal law only for monasteries of nuns; for other religious institutes it was to be governed by the *ius proprium*.

The fourth principle asserts that some norms in a juridic document can integrally reorder, and thereby revoke, the norms in a previous document while leaving others intact. It distinguishes levels of the hierarchy of documents and the norms within them. This principle is borne out in the survey of the documents presented above. While cc. 29-34 upon which this principle is based were new to the code, and as such are not retroactive, nonetheless, they were rooted in the Church's experience of differentiating the weight of ecclesiastical documents during the postconciliar years and even before. In effect, the basic concepts of both general decrees and instructions, while not included in *CIC/17*, were alluded to in the motu proprio that established the Code Commission after the promulgation of the initial code.[129] *Cum iuris canonici* made clear that the Roman congregations were not to publish general decrees unless required to do so by grave necessity. Rather they were to issue instructions whose purpose was to complement the law by providing further explanation and helping to enforce it.[130] This need became a reality, especially in the years following the Second Vatican Council, as various dicasteries sought to implement the conciliar decrees. Thus, the schema put forth in this fourth principle has been applied to the documents that were examined.

Overall, the documents cited provide examples of a level one document, the *Code of Canon Law*, integrally reordering other level one or lower level documents or the norms within them For example, both *Pastorale munus* and *Cum admotae*

---

[129] See J. RISK, "Title III: General Decrees and Instructions," in *CLSA Commentary*, p. 46.
[130] See BENEDICT XV, Motu proprio, *Cum iuris canonici*, 15 September 1917, in *AAS*, 9 (1917), p. 484. English translation in *Canon Law Digest* 1, pp. 56: "Sacrae Romanae congregationes nova *Decreta Generalis* iam nunc ne ferant, nisi qua gravis Ecclesiae universae necessitas aliud suadeat. Ordinarium igitur earum munus in hoc genere erit tum curare ut Codicis praescripta religiose serventur, tum *Instructiones*, si res ferat, edere quae iisdem Codicis praeceptis maiorem et lucem afferant et efficientiam pariant."

144

were decrees of the supreme legislator capable of being revoked only by comparable universal laws. The SCRIS declaration, *Clausuram papalem*, and *Mutuae relationes*, issued jointly by SCRIS and the Sacred Congregation for Bishops, representing a level two and three document, respectively, were abrogated or derogated by the code.

The only example of a document being integrally reordered other than by the code is the instruction, *Venite seorsum*, a level three document. As alluded to previously, this was integrally reordered by *Verbi sponsa*, another level three document.

The fifth principle emphasizes that integral reordering cannot be presumed but must be proven. This was substantiated throughout the examples cited. Whether an entire document, or some of the norms within a document, are integrally reordered by a later document, the abrogation or derogation must be demonstrated. If there is a doubt as to whether revocation has occurred, then the later law must be harmonized with the former.[131] Examples of such doubt were presented with respect to certain norms of *Mutuae relationes*.[132] In these cases those norms of *MR* retain their force. However, in the case of *MR*, the doubtful reordering stems from *lex*, not the same level document. Thus c. 21 is not directly applicable. The norms of *MR* are to be reconciled with those of *CIC/83*, not the other way around.

Principles 6 and 7 deal with the practical means of integral reordering Principle 6 has been authenticated in several ways in this overview of religious documents. This tenet maintains that in order to determine whether integral reordering has taken place, the tenor and circumstances of the norms as well as the mind of the legislator must be considered. Several models have emerged in this survey. The examples cited have led to observations regarding indications or patterns of integral reordering. These include: 1) the integration of an earlier law into a later legislative

---

[131] As indicated in discussing this possibility earlier in this study, doubt of revocation can exist only when there is a doubt concerning whether a law or norm has truly been integrally reordered. Doubt does not exist where the law is expressly revoked; nor is there doubt if two laws are directly contrary.

[132] See pp. 128-131 above.

text; 2) the incorporation of an administrative norm into a legislative text; 3) the substitution of the *ius proprium* of the religious institute as the norm, rather than universal *lex*; 4) the addition of a further stipulation to a previous norm; 5) a change in the authority responsible for the directive put forth in the norm.

Concerning the first observation, *Cum superiores generales* was a legislative text that was incorporated into the code. Thus it was integrally reordered; the decree has no juridic force of itself. *CIC/83* is the *ius vigens*.

Regarding the second observation, many of the documents and norms that were integrally reordered by the code reflect a change in the weight of the document or norm in that what had been experimental norms now became a stable part of the ecclesiastical law. This is exemplified in some of the norms of the decree, *Religionem laicalium*, issued by SCRIS, as well as *Mutuae relationes*, issued by SCRIS and the Sacred Congregation of Bishops, that were incorporated into the code, elevating their juridic value by making them *lex*.

The third observation indicative of integral reordering reveals that the norms of many pre-code documents were revoked by *CIC/83* in that their subject matter was relegated to the *ius proprium* of the individual religious institute. This is exemplified in the first three norms of *Clericalia instituta*.[133] Such was also the case with the declaration, *Clausuram papalem*. Canon 667, §1 left the determination of the cloister to the dictates of the institute's proper law.[134]

The fourth pattern that emerges is that frequently an additional stipulation to a norm indicates integral reordering in that it changes the tenor of the law, or the circumstances that the law requires, or determines more precisely the mind of the legislator. Examples of this appeared in *Pastorale munus* and *Cum admotae*. *PM*, n. 34 was integrally reordered by c. 667, §4. The canon added the stipulation of the consent of the superior along with the bishop's permission for others to enter the

---

[133] See pp. 121-123 above.
[134] See p. 123 above.

cloister or nuns to leave the cloister.[135] Likewise, *CA*, n. 9 was integrally reordered by the additional specifications of c. 638, §3 in regard to alienation of any affair that would worsen the patrimonial condition of the religious institute.[136]

The fifth observation indicates that a norm is integrally reordered when the authority competent for an act is changed. *CIC/83* accomplished this in numerous instances. This was obvious in *Pastorale munus*, nn. 33 and 38. These norms were integrally reordered by cc. 630, §§1 and 2 and 684, §1, respectively. Canon 630, §§1 and 2 gives superiors, rather than the bishop, the responsibility to see that confessors are available for members of the religious institute; 684, §1 allows the supreme moderator, rather than the bishop, to permit religious to transfer to another religious institute.[137] Such is also the case with *Cum admotae*, nn. 13, 15 and 17, *Religionum laicalium*, nn. 4 and 5, and *MR*, n. 57 that were integrally reordered by the code in terms of a change in the competent authority for various faculties.[138]

Principle 7 speaks of the change in tone or the forcefulness of a law as a sign of integral reordering. This indicator was not frequently evident in the norms of the documents that were studied. Perhaps this can be attributed to the nature of religious law itself as well as the principles that guided the *coetus* that worked in this area of the code.[139] However, there were a couple of indications of its use. Although *Verbi*

---

[135] See pp. 111-112 above.
[136] See p. 114 above.
[137] See pp. 111-112 above.
[138] See pp. 113, 115, n. 43 and 126-128 above.
[139] In addition to the ten principles drawn up for the revision of the *Code of Canon Law* (see *Communicationes*, 1 (1969), pp. 55-56 and 77-85), the *coetus* that dealt with religious life was guided by directives that would be applicable to the law regarding consecrated life. See *Communicationes*, 2 (1970), pp. 170-176. These included a reflection of the spiritual dimension that should undergird the juridical norms; a respect for the special characteristics of each institute, its mission and charism as well as the principle of subsidiarity in the use of the proper law in many areas; a flexibility that would adapt norms to the diversity of the institutes; and the concept of co-responsibility in the government of institutes and equality between institutes of men and women. These directives allow for a more open-ended approach to renewing the law that would not be reflected in changing the forcefulness of the law. These directives led to other ways of integrally reordering the law as has been described throughout this study. See also PONTIFICAL COMMISSION FOR THE REVISION OF THE CODE OF CANON LAW, *Schema of Canons on Institutes of Life Consecrated by Profession of the Evangelical Counsels*, draft, Washington, DC, United States Catholic Conference, 1977, pp. 8-17.

sponsa integrally reordered *Venite seorsum* in its entirety, the change in tone of the later document was indicated in regard to social communication.[140] An additional example was provided by *MR,* n. 58 that was integrally reordered by c. 682, §1. The earlier norm demanded "a grave cause" for the bishop to remove a religious from an office entrusted to him. The code relaxes this, stating that removal can occur at the discretion of the bishop or of the religious superior.[141] This pattern, although not frequently used in religious law, was demonstrated in the examples concerning the liturgical emendations presented in the previous chapter.

The eighth and final principle, which is an outcome of all the principles, states that a law that has integrally reordered an earlier law does not depend on the prior law; the new law stands on its own. If a given norm needs to be interpreted in light of a prior one on the same subject matter, or if significant content in the earlier norm has not been restated in the later norm, then doubt of its revocation exists. Accordingly, the rule of c. 21 must be applied. However, when integral reordering occurs, the earlier juridic document, institute or norm loses juridic force. The prior law exists as part of the *traditio canonica,* but without force. While the former may help in understanding the source or history of the later law, and make the nature of the law itself clearer, the *ius vigens* is found only in the later law.

The examples provided in this chapter demonstrate the revocation of earlier documents, institutes and norms by the integral reordering of their subject matter. The application of the principles for determining the integral reordering of law enables one to ascertain the universal *ius vigens* for religious as it now exists.

This chapter has afforded the opportunity to apply the principles of integral reordering that were delineated in the previous chapter to ecclesiastical documents affecting religious issued by the Holy See since the time of the Second Vatican Council. As noted, some of these documents, although applicable to the universal Latin Church and supportive of the law, are not juridic in nature. Those that were

---

[140] See pp. 120-121 above.
[141] See pp. 127-128 above.

juridic in nature had been or currently serve as the *ius vigens* for religious. With the exception of the six documents that contained within them revoking clauses, none of the remaining documents was expressly revoked. However, as has been demonstrated, the majority of these documents is no longer part of the *ius vigens* due to the fact that their subject matter was integrally reordered.

Pivotal to this study has been the revised *Code of Canon Law*. All documents issued before the code were measured against it to determine whether the document itself had been revoked by integral reordering or whether any of its norms were revoked by their being directly contrary to *CIC/83* or integrally reordered by it.

Throughout the survey of documents pertaining to religious law, the principles presented in Chapter 2 were applied to determine the status of the document or of individual norms within it. The methodology employed has demonstrated that integral reordering is a chief way in which revocation of ecclesiastical law occurs. It has shown the scope of integral reordering as a means of revocation by corroborating the principles put forth in Chapter 2. The principles, which serve as indicators of or guides for assessing integral reordering, provide an analytical tool for canonists in determining the *ius vigens*. Their application to the documents regarding religious law has highlighted in a practical way the importance and efficiency of this common means of revocation of law.

AFTERWORD

The integral reordering of a law is its tacit revocation by a later law that treats anew the entire matter of the earlier law, thus resulting in an incompatibility between the two laws. In this definition, the term "law" refers to both legislative norms (*leges*) and general administrative norms in documents of executive power. The law in question may consist of all the norms of an entire document, all the norms governing a distinct juridic institute, or one or more individual norms. The term "revocation" connotes abrogation or derogation. Usually integral reordering results in abrogation of the previous law. However, when the law in question is part of a document still in force, such as the *Code of Canon Law* or a liturgical book, the reordering may involve either abrogation or derogation. Incompatibility means that the two laws cannot coexist. This can be due to an actual change in the law itself, or the fact that the earlier law or administrative norm, though unchanged, has been incorporated into a later legislative document. In the first instance, the incompatibility results from the general administrative norm assuming a higher juridic value. In the second instance, the incompatibility is simply the result of a later law taking precedence over the earlier law. The incompatibility in this case lies in the fact that two laws are not needed on the same subject matter.

With few exceptions, commentators on the initial code applied integral reordering only to juridic documents and institutes. While acknowledging it as a means of tacit or implicit revocation of law, they nonetheless resorted to contrariety between two laws as the more common way of ascertaining the tacit revocation of a former law by a later one. Commentators broadened the notion of direct contrariety by developing distinctions between direct and indirect contrariety. The latter was said to occur when the new law was opposed to the former law only obliquely, that is, although the object of both laws was formally diverse, there was between them a certain connection of effective dependency. However, this research contends that indirect contrariety should have been viewed more properly as a type of integral reordering of the law, but the commentators at that time did not make this connection.

Part of the reluctance for the authors to invoke integral reordering was rooted in their concern to determine accurately the extent of what was reordered, since that which was whole from one perspective could be considered partial from another. Thus after its inclusion in *CIC/17*, integral reordering was exemplified by commentators primarily in regard to entire documents and institutes; its relevance to singular laws or general administrative norms as a means of revocation was seldom acknowledged or illustrated by means of concrete examples.

As a result of the disciplinary reforms mandated by the Second Vatican Council, integral reordering as a means of abrogation and derogation of law acquired greater importance. Ecclesiastical law, which for the most part had stabilized since its codification, was integrally reordered by the documents that emanated from the council. The canons of *CIC/17* as well as other laws not contained in the code were further impacted by the implementation of the council, which generated a multitude of documents of a juridic nature.

This period of *aggiornamento* and experimentation in the Church that resulted from Vatican II culminated in the promulgation of the revised *Code of Canon Law* in 1983. Integral reordering was introduced into c. 6 as a means of revoking laws already in existence; it was retained in c. 20 in regard to the future abrogation or derogation of law. *CIC/83* did not have the same objective as its predecessor. Rather, the later code sought to revise ecclesiastical law in light of the Second Vatican Council. Unlike the 1917 codification, *CIC/83* made no pretense of embracing the totality of the law. Thus, the principle of integral reordering became highly significant for determining which postconciliar documents were abrogated or derogated by *CIC/83* and which documents or norms within them remained part of the *ius vigens*.

151

The integral reordering of the subject matter of a law is a very common means of revocation today. Yet, canonists recognize the difficulties involved in determining the extent of integral reordering. In addition, commentators seldom apply the concept to individual norms within juridic documents. This deficiency in canonical doctrine is addressed in this study by a thorough examination of integral reordering as a means of revocation.

This study approaches integral reordering, not only from the perspective of juridic documents or institutes, but from the norms within them as well. The principal result of this research is the formulation of the following principles, which serve as indicators or guides to assist in assessing whether the subject matter of a juridic document, institute or norm has been integrally reordered.

1. Integral reordering results in abrogation or derogation; thus, it is necessary to determine the extent of the reordering.

2. Integral reordering is distinct from revocation of law by means of direct contrariety.

3. An entire document on a given juridic matter can integrally reorder a previous document on that same subject; a juridic institute can be integrally reordered by a later document or law(s).

4. Some norms in a juridic document can integrally reorder, and thereby revoke, some of the norms in a previous document while leaving others intact. This occurs in various ways according to the hierarchy of juridical documents and the norms within them:

   a. <u>Level one documents</u>
   Laws (*leges*) in legislative documents can integrally reorder:
   1. other laws of the same legislator (universal, conference of bishops, diocesan bishop, etc); and
   2. general administrative norms issued by an executive authority of that legislator (e.g., a Roman congregation).

   b. <u>Level two documents</u>
   General administrative norms contained in documents issued for the community can reorder other such norms as well as the norms in documents issued for the executors of the law.

c. <u>Level three documents</u>
General administrative norms in documents issued for the executors of the law can only reorder other such norms.

5. Integral reordering cannot be presumed; it must be proven.

6. It is necessary to consider the tenor and circumstances of the norms as well as the mind of the legislator to determine whether integral reordering has taken place.

7. Integral reordering can occur through a change in the tone or forcefulness of a given law or general administrative norm.

8. A law that has integrally reordered an earlier law does not depend on the prior law for its juridic force or its meaning.

These principles are validated through a study of the liturgical emendations made by the Apostolic See that were necessitated at the time the code was revised. Likewise their effectiveness is evident in their application to religious law in light of postconciliar and post-code documents, demonstrating how one can attain clarity in regard to the *ius vigens*.

Integral reordering results in abrogation or derogation; thus, it is necessary to determine the extent of the reordering. This study illustrates the versatility of integral reordering in regard to the revocation of juridic documents, institutes and individual norms. Integral reordering always involves a total reworking of the subject matter of the previous law. This results in the abrogation of an entire document or the abrogation of a norm or norms within the document. Likewise, integral reordering can bring about the derogation of a document or a single norm or norms. Thus, the concern of what is whole and what is partial is no longer an issue, for integral reordering is applicable to both total and partial revocation.

Integral reordering is distinct from revocation of law by means of direct contrariety. This study contrasts the difference between direct contrariety and integral reordering as means of revocation. Both imply incompatibility. However, direct contrariety has a more limited application. Commentators today no longer speak of direct and indirect contrariety. If the incompatibility between an earlier law that has not been expressly revoked and a later law is not the result of direct opposition, then the only alternative is that the incompatibility has been brought about by the integral reordering of the subject matter. Direct contrariety is not a broadly applicable means of revocation. It is applicable only to individual norms and, unlike integral reordering, applies neither to entire juridic documents nor institutes.

An entire document on a given juridic matter can integrally reorder a previous document on that same subject; a juridic institute can be integrally reordered by a later document or law(s). Juridic documents and institutes are only revoked tacitly, or implicitly, by integral reordering; although, as has been established, a juridic document that is totally reordered may include some norms that are directly contrary to the earlier ones.

Based on the analysis of the canonical theory and the examples presented in this study, direct contrariety can, in fact, be understood as a form of integral reordering. t is one way of integrally reordering the subject matter of the law or of an administrative norm, so as to bring about revocation. Thus, extrinsic revocation might better be categorized in two ways: that which is expressly stated by the legislator and that which is brought about by the integral reordering of the subject matter of a law. The category of direct contrariety is not necessary, because it is included in the notion of integral reordering.

Some norms in a juridic document can integrally reorder, and thereby revoke, some of the norms in a previous document while leaving others intact. This occurs in various ways according to the hierarchy of juridical documents and the norms within them. It is important to identify the nature of the juridic matter that is being integrally reordered (the earlier norm) as well as the nature of that which brings about integral reordering (the later norm). The hierarchy of documents and the norms within them, based on cc. 29-34, provides a framework for such assessment. It is possible for integral reordering to occur without materially changing the subject matter of the norm. This happens, for example, when an earlier law is incorporated into a later law or when a general administrative norm is later promulgated in the form of legislation. An administrative norm, on the other hand, cannot reorder a legislative norm (*lex*).

Integral reordering cannot be presumed; it must be proven. This entails a critical study of the new law in light of the earlier one. Once it is determined that a document or norm has been integrally reordered, there can be no doubt about its revocation. If there is uncertainty regarding whether the legislator intended to reorder the former juridic document, institute or law, then, in keeping with c. 21, the later must be reconciled with the earlier; the former is not revoked.

It is necessary to consider the tenor and circumstances of the law as well as the mind of the legislator to determine whether integral reordering has taken place. Likewise, integral reordering can occur through a change in the tone or forcefulness of a given law. A substantive addition to a new law renders the former law incomplete so that it cannot stand on its own as the *ius vigens*. Likewise, a change in the tenor or circumstances of the law, or a change that reveals more precisely the mind of the legislator, or a change in the authority cited in a determined law, or a relaxation or strengthening of the tone or forcefulness of a former law are indications of integral reordering. An authentic interpretation of a law that is extensive or restrictive is a type of integral reordering, revealing more precisely the *mens legislatoris*. Although the law appears to be the same, the literal meaning of the text is changed to something new. In effect, a tacit revocation occurs.

A law that has integrally reordered an earlier law does not depend on the prior law for its juridic force or its meaning. In all cases of integral reordering, the later law is not dependent on the former for its meaning or force.

The theoretical considerations and the practical examples presented in this study lay the groundwork for continued exploration and development of the concept of integral reordering. Moreover, several questions still need to be addressed that are beyond the scope of this study.

First, throughout this work integral reordering has been approached only from the perspective of tacit revocation. Yet integral reordering of the subject matter of a law appears to be the basis of most expressly revoked laws as well. This was exemplified in those postconciliar documents addressed in Chapter 3 that contained revoking clauses within them. Despite the fact that they were expressly revoked, they are still considered by some canonists as having been integrally reordered by the code. Given that direct contrariety is a form of integral reordering, might integral reordering itself be the sole means necessary for the revocation of most laws? Is there a need for the legislator expressly to revoke a law or would not the integral reordering of the subject matter of a given juridic document, institute or norm be sufficient? If the universal legislator resorted more to integral reordering and less to express revocation, would this have a positive or negative impact on the life of the Church, in that particular laws and customs cannot be revoked by integral reordering?

Second, a question arises regarding the liturgical emendations discussed in Chapter 2. As indicated, these were made in light of c. 20 of *CIC/83*. Yet c. 2 states that "liturgical laws in force until now retain their force unless one of them is contrary to the canons of the code." Since it does not refer to integral reordering, there appears to be a discrepancy between c. 2 and the process used by the committee that prepared the emendations for the legislator. For this group used both direct contrariety and integral reordering in accord with c. 20 in assessing which norms were abrogated or derogated. This could be reconciled in that the emendations were, in fact, a form of express revocation. However, one might also explore whether or not c. 2 is incomplete, in that it does not mention integral reordering, or whether this canon is even necessary, given the rule of c. 6, §1, nn. 2 and 4. Why would liturgical law only be revoked by direct contrariety?

Third, a key area for further research proceeds from the assessment of religious law presented in Chapter 3. In actuality, the universal *ius vigens* for religious when examined in light of the principles formulated is quite limited. For the most part, universal law specifically for religious is found in *CIC/83* itself. The number of juridic documents that complement the code is relatively small. Is this equally true for other law in the code, or are there areas of ecclesiastical law for which the pre-code juridical documents and norms still are largely in force? Likewise, the application of the principles to recently published documents could help clarify their status as well as the status of earlier laws to which they might refer.

Finally, the principles that emerged in this study, through their use and application, could in time become more refined and developed. For example, the hierarchy of documents as well as the nature of juridic norms themselves are topics that are being addressed by canonists today. The complexity involved in assessing the juridic value of different kinds of documents or the norms within them poses a problem for both interpreters of the law and those required to observe it. Further simplification in these areas, which would be welcome, could impact the principles developed in this work.

This study represents an initial attempt to deal comprehensively with the concept of the integral reordering of law and provides a foundation upon which canonists can continue to build. Hopefully it will serve as a catalyst for further research and discussion.

APPENDIX

ASSESSMENT OF THE NORMS OF *MUTUAE RELATIONES*

The chart below is a summary of the status of the articles of *Mutuae relationes*, Part II, "Directives and Norms." Based on the research done for Chapter 3, these norms have been categorized into five sections. The first two columns, "Pertains to Bishops" and "Other Books of *CIC/83*" have not been evaluated as to whether they are currently *ius vigens* in that they did not concern religious law as defined in this study. Those norms that have been integrally reordered have been revoked. Those that appear in the last two columns, "Doubt of revocation" and "*Ius vigens*" remain in force.

Article	Pertains to Bishops	Other Books of *CIC/83*	Integrally reordered	Doubt of revocation	*Ius vigens*
24	X				
25					X
26					X
27					X
28	X				
29					X
30	"b"				"a"
31		X			
32	X				

Article	Pertains to Bishops	Other Books of *CIC/83*	Integrally reordered	Doubt of revocation	*Ius vigens*
33		X			
34					X
35					X
36		X			
37				X	
38					X
39					X
40	X				
41					X
42					X
43		X			
44	X				
45					X
46					X
47					X
48					X
49					X
50					X
51				X	
52	"a"				"b"
53		"b"	"a"		
54					X
55	X				
56		X			

Article	Pertains to Bishops	Other Books of CIC/83	Integrally reordered	Doubt of revocation	*Ius vigens*
57			X		
58			X		
59				X	
60	X				
61					X
62					X
63					X
64					X
65					X
66					X
67		X			

SOURCES AND SELECT BIBLIOGRAPHY

PRIMARY SOURCES:

Acta Apostolicae Sedis: Commentarium officiale, 1909-.

Acta Sanctae Sedis, 1865-1909, 41 vols.

BENEDICT XV, Apostolic Constitution, *Providentissima Mater Ecclesia*, 27 May 1917, in *AAS*, 9, Part II (1917), pp. 5-8.

____, Motu proprio, *Cum iuris canonici*, 15 September 1917, in *AAS*, 9 (1917), pp. 483-484. English translation in *Canon Law Digest* 1, pp. 55-57.

Canon Law Digest, T.L. BOUSCAREN (ed.), vols. 1-3; vols. 4-6: T.L. BOUSCAREN and J.I. O'CONNOR (eds.), Milwaukee, Bruce Publishing Company, New York; vols. 7-10: J.I. O'CONNOR (ed.), Mundelein, IL, Chicago Province, S.J.; vol. 11: E. PFNAUSCH (ed.), Washington, DC, CLSA, 1934-.

Canonical Documentation on Consecrated Life (1963-1976), M.J. DINN (ed.), Ottawa, Faculty of Canon Law, Saint Paul University, 1977.

Codex canonum ecclesiarum orientalium, Ioannis Pauli PP. II auctoritate promulgatus, Typis polyglottis Vaticanis, 1990; English translation prepared under the auspices of the CLSA, Washington, DC, CLSA, 1992.

Codex iuris canonici, Pii X Pontificis Maximi iussu digestus, Benedicti Papae XV auctoritate promulgatus, Romae, Typis polyglottis Vaticanis, 1917.

Codex iuris canonici, Pii X Pontificis Maximi iussu digestus, Benedicti Papae XV auctoritate promulgatus, praefatione, fontium annotatione et indice analytico-alphabetico, P. GASPARRI (ed.), Romae, Typis polyglottis Vaticanis, 1917.

Codex iuris canonici, auctoritate Ioannis Pauli PP. II promulgatus, Vatican City, Libreria editrice Vaticana, 1983.

American version of the English-language translation: *Code of Canon Law*, Latin-English Edition, translation prepared under the auspices of the CLSA, Washington, DC, CLSA, 1983.

Codex iurus canonici,

French translation: *Code de droit canonique, texte officiel et traduction française par La Société internationale de droit canonique et de législations religieuses comparées avec le concours de Faculté de droit canonique de l'Université Saint-Paul d'Ottawa, Faculté de droit canonique de l'Institut catholique de Paris,* Paris, Éditions Centurion, Cerf, Tardy, 1984.

German translation: *Codex des kanonischen Rechtes*: Lateinisch-deutsche Ausgabe, mit Sachverzeichnis herausgegeben im Auftrag der deutschen und der berliner Bischofskonferenz, der österreichischen Bischofskonferenz, der schweizer Bischofskonferenz sowie der Bischöfe von Bozen-Brixen, von Luxemburg, von Lüttich, von Metz und von Straßburg; die deutsche Übersetzung und die Erarbeitung des Sachverzeichnesses besorgte im Auftrag der deutschen Bischofskonferenz die folgende von ihr berufene Übersetzergruppe, Butzon & Bercker, Keverlaer, 1984.

Italian translation: *Codice di diritto canonico, testo ufficiale e versione italiana, sotto il patrocinio della Pontificia Università Lateranesnse e della Pontificia Università Salesiana,* Roma, Unione editori cattolici italiani, 1983.

Codex iurus canonici, auctoritate Ioannis Pauli PP. II promulgatus, fontium annotatione et indice analytico — alphabetico auctus, Libreria editrice Vaticana, 1989.

Code of Canon Law, Latin-English edition, new English translation, prepared under the auspices of the CLSA, Washington, DC, CLSA, 1999.

Communicationes, Romae, PONTIFICIA COMMISSIO CODICI IURIS CANONICI RECOGNOSCENDO [vols.1-15 (1969-1983)], PONTIFICIA COMMISSIO CODICI IURIS CANONICI AUTHENTICE INTERPRETANDO [vols. 16-20, (1984-1988)], PONTIFICUM CONSILIUM DE LEGUM TEXTIBUS INTERPRETANDIS [vols. 21 -, (1989-)].

CONGREGATION FOR INSTITUTES OF CONSECRATED LIFE AND SOCIETIES OF APOSTOLIC LIFE, Directives, *Potissimum institutione,* 2 February 1990, in *AAS,* 82 (1990), pp. 470-532. English translation in *Origins,* 19 (1989-1990), pp. 667-699.

_____,Instruction, *Verbi Sponsa,* 13 May 1999, at ⟨http://www.vatican.va/ romancuria/congregations/ccscrlife/documents/rc_con_ccscrlife_doc_13051999 verbisponsa_lt.html⟩. English translation in *Origins,* 29 (1999-2000), pp. 155-164.

_____, "Fraternal Life in Community," 19 February 1994, in *Origins,* 23 (1993-1994), pp. 693-712.

CONGREGATION FOR INSTITUTES OF CONSECRATED LIFE AND SOCIETIES OF APOSTOLIC LIFE, "Procédure pour la séparation d'un membre de son institut," June 1984 (no day given), in *EV*, 9 (1983-1985), pp. 848-860. English translation in *CLD*, 11, pp. 92-98.

CONGREGATION FOR RELIGIOUS AND FOR SECULAR INSTITUTES, Decree, *Iuris canonici Codici*, 2 February 1984, in *AAS*, 76 (1984), pp. 498-499. English translation in *CLD*, 11, pp. 84-85.

_____, Decree, *Praescriptis canonum*, 2 February 1984, in *AAS*, 76 (1984), p. 500. English translation in *CLD*, 11, pp. 91-92.

Corpus iuris canonici, editio lipsiensis secunda, A.L. RICHTERI, 1879, A. FRIEDBURG, (ed.), Graz, Akademische Druck, 1959.

Enchiridion documentorum instaurationis liturgicae, R. KACZYNSKI (ed.), vol. 1: Torino, Marietti, 1976; vols. 2-3: Roma, Edizioni Liturgiche, 1988 and 1997.

Enchiridion Vaticanum testo ufficiale e versione italiana, Bologna, Edizione Dehoniane, 1963-.

FLANNERY, A. (gen. ed.), *Vatican Council II: The Basic Sixteen Documents*, rev. translation in inclusive language (= FLANNERY), Northport, New York, Costello Publishing Company, 1996.

_____, *Vatican Council II: the Conciliar and Postconciliar Documents*, vol. 1, new revised edition (= FLANNERY I), Northport, New York, vol. 1, 1996.

GASPARRI, P., *Codex Iuris canonici cum notis schema Codicis canonici*, Romae, Typis Polyglottis Vaticanis, 1916.

_____, *Sanctissimi Domini Nostri PII PP. X, Codex iuris canonici schema Codicis iuris canonici sub secreto pontificio*, Romae, Typis Polyglottis Vaticanis, 1912.

JOHN XXIII, Allocution, *Ad emos patres cardinales in urbe praesentes habita*, 25 January 1959, in *AAS*, 51 (1959), pp. 65-69. English translation in *The Pope Speaks*, 5 (1958-1959), pp. 398-401.

JOHN PAUL II, Apostolic Constitution, *Pastor bonus*, 28 June 1988, in *AAS*, 80 (1988), pp. 841-924. English translation in *Code of Canon Law Annotated*, pp. 1167-1279.

_____, Apostolic Constitution, *Sacræ disciplinæ leges*, 25 January 1983, in *AAS*, 75, Part II (1983), pp. vii-xiv. English translation in *Code of Canon Law Annotated*, pp. 47-57.

_____, Apostolic Exhortation, *Redemptionis donum*, 25 March 1984, in *AAS*, 76 (1984), pp. 513-546. English translation in *Origins*, 13 (1983-1984), pp. 721-731.

JOHN PAUL II, Apostolic Exhortation, *Vita consecrata*, 25 March 1996, in *AAS*, 88 (1996), pp. 377-486. English translation in *The Pope Speaks*, 41 (1996), pp. 257-338.

_____, Encyclical, *Redemptoris missio*, 22 January 1991, in *AAS*, 83 (1991), pp. 249-340. English translation in *Origins*, 20 (1990-1991), pp. 541-568.

PAUL VI, Allocution to the International Congress of Canonists, 25 May 1968, in *AAS*, 60 (1968), pp. 337-342. English translation in *CLD*, 7, pp. 63-68.

_____, Apostolic Constitution, *Paenitemini*, 17 February 1966, in *AAS*, 58 (1966), pp. 177-198. English translation in *The Pope Speaks*, 11 (1966), pp. 362-371.

_____, Apostolic Constitution, *Regimini Ecclesiae universae*, 15 August 1967, in *AAS*, 59 (1967), pp. 885-928. English translation in *The Pope Speaks*, 12 (1967), pp. 393-420.

_____, Apostolic Exhortation, *Evangelica testificatio*, 29 June 1971, in *AAS*, 63 (1971), pp. 497-526. English translation in *CLD*, 7, pp. 425-449.

_____, Motu proprio, *De episcoporum muneribus*, 15 June 1966, in *AAS*, 58 (1966), pp. 467-472. English translation in *CLD*, 6, pp. 394-400.

_____, Motu proprio, *Ecclesiae sanctae*, 6 August 1966, in *AAS*, 58 (1966), pp. 264-298. English translation in *CLD*, 6, pp. 264-298.

_____, Motu proprio, *Pastorale munus*, 30 November 1963, in *AAS*, 56 (1964), pp. 5-12. English translation in *CLD*, 6, pp. 370-378.

PIUS X, Motu proprio, *Arduum sane munus*, 19 March 1904, in *ASS*, 36 (1903-1904), pp. 549-551.

PONTIFICAL COMMISSION FOR THE REVISION OF THE CODE OF CANON LAW, *Draft of the Canons of Book One: General Norms*, translated under the auspices of the CLSA by D. BURNS, Rome, The Vatican Polyglot Press, 1977.

PONTIFICIA COMMISSIO CODICI IURIS CANONICI ORIENTALIS RECOGNOSCENDO, *Nuntia*, Roma, Libreria Editrice Vaticana.

PONTIFICIA COMMISSIO CODICI IURIS CANONICI RECOGNOSCENDO, *Schema canonum libri I, de normis generalibus*, Romae, Typis polyglottis Vaticanis, 1977.

_____, *Codex iuris canonici: schema Patribus commissionis reservatum*, Romae, Città del Vaticano, Liberia editrice Vaticana, 1980.

_____, *Codex iuris canonici: Schema novissimum iuxta placita Patrum commissionis emendatum atque Summo Pontifici praesentatum*, Civitate Vaticana, Typis polyglottis Vaticanis, 1982.

PONTIFICAL COMMISSION FOR THE REVISION OF THE CODE OF CANON LAW, *Schema of Canons on Institutes of Life Consecrated by Profession of the Evangelical Counsels*, draft, Washington, DC, United States Catholic Conference, 1977.

PONTIFICAL COUNCIL FOR THE PROMOTION OF CHRISTIAN UNITY, *Directorium oecumenicum noviter compositum*, original in French, *Directoire pour l'application des principes et des normes sur l'oecuménisme*, 25 March 1993, in *AAS*, 85 (1993), pp. 1039-1119. English translation in *Origins*, 23 (1993-1994), pp.129-160.

SACRED CONGREGATION FOR RELIGIOUS, Decree, *Religionem laicalium*, 31 May 1966, in *AAS*, 59 (1967), pp. 362-364. English translation in *CLD*, 6, pp. 153-156.

SACRED CONGREGATION FOR RELIGIOUS AND FOR SECULAR INSTITUTES, Declaration, *Clausuram papalem*, 4 June 1970, in *AAS*, 62 (1970), pp. 548-549. English translation in *CLD*, 7, p. 536.

____, Decree, *Ad instituenda*, 4 June 1970, in *AAS*, 62 (1970), pp. 549-550. English translation in *CLD*, 7, pp. 80-82.

____, Decree, *Cum superiores generales*, 27 November 1969, in *AAS*, 61 (1969), pp. 738-739. English translation in *CLD*, 7, p. 77.

____, Decree, *Dum canonicarum legum*, 8 December 1970, in *AAS*, 63 (1971), pp. 318-319. English translation in *CLD*, 7, pp. 531-533.

____, Decree, *Clericalia instituta*, 27 November 1969, in *AAS*, 61 (1969), pp. 739-740. English translation in *CLD*, 7, pp. 468-471.

____, Decree, *Experimenta circa regiminis rationem*, 2 February 1972, in *AAS*, 64 (1972), pp. 393-394. English translation in *CLD*, 7, pp. 484-485.

____, Decree, *Processus judicialis*, 2 March 1974, in *AAS*, 66 (1974), pp. 215-216. English translation in *CLD*, Supplement 1974, pp. 2-3.

____, "Essential Elements in Church Teaching on Religious Life," in *The Pope Speaks*, 28 (1983), pp. 304-322; *Origins*, 13 (1983-1984), pp. 139-142; in *EV*, 9 (1983-1985), pp. 162-259.

____, Instruction, *Renovationis causam*, 6 January 1969, in *AAS*, 61 (1969), pp. 103-120. English translation in *CLD*, 7, pp. 489-508.

____, Instruction, *Venite seorsum*, 15 August 1969, in *AAS*, 61 (1969), pp. 674-690. English translation in *CLD*, 7, pp. 536-541.

____, "Religious and Human Promotion," in *The Pope Speaks*, 26 (1981), pp. 97-122.

____, "The Contemplative Dimension of Religious Life," in *The Pope Speaks*, 26 (1981), pp. 123-139.

SACRED CONGREGATION FOR RELIGIOUS AND FOR SECULAR INSTITUTES AND SACRED CONGREGATION FOR BISHOPS, Directives, *Mutuae relationes*, 14 May 1978, in *AAS*, 70 (1978), pp. 473-506. English translation in *CLD*, 9, pp. 296-339.

SACRED CONGREGATION FOR THE SACRAMENTS AND DIVINE WORSHIP, "Variationes in novas editiones librorum liturgicorum ad normam Codicis iuris canonici nuper promulgati introducendae," 12 September 1983, in *Notitiae,* 19 (1983), pp. 540-555. English translation in "Emendations in the Liturgical Books Following Upon the New Code of Canon Law," prepared by the INTERNATIONAL COMMISSION ON ENGLISH IN THE LITURGY, Washington, DC, 1984.

Schema Codicis iuris canonici orientalis 1986, Code of Eastern Canon Law 1986 Draft, English translation, preliminary edition for restricted distribution, Brooklyn, New York, United States Eastern Catholic Bishops Consultation, 1987.

SECOND VATICAN COUNCIL, Dogmatic Constitution on the Church, *Lumen gentium,* 21 November 1964, in *AAS,* 57 (1965), pp. 5-67. English translation in FLANNERY, pp. 1-96.

_____, Constitution on the Sacred Liturgy, *Sacrosanctum concilium,* 4 December 1963, in *AAS,* 56 (1964), pp. 97-138. English translation in FLANNERY, pp. 117-161.

_____, Decree on the Church's Missionary Activity, *Ad gentes divinitus,* 7 December 1965, in *AAS,* 58 (1966), pp. 947-990. English translation in FLANNERY, pp. 443-497.

_____, Decree on Ecumenism, *Unitatis redintegratio,* 21 November 1964, in *AAS,* 57 (1965), pp. 90-112. English translation in FLANNERY, pp. 499- 523.

_____, Decree on the Pastoral Office of Bishops in the Church, *Christus Dominus,* 28 October 1965, in *AAS,* 58 (1966), pp. 673-701. English translation in FLANNERY, pp. 283-315.

_____, Decree on the Up-to-date Renewal of Religious Life, *Perfectae caritatis,* 28 October 1965, in *AAS,* 58 (1966), pp. 637-696. English translation in FLANNERY, pp. 385-401.

SECRETARIAT FOR THE PROMOTION OF THE UNITY OF CHRISTIANS, Directory concerning Ecumenical Matters: Part One, *Ad totam Ecclesiam,* 14 May 1967, in *AAS,* 59 (1967), pp. 574-592. English translation in FLANNERY I, pp. 483-501.

_____, Directory concerning Ecumenical Matters: Part Two, *Spiritus domini,* 16 April 1970, in *AAS,* 62 (1970), pp. 705-724. English translation in FLANNERY I, pp. 515-532.

_____, Instruction, *In quibus rerum circumstantiis,* 1 June 1972, in *AAS,* 64 (1972), pp. 518-525. English translation in *CLD,* 7, pp. 583-590.

_____, *Dopo la publicazione,* 17 October 1973, in *AAS* 55 (1973), pp. 616-619. English translation in FLANNERY I, pp. 560-563.

SECRETARY OF STATE, Pontifical Rescript, *Cum admotae*, 6 November 1964, *AAS*, 59 (1967), pp. 374-378. English translation in *CLD*, 6, pp. 147-152.

BOOKS:

ABBO, J.A. and J.D. HANNAN, *The Sacred Canons: A Concise Presentation of the Current Disciplinary Norms of the Church*, rev. edition, St. Louis, MO, B. Herder Book Co., 1957, 2 vols.

AUGUSTINE, C., *A Commentary on the New Code of Canon Law*, St. Louis, MO, Herder, 1925-1936, 8 vols.

BEAL, J.P., J.A. CORIDEN, and T.J. GREEN (eds.), *New Commentary on the Code of Canon Law*, commissioned by the CLSA, New York/Mahwah, NJ, Paulist Press, 2000.

BERUTTI, C., *Institutiones iuris canonici*, Taurini, Romae, Marietti, 1936-1943, 6 vols.

BESTE, U., *Introductio in Codicem*, 5th edition, Napoli (Italia), M. D'Auria Pontificius Editor, 1961.

BEYER, J., *Dal Concilio al Codice: il nuovo Codice e le istanze del Concilio Vaticano II*, Bologna, Edizione Dehoniane, 1984.

BLANCO NÁJERA, F., *Código de derecho canónico traducido y comentado*, Cadiz, Establecimientos Cerón y Libreria Cervantes, S.L., 1942-1945, 2 vols.

BLAT, A., *Commentarium textus Codicis iuris canonici*, Romae, Typographia Pontificia in Instituto Pii IX, 1921-1938, 5 t. in 6 vols.

BOLOGNINI, F., *Lineamenti di diritto canonico*, Torino, G. Giappichelli, 1993.

BOUSCAREN, T.L., A.C. ELLIS and F.N. KORTH, *Canon Law: A Text and Commentary*, 4th rev. edition, Milwaukee, The Bruce Publishing Company, 1966.

BOUUAERT, F.C. and G. SIMENON, *Manuale iuris canonici ad usum seminariorum*, 5th edition, Gandae et Leodii, Prostat apud auctores in Seminariis Gandavensi et Leodiensi, 1934-1935, 3 vols.

BRYS, J., *Juris canonici compendium*, 10th edition, Bruges, Desclée de Brouwer, 1947-1949, 2 vols.

CABREROS DE ANTA, M., *Derecho canónico fundamental*, Madrid, Editorial y Libería Co., Cul. S.A., 1960.

_____, *Estudios canónicos*, Madrid, Editorial Coculsa, 1956.

_____, *Nuevos estudios canónicos*, Victoria, Editorial Eset, 1966.

CABREROS DE ANTA, M., *Vigencia y estado actual de la legislacion canónica*, Pamplona, Ediciones Universidad de Navarra, S.A., 1974.

CABREROS DE ANTA, M., A. ALONSO LOBO and S. ALONSO MORAN, *Comentarios al Código de derecho canónico*, Madrid, Biblioteca de Autores Cristianos, 1963-1964, 4 vols.

CANCE, A., *Le Code de droit canonique: commentaire succinct et pratique*, Paris, J. Gabalda et Cie, 1933-1949, 4 vols.

CAPARROS, E., M. THÉRIAULT and J. THORN (eds.), *Code of Canon Law Annotated, Latin-English Edition of the Code of Canon Law and English-language Translation of the Spanish-language of the 5th Spanish-language Edition of the Commentary Prepared under the Responsibility of the Instituto Martín de Azpilcueta*, Montréal, Wilson & Lafleur Limitée, 1993.

CAPPELLO, F.M., *Summa iuris canonici in usum scholarum concinnata*, 4th edition, Romae, Apud Aedes Universitatis Gregorianae, 1945, 3 vols.

CHIAPPETTA, L., *Il Codice di diritto canonico: commento giuridico-pastorale*, 2nd edition, Roma, Edizione Dehoniane, 1996, 3 vols.

CICOGNANI, A.G., *Canon Law*, authorized version by J. O'HARA and F. BRENNAN from the Latin original, 2nd rev. edition, Philadelphia, Dolphin Press, 1935.

Cocchi, G., *Commentarium in Codicem iuris canonici ad usum scholarum*, 5th ed., Taurinorum, Augustae, Marietti, 1931-1942, 8 vols.

COGAN, P.J. (ed.), *CLSA Advisory Opinions 1984-1993*, Washington, DC, The Catholic University of America, 1995.

CORIDEN, J.A., T.J. GREEN and D.E. HEINTSCHEL (eds.), *The Code of Canon Law: A Text and Commentary*, commissioned by the CLSA, New York/Mahwah, New Jersey, Paulist Press, 1985.

CORONATA, M.C., *Compendium iuris canonici ad usum scholarum*, Taurini, Marii E. Marietti, 1937, 5 vols.

CRNICA, A., *Commentarium theoretico - practicum Codicis iuris canonici*, Sibenik, Typis Typographie, 1940, 2 vols.

DE ECHEVERRIA, L. (ed.), *Código de derecho canónico, edición bilingüe comentada por los professores de la Facultad de Derecho canónico de la Universidad Pontificia de Salamanca*, 7th rev. edition, Madrid, Biblioteca de autores cristianos, 1986.

DELLA ROCCA, F., *Manual of Canon Law*, translated by A. THATCHER, Milwaukee, The Bruce Publishing Company, 1959.

EICHMANN, E., *Manual de derecho eclesiástico a tenor del Codex juris canonici*, translated by T. GÓMEZ PIÑÁN, 3rd edition, Barcelona, Librería Bosch, 1931, 2 vols.

FALCO, M., *Corso di diritto ecclesiastico*, 2nd edition, Padova, Casa Editrice Dott., Antonio Milani, 1935.

_____, *Introduzione allo studio del "Codex iuris canonici,"* Torino, Fratelli Bocca, Editori, 1925.

FARIS, J.D., *Eastern Catholic Churches: Constitution and Governance According to the Code of Canons of the Eastern Churches*, New York, Saint Maron Publications, 1992.

GAUDEMET, J., *La doctrine canonique médiévale*, Brookfield, Vermont, Ashgate Publishing Company, 1994.

GLARE, P. et al., *Oxford Latin Dictionary*, Oxford, Clarendon Press, 1968.

GHIRLANDA, G., *Il diritto nella Chiesa, mistero di communione, compendio di diritto ecclesiale*, Milan, Edizione Paoline, Editrice Pontificia Università Gregoriana, 1990.

HERRANZ, J., *Studi sulla nuova legislazione della Chiesa*, Milano, Guiffrè Editore, 1990.

HERVADA, J., *Vetera et nova — cuestiones de derecho canónico y afines (1958-1991)*, Pamplona, Servicio de Publicaciones de la Universidad de Navarra, S.A., 1991, 2 vols.

JOMBART, E., *Manuel de droit canonique conforme au Code de 1917 et aux plus récentes décisions du Saint-Siège*, Paris, Beauchesne, 1958.

_____, *Memento de droit canon*, translated by R. BÉGIN, New York, NY, Benzinger, 1960.

JONE, H., *Commentarium in Codicem iuris canonici*, Paderborn, Officina Libraria F. Schöningh, 1950-1955, 3 vols.

LABANDEIRA, E., *Tratado de derecho administrativo canónico*, 2nd edition, Pamplona, Ediciónes Universidad Navarra, S.A., 1993.

_____, *Trattato di diritto amministrativo canonico*, 2nd edition, translated by L. GRAZIANO, Milano, Guiffrè, 1994.

LOMBARDÍA, P. and J.I. ARRIETA, *Codice di diritto canonico: edizione bilingue comentata*, Italian edition by L. CASTIGLIONE, Rome, Logos, 1986-1987, 3 vols.

LÜDICKE, K. et al. (eds.), *Münsterischer Kommentar zum Codex Iuris Canonici*, Essen, Ludgerus, 1985, 4 vols.

MARZOA, A., J. MIRAS and R. RODRÍGUEZ-OSCAÑA (eds.), *Comentario exegético al Código de derecho canónico*, segunda edición, Pamplona, Ediciones Universidad de Navarra, S.A., 1997, 8t in 5 vols.

MAROTO, P., *Institutiones iuris canonici ad normam novi Codicis*, 3rd edition, Romae, Apud Commentarium pro Religiosis, 1919-1921, 2 vols.

MARTINS GIGANTE, J.A., *Instituiçoes de direito canónico*, 3rd edition, Braga, Escola Tip. De Oficiana de S. José, 1955.

MICHIELS, G., *Normae generales juris canonici: commentarius libri I Codicis juris canonici*, editio altera, Tournai, Desclée, 1949, 2 vols.

MIGUÉLEZ DOMINGUEZ, L., S. ALONSO MORÁN and M. CABREROS DE ANTA, *Código de derecho canónico y legislación complementaria, texto latino y versión castellana, con jurisprudencia y comentarios*, 9th edition, Madrid, Biblioteca de autores cristianos, 1974.

MIGUÉLEZ DOMINGUEZ, L., *Derecho canónico postconciliar suplemento al Código de derecho canónico bilingüe de la biblioteca de autores cristianos*, Madrid, Biblioteca de Autores Cristianos, 1967.

MORRISEY, F.G., *Papal and Curial Pronouncements: Their Canonical Significance in Light of the Code of Canon Law*, 2nd edition, rev. by M. THÉRIAULT, Ottawa, Faculty of Canon Law, Saint Paul University, 1995.

NAZ, R. (ed.), *Dictionnaire de droit canonique*, Paris, Letouzey et Ané, 1935-1965, 7 vols.

NAZ, R. et al., *Traité de droit canonique*, Paris, Letouzey et Ané, 1947-1949, 4 vols.

NEUBERGER, N.J., *Canon 6*, Canon Law Studies, no. 44, Washington, DC, Catholic University of America, 1927.

OCHOA, X., *Index verborum ac locutionum Codicis iuris canonici*, 2nd edition, Roma, Commentarium pro Religiosis, 1984.

OJETTI, B., *Commentarium in Codicem iuris canonici*, Romae, Apud Aedes Universitatis Gregorianae, 1927-1931, 2 t. in 4 vols.

ÖRSY, L., *From Vision to Legislation: From the Council to a Code of Laws*, The Père Marquette Theology Lecture, Milwaukee, WI, Marquette University Press, 1985.

_____, *Theology and Canon Law: New Horizons for Legislation and Interpretation*, Collegeville, Minnesota, A Michael Glazier Book, The Liturgical Press, 1992.

PINTO, P.V., *Commento al Codice di diritto canonico*, Roma, Urbaniana University Press, 1985.

POSPISHIL, V.J., *Eastern Catholic Church Law*, 2nd rev. and augmented edition, Staten Island, New York, Saint Maron Publications, 1996.

PUGLIESE, A., *Iuris canonici publici et privati summa lineamenta*, Augustae Taurinorum, Typis Scholae Typographicae, 1936-1939, 2 vols.

PUNZI NICOLÒ, A.M., *Gli enti nell'ordinamento canonico*. I — *Gli enti di strutura*, Pavoda, Casa Editrice Dott. Antonio Milani, 1983.

RAMSTEIN, M., *A Manual of Canon Law*, Hoboken, NJ, Terminal Printing and Publishing Co., 1947.

REGATILLO, E.F., *Institutiones iuris canonici*, Santander, Sal Terrae, 1941-1942, 2 vols.

ROMANI, S., *De norma juris, De normae juris natura deque virtute*, Romae, Rassegna di Morale e Diritto, 1937.

_____, *Institutiones juris canonici*, Romae, Editrice Iustitia, 1941-1945, 2 t. in 3 vols.

SANTI, F., *Prælectiones iuris canonici*, 4th ed., Romae, Sumptibus et typis Friderici Pustet, 1904, 5 vols.

SHEEHY, G. et al. (eds.), *The Canon Law: Letter & Spirit: A Practical Guide to the Code of Canon Law*, prepared by the Canon Law Society of Great Britain and Ireland in association with the Canadian Canon Law Society, Collegeville, MN, Liturgical Press, 1995.

URRUTIA, F.J., *De normis generalibus adnotationes in Codicem: liber I*, Romae, Pontificia Universitas Gregoriana, 1983.

URRUTIA, F.J., *Les normes générales: commentaire des canons 1-203*, Paris, Éditions Tardy, 1992.

VALDRINI, P. et al., *Droit canonique*, Paris, Dalloz, 1989.

VAN HOVE, A., *De legibus ecclesiasticis*, Romae, H. Dessain, 1930-1945, t. 2 in 1 vol.

VERMEERSCH, A. and I. CREUSEN, *Epitome iuris canonici cum commentariis ad scholas et ad usum privatum*, 8th edition, rev. by A. BERGH and I. GRECO, Museum Lessianum, Section Théologique, no. 5, Mechliniae, H. Dessain, 1963.

WÄCHTER, L., *Gesetz im kanonischen Recht: eine rechtssprachliche und systematisch-normative Untersuchung zu Grundproblemen der Erfassung des Gesetzes im katholischen Kirchenrecht*, Münchener theologische Studien, III, Kanonistische Abteilung, Bd. 43, St. Otilien, EOS Verlag, 1989.

WERNZ, F.X. and P. VIDAL, *Ius canonicum*, 3rd edition, Romae, Pontificia Universitas Gregoriana, 1927-1946, 7 t. in 8 vols.

WOYWOD, S., *The New Canon Law: A Commentary and Summary of the New Code of Canon Law*, 3rd edition, New York, NY, J.F. Wagner, 1918.

WOYWOD, S., *A Practical Commentary on the Code of Canon Law,* rev. by C. SMITH, New York, NY, J.F. Wagner, 1948, 2 vols.

WRENN, L., *Authentic Interpretations on the 1983 Code,* Washington, DC, CLSA, 1993.

ARTICLES:

ALESANDRO, J.A., "Background on the Canon Law Code's Revision," in *Origins,* 12 (1982-1983), pp. 541-544.

_____, "The Revision of the Code of Canon Law: a Background Study," in *Studia canonica,* 24 (1990), pp. 91-146.

ARIAS GOMEZ, J., "Revocación, irretroactividad y derechos adquiridos," in *Ius canonicum,* 21 (1981), pp. 723-737.

AUSTIN, R., "An Overview of the New Code of Canon Law," in G. ROBINSON (ed.), *Introduction to the New Code of Canon Law,* Sydney, The Canon Law Society of Australia and New Zealand, 1982, pp. 18-43.

BASSETT, W.W., "Civil Metaphors and Canonical Judgment," in J.H. PROVOST and K. WALF (eds.), *Studies in Canon Law Presented to P.J.M. Huizing,* Leuven, University Press, 1991, pp. 208-229.

_____, "A New Canon Law and the Crisis of Reform," in *Journal of Ecumenical Studies,* 10 (1973), pp. 233-258.

BEYER, J., "Norma e libertà nella visione post-conciliare," in *Vita consecrata,* 25 (1989), pp. 606-611.

_____, "Le nouveau Code de droit canonique esprit et structures," in *Nouvelle revue théologique,* 106 (1984), pp. 360-382.

CIÁURRIZ, J., "Titulus III: De decretis generalibus et de instructionibus," in *Comentario exegético,* vol. 1, pp. 471-496.

COOMBS, J.V., "Réforme du droit et changements dans le Code de 1983," in *Praxis juridique et religion,* 2 (1985), pp. 289-290.

CORECCO, E., "Aspects of Reception of Vatican II in the *Code of Canon Law,*" translated by M. O'CONNELL, in G. ALBERIGO, J.P. JOSSUA and J. KOMONCHAK (eds.), *The Reception of Vatican II,* Washington, DC, Catholic University Press, 1987, pp. 249-296.

_____, "Theological Justifications of the Codification of the Latin Canon Law," in M. THÉRIAULT and J. THORN (eds.), *The New Code of Canon Law, Proceedings of the 5th International Congress of Canon Law Organized by Saint Paul University and Held at the University of Ottawa, August 19-25, 1984,* vol. 1, Ottawa, Faculty of Canon Law, Saint Paul University, 1986, pp. 69-96.

CORIDEN, J.A., "Laws and Non-Laws," in *CLSA Proceedings of the Forty-fifth Annual Convention*, Washington, DC, CLSA, Catholic University, 1983, pp. 79-91.

_____, "Laws in Service to the People of God," in *The Jurist*, 41 (1981), pp. 1-20.

CREUSEN, J., "L'abrogation de l'ancien droit," in *Nouvelle revue théologique*, 50 (1923), pp. 196-207.

CUNNINGHAM, R., "The Principles Guiding the Revision of the Code of Canon Law," in *The Jurist*, 30 (1970), pp. 447-455.

DEUTSCH, B.F., "Ancient Roman Law and Modern Canon Law: Introduction," in *The Jurist*, 27 (1967), pp. 297-309.

_____, "Ancient Roman Law and Modern Canon Law: Summary and Conclusions," in *The Jurist*, 30 (1970), pp. 75-84.

D'ORS, A., "Sobre la palabra 'norma' en derecho canónico," in *Ius canonicum*, 16 (1976), pp. 103-107.

EIJSINK, H., "Some Striking Changes in the Code of Canon Law since April 1982," in *Studies in Canon Law*, 1991, pp. 1-20.

FOX, J., "A General Synthesis of the Work of the Pontifical Commission for the Revision of the Code of Canon Law," in *The Jurist*, 48 (1988), pp. 800-840.

GARCIA Y GARCIA, A., "Las codificaciones y su impacto en la iglesia a través de la historia," in *Temas fundamentales en el nuevo Código*, Bibliotheca Salmanticensis Estudios 65, Salamanca, Universidad Pontificia, 1984, pp. 35-62.

GAUDEMET, J., "La Hiérarchie des normes dans le nouveau Code de droit canonique," in H. Schambeck (ed.), *Pro fide et iustitia*, Berlin, Duncker & Humblot, 1984, pp. 205-218.

GONZÁLEZ DEL VALLE, J.M., "Los actos pontificios como fuente del derecho canónico," in *Ius canonicum*, 16 (1976), pp. 245-292.

GONZÁLEZ DEL VALLE, J.M., "The Method of the *Codex iuris canonici*," in *Proceedings, 5th International Congress*, pp. 141-154.

GY, P., "Commentarium: Les changements dans les Praenotanda des livres liturgiques à la suite du Code de droit canonique," in *Notitiae*, 19 (1983), pp. 556-561.

HERRANZ, J., "Prolegómenos II – génesis y elaboración del nuevo Código de derecho canónico," in *Comentario exegético*, pp. 157-205.

HITE, J.F., "Book II, The People of God: Part III, Title II: Religious Institutes (cc. 607-709)," in *CLSA Commentary*, pp. 470-524.

HOLLAND, S.L., "The Code and *Essential Elements*," in *The Jurist*, 44 (1984), pp. 304-338.

HUELS, J.M., "Back to the Future: the Role of Custom in a World Church," in *CLSA Proceedings of the Fifty-ninth Annual Convention*, Washington, DC, CLSA, Catholic University of America, 1997, pp. 1-25.

_____, "Liturgical Law: An Introduction," in E. FOLEY (ed.), *American Essays in Liturgy*, n. 4, The Pastoral Press, Washington, DC, 1987.

_____, A Theory of Juridical Documents Based on Canons 29-34," in *Studia canonica*, 32 (1998), pp. 337-370.

JIMÉNEZ URRESTI, T.I., "Libro I: cc. 1-123," in L. DE ECHEVERRIA (ed.), *Código de derecho canónico, edición bilingüe comentada por los professores de la Facultad de Derecho canónico de la Universidad Pontificia de Salamanca*, 7th rev. edition, Madrid, Biblioteca de autores cristianos, 1986, pp. 11-99.

LABANDEIRA, E., "Clasificación de las normas escritas canónicas," in *Ius canonicum*, 29 (1989), pp. 679-693.

LO CASTRO, G., "De las normas generales: introducción," in *Comentario exegético*, vol. 1, pp. 229-254.

MARINI, P., "Codice di diritto canonico e legislazione liturgica," in *Notitiae*, 19 (1983), pp. 280-281.

MAZZONI, G., "Le norme generali," in E. CAPPELLINI (ed.), *La normativa del nuovo Codice*, 2nd edition, Brescia, Queriniana, 1985, pp. 29-66.

MENDONÇA, A. "Book I: General Norms, Canons 1-95," in *Letter & Spirit*, pp. 1-54.

MCDONOUGH, E., "The *Potestas* of Canon 596," in *Antonium*, 63 (1988), pp. 551-606.

METZ, R., "Les deux codifications du droit de l'Église au XXe siècle, 1917 et 1983," in W. SCHULZ and G. FELICIANI (eds.), *Vitam impendere vero, studi in onore di Pio Ciprotti*, Roma, Liberia editrice Vaticana, 1986, pp. 185-208.

MORRISEY, F.G., "Introduction," in J. HITE, S. HOLLAND, and D. WARD (eds.), *A Handbook on Canons 573-746*, Collegeville, MN, The Liturgical Press, 1985, pp. 13-30.

_____, "Recent Ecclesiastical Legislation and the Code of Canon Law," in *Studia canonica*, 6 (1972), pp. 3-78.

_____, "The Role of Canon Law Today," in *Chicago Studies*, 15 (1976), pp. 236-254.

ÖRSY, L., "Book I, General Norms (cc. 1-203), Introduction," in *CLSA Commentary*, 1985, pp. 23-29.

———, "Longergan's Cognitional Theory and Foundational Issues in Canon Law," in *Studia canonica*, 13 (1979), pp. 177-243.

———, "Quantity and Quality of Laws after Vatican II," in *The Jurist*, 27 (1967), pp. 385-412.

———, "General Norms, Title I: Ecclesiastical Laws," in *CLSA Commentary*, pp. 29-37.

OTADUY, J.G., "De las normas generales: título I de las leyes eclesiásticas," in *Comentario exegético*, pp. 289-417.

———, "El derecho canónico postconciliar como *ius vetus* (c. 6 §1)," in *Proceedings, 5th International Congress*, pp. 115-129.

———, "El sentido de la ley canónica a la luz del libro I del nuevo Código," in *La nueva codificación canónica*, vol. 1, *Temas fundamentales en el nuevo Código*, Salamanca, Universidad Pontificia Salamanca, pp. 63-80.

———, "Funciones del Código en la recepción de la legislación postconciliar," in *Ius canonicum*, 25 (1985), pp. 479-516.

———, "Introducción: cc. 1-6," in *Comentario exegético*, pp. 255-288.

———, "Normas y actos jurídicos," in *Manuale de derecho canónico*, obra a cargo del INSTITUTO MARTÍN DE AZPILCUETA, Pamplona, Ediciones Universidad de Navarra, 1988, pp. 229-264.

PAGÉ, R., "'Variationes:' Réflexions d'un canoniste," in *Bulletin national de liturgie*, 18 (1984), pp. 56-60.

POTZ, R., "The Concept and Development of Law According to 1983 CIC," in *Concilium*, 185 (1986), pp. 14-22.

PREE, H., "Traditio canonica: La norma de interpretación del c. 6, §2 del CIC," in *Ius canonicum*, 35 (1995), pp. 423-446.

PROVOST, J. and K. WALF, "Editorial: Church Law — Church Reality," in *Concilium*, 185 (1986), pp. ix-xvii.

REDAELLI, C., "Il metodo esegetico applicato al Codice di diritto canonico del 1917 e a quello del 1983," in *Periodica*, 86 (1997), pp. 57-100.

RISK, J., "Title III: General Decrees and Instructions," in *CLSA Commentary*, pp. 46-48.

SCHWENDENWEIN, H., "Zur Frage der Weitergeltung kirchlicher Vorschriften bei Inkrafttreten des neues kirchlichen Gesetzbuches," in F. POTATSCHNIG and A. RINNERTHALER (eds.), *Im Dienst von Kirche und Staat: In memoriam Carl Holböeck, Kirche und Recht,* vol. 17, Wein Verlag des Verbands der wissenschaftlichen Gesellschaften Öesterreichs, 1985, pp. 403-419.

TEGELS, A., "Chronicle," in *Worship,* 58 (1984), pp. 55-59.

URRUTIA, F.J., "Adnotationes quaedam ad propositam reformationem libri primi Codicis iuris canonici," in *Periodica,* 64 (1975), pp. 633-659.

_____, "Canones praeliminares Codicis (CIC). Comparatio cum canonibus praeliminaribus Codicis canonum ecclesiarum orientalium (CC)," in *Periodica,* 81 (1992), pp. 153-177.

_____, "De quibusdam quaestionibus ad librum primum Codicis pertinentibus," in *Periodica,* 73 (1984), pp. 292-382.

_____, "Il libro I: le norme generali," in J. BEYER et al. (eds.), *Il nuovo Codice di diritto canonico,* Leumann (Torino), Editrice Elle di CI, 1985, pp. 32-59.

GENERAL INDEX

abrogation, 7, 10, 17, 21, 24, 26, 28, 29, 32, 33, 36, 37, 39, 44, 46, 47, 63-65, 68, 69, 76, 81, 87, 196, 112, 149-152
Ad totam Ecclesiam, see Ecumenical Directory
Ad instituendo, 104, 106
cessation of law, 1, 2, 7, 31-33, 54, 55, 59, 70, 80
Clausuram papalem, 104, 123, 142-145
Clementinae, 2
Clericalia institutia (CI), 104, 121, 142, 145
Code commission, 3, 12, 22, 29, 46, 48, 60, 143
communicatio in sacris, 41, 42, 67
concelebration, 92, 93, 97
Congregation for Consecrated Life and Societies of Apostolic Life, (CICLSAL), 102, 104, 106, 117, 132, 137, 139, 140, 142
Congregation for Religious and Secular Institutes (CRIS), 102, 104, 106, 120, 132
Congregation for the Sacraments and Divine Worship, 80, 81, 96
Congregation for the Evangelization of Peoples, 104
Contemplative Dimension of Religious Life, 104, 132-134, 137, 140
Corpus juris canonici, 2
Council of Trent, 7, 75
Cum admotae (CA), 104, 109, 112, 114, 115, 141, 143, 145, 146
Cum iuris canonici, 3, 143
Cum superiores generales (CSG), 104, 115-117, 142, 145
derogation, 2, 4, 10, 29, 32, 33, 36, 42, 37, 44, 63-65, 68, 69, 76, 81, 84, 87, 93, 109, 118, 132, 137, 141, 144, 149-152

direct contrariety, 2, 4, 25, 33-35, 59, 65, 66, 80, 81, 84-88, 90, 93, 96, 108, 142, 149-153, 155
Dopo le publicazione, 71
Dum canonicarum legum, 104, 106, 107
Ecclesiae sanctae (ES), 104-107, 124, 127
Ecumenical Directory, 40-42, 45, 67, 72, 73, 96
Emendations in Liturgical Books following the New Code, 80, 83, 91, 94, 96-99, 142
 liturgical emendations, 5, 80-87, 97, 98, 147, 152, 155, 156
Essential Elements in Church Teaching on Religious Life, 102, 104, 107, 134, 135, 137, 140
executive power, 50-53, 113, 149
Extravagantes, 2
Extravagantes communes, 2
Fraternal Life in Community, 104, 140, 141
general administrative norms, 13, 52, 55, 57, 58, 60-63, 68-72, 149-152
general executory decrees, 51, 53, 54, 69, 70
General Instruction of the Roman Missal, 82, 87, 89, 92
godparent, 94-97
in forma specifica, 53, 68
incompatibility, 75, 81, 83, 87, 88, 97, 149, 152, 153, 155
instructions, 11, 43, 47, 51, 54, 59, 70, 71, 76, 137, 140, 143
integral reordering, 2, 4, 5, 7, 8, 10, 14, 18, 24-28, 33-40, 42-46, 48, 50, 54-81, 83, 84, 86, 87, 89, 91-93, 96-99, 102, 103, 106, 108, 115, 117, 126, 133, 141-156
 definition, 4, 151
 ex/de integro 9, 10, 14, 21-23, 26, 32, 38, 60-64
 extent of integrity, 38, 61, 64, 153
 formal integrity, 38, 39, 41-43, 45, 76

Italian civil code, 28, 34
Iuris canonici Codice, 104, 135, 136
ius, 9, 11-15, 28, 39, 42, 47, 49, 58, 60
    ius canonicum, 12, 34, 43, 45, 48, 49
    ius commune, 26
    ius particulare, 26, 29
    ius peculiare, 11, 29
    ius proprium, 30, 103, 122, 123, 136, 143, 145, 146
    ius religionis, 103, 108
    ius speciale, 14, 29-31
    ius vetus, 11, 16, 20, 21, 23, 24, 60, 63, 65
    ius vigens, 2-4, 7, 14, 15, 22, 23, 25-27, 36, 41, 46, 55, 56, 60, 65, 67, 73, 79, 81, 99, 103, 108-110, 112, 115, 117, 118, 123, 126, 128, 129, 132, 134-141, 143, 147, 148, 151, 152, 154, 155, 157
juridic document, 3-8, 35, 45, 48-51, 53-56, 58, 62-67, 79, 81, 83, 95, 97, 99, 103, 105, 108, 109, 137, 140, 141, 143, 147, 149, 151-155
juridic institute, 13, 35-37, 58-67, 74, 78, 86, 92, 94, 97, 102, 142, 151, 153
juridic norm, 4, 42, 48, 51, 54, 62, 63, 79, 80, 86, 89, 101, 147, 151, 154-158
juridic person, 30, 31, 132
lex/leges, 9, 11-14, 17, 24, 26, 29, 31, 47, 48, 51, 52, 54, 57-62, 68-72, 75, 76, 83, 97, 133, 145, 146, 151, 153, 156
liturgical law, 58, 80, 81-84, 87, 89, 90, 96, 157, 158
Lumen gentium, 102, 124
mind of legislator, 9, 37, 74, 75, 79, 83, 87, 98, 117, 144, 145, 152, 154
Mutuae relationes (MR), 104, 123-134, 138-141, 144, 145, 157-159
obrogate/*obrogare*, 27, 29, 64
Pastor bonus, 45, 51, 67, 72, 102
Pastorale munus (PM), 104, 109-112, 143, 145, 146
Perfectae caritatis, 102, 105
Potissimum institutione (PI), 104, 107, 108, 137-140
praenotanda, 81-85, 88-92, 96, 97
Praescriptis canonum, 104, 137

Procedures for the Separation of Members from Institute, 104, 136, 140
Processus juricialis, 104, 107
Providentissima mater Ecclesia, 1, 15, 16
Regimini Ecclesiae universae, 45, 67, 72
Religionum laicalium, 104, 115, 142, 146
Religious and Human Promotion, 104, 132-134, 137
religious law, 5, 57, 79, 99, 102, 103, 109, 112, 115, 125, 126, 132, 140, 141, 146-148, 152, 155, 157
Renovationis causam, 104, 105, 107, 138
revocation, 4, 7, 8, 17, 27, 29-38, 42-46, 54-66, 69-72, 82, 91, 96, 106, 112, 128-130, 136, 142, 143, 144, 147-159
    doubt of, 8, 44, 45, 812, 97, 128, 130, 144, 147, 157-159
    explicit, 54, 59, 69, 70, 99
    express, 1, 2, 4, 31, 33-35, 65, 80-82, 96, 155
    explicit, 54, 59, 69, 70, 99, 151
    implicit, 25, 33, 34, 36, 54, 59, 60, 69, 70, 96, 149
    tacit, 4, 25, 33-36, 54, 55, 65, 66, 96, 142, 149, 154, 157
Sacred Congregation for Religious (SCR), 102, 104, 105, 115
Sacred Congregation for Religious and Secular Institutes (SCRIS), 102, 104, 106, 116, 117, 120, 121, 124, 133, 135, 144, 146
Secretariat for the Promotion of Christian Unity, 40, 71
Spiritus Domini, see Ecumenical Directory
subrogation, 29, 64
tenor of law, 38, 39, 45, 74, 76, 79, 83, 87, 97, 145, 152, 154
tone of law, 42, 43, 64, 76, 77, 79, 86, 89-91, 97, 98, 121, 146, 147, 152, 154
traditio canonica, 3, 23, 24, 45, 58, 117, 147
Unitatis redintegratio, 40, 67
Vatican Council,
    First, 14, 20
    Second, 3, 7, 8, 18-20, 22, 25, 35, 40, 47, 49, 55, 60, 64, 66, 69, 75, 77, U 103, 107, 112, 137, 142, 143, 147, 150
Venite seorsum, 104, 117-121, 140, 142, 144, 147
Verbi sponsa, 104, 117-121, 140, 142, 144, 147

INDEX OF AUTHORS

ABBO, J.A., 33, 37, 75
ALESANDRO, J., 20, 43, 77
ARIAS GOMEZ, J., 33, 34
BENEDICT XV, 1, 3, 144
BERUTTI, C., 28, 58, 66
BLANCO NAJERA, F., 17
BLAT, A., 37
BONIFACE VII, 2, 17, 28
CABREROS DE ANTA, M., 8, 15-17, 32-36, 45, 58, 59, 78, 97
CAPPELLO, F.M., 32, 33
CHIAPPETTA, L., 19, 25, 31-34, 37, 44, 49
CICOGNANI, A.G., 7, 12, 18, 28, 29, 33, 34, 45, 58, 61, 112
CIÁURRIZ, M.J., 49, 60, 71
CORECCO, E., 18, 19, 39, 54, 78
CREUSEN, J., 17
CRNICA, A., 15, 58
CUNNINGHAM, R., 43, 77
DELLA ROCCA, F., 32, 33
EICHMANN, E., 15
EIJSINK, H., 11
FALCO, M., 21
FARRIS, J.D., 26
GAUDAMET, J., 7, 50
GARCIA Y GARCIA, A., 54
GHIRLANDA, G., 36, 37
GLARE, P., 9, 10, 33
GREGORY IX, 1, 2, 7
GY, P., 81, 83, 85, 90
HERVADA, J., 19
HERRANZ, J., 20
HITE, J.F., 119
HOLLAND, S., 135
HUELS, J.M., 12, 13, 49-53, 68, 69, 89
JIMÉNEZ URRESTI, T.I., 75

JOMBART, E., 14
JOHN XXIII, 18
JOHN PAUL II, 19, 49, 67, 105, 109, 134
LABANDEIRA, E., 49-53, 71
LOMBARDÍA, P., 19
MARINI, P., 81
MARTINS, J.A., 28
MCDONOUGH, E., 117
MENDONÇA, A., 19, 25, 34, 44, 60, 62
MICHIELS, G., 18, 33, 35, 38, 45, 61, 64, 74
MIG L., 15
MORRISEY, F.G., 49, 118
NEUBERGER, N., 2, 15, 17
OCHOA, X., 9, 11, 13, 29
OJETTI, B., 15, 37, 63
ÖRSY, L., 23-25, 31, 33, 35, 36, 45, 55, 62, 73, 74, 77
OTADUY, J., 8, 14, 20, 21, 24, 25, 28-36 39-43, 45-47, 57, 61-64, 67, 72-76, 79, 97, 102, 106, 112
PAGÉ, R., 82
PAUL VI, 45, 67, 72, 75, 102, 104, 105, 109, 112
PIUS IX, 14, 45, 58, 72
PIUS X, 1, 15, 72
PIUS XII, 59, 75
POTZ, 19, 98
PROVOST, J., 41, 42
REGATILLO, E.F., 32, 38, 39, 61, 64
RISK, J., 143
TEGELS, A., 82, 83
URRUTIA, F., 19, 25, 26, 30, 33, 34
VAN HOVE, A. , 14, 28, 35, 37, 41, 46, 74
WÄCHTER, L., 12, 13, 30, 49
WOYWOD, S., 7, 16
WRENN, L., 75, 76

ROMAN CATHOLIC STUDIES

1. L. Thomas Snyderwine (ed.), **Researching the Development of Lay Leadership in the Catholic Church Since Vatican II: Bibliographical Abstracts**
2. Frank Przetacznik, **The Catholic Concept of Genuine and Just Peace as a Basic Collective Human Right**
3. Andrew Cuschieri, **Introductory Readings in Canon**
4. Ernest Skublics, **How Eastern Orthodoxy Can Contribute to Roman Catholic Renewal: A Theological and Pastoral Proposition**
5. Robert J. Kaslyn, **"Communion with the Church" and the Code of Canon Law: An Analysis of the Foundation and Implications of the Canonical Obligation to Maintain Communion with the Catholic Church**
6. Patricia Voydanoff and Thomas M. Martin (eds.), **Using a Family Perspective in Catholic Social Justice and Family Ministries**
7. Michael Sundermeier and Robert Churchill (eds.), **The Literary and Educational Effects of the Thought of John Henry Newman**
8. Ross A. Shecterle, **The Theology of Revelation of Avery Dulles, 1980-1994: Symbolic Mediation**
9. Filippo Maria Toscano, **El Universalismo Del Pensamiento Cristiano De Don Luigi Sturzo**
10. James L. MacNeil, **A Study of Gaudium et Spes 19-22, The Second Vatican Council Response to Contemporary Atheism**
11. David B. Perrin, **The Sacrament of Reconciliation: An Existential Approach**
12. Stephen R. Duncan, **A Genre in Hindusthani Music (Bhajans) as Used in the Roman Catholic Church**
13. Maria G. McClelland, **The Sisters of Mercy, Popular Politics and the Growth of the Roman Catholic Community in Hull, 1855-1930**
14. Robert Berchmans, **A Study of Lonergan's Self-Transcending Subject and Kegan's Evolving Self: A Framework for Christian Anthropology**
15. Larry Hostetter, **The Ecclesial Dimension of Personal and Social Reform in the Writings of Isaac Thomas Hecker**
16. Patricia Smith, **Theoretical and Practical Understanding of the Integral Reordering of Canon Law**